Personal Testimonies

God used *Praying Scripture for Your Marriage* early on in my marriage to teach me to put my hopes, fears, worries, and deepest needs in His hands. My marriage was changed because God changed me! I experienced firsthand the power of standing on God's Word even when it looked as though my prayers weren't being answered. Through learning the principle and application of praying Scripture, agreeing with God, I had hope where before there was despair, peace replaced chaos, and love dissolved resentment. I could not be more thankful for learning how to agree with God for my marriage, and I haven't stopped yet. You will not want to miss this! Be richly blessed by all of His glorious gifts, dear sister, and I assure you this teaching is one of them!

~ Jenna

My husband and I had an extremely rocky seven years of marriage. In desperation I cried out to God for help! Not knowing how desperate I was, Tammy told me about *Praying Scripture for Your Marriage* just a few days later! It was exactly what I needed to not only save my marriage but grow it into all that God intended it to be. It taught me how to pray God's Word over myself and my family, and now my husband and I even use it to pray together. It truly is a gift from God!

~ Gretchen

In biblical times, cities would build walls or fortresses around the city to protect them from attacks and invasions. Each city had watchtowers that would be on the lookout for potential invasions as well as protecting its people from leaving when the gates were closed.

Here is my heart on what praying Scripture for my marriage does for me: Praying God's Word is the building and reinforcing of the wall around my marriage. God sends His soldiers to guard the wall. Each week that we pray Scripture, the wall is repaired and strengthened. If the "wall" is neglected, then it begins to crumble and weaknesses become present. If this continues, then the wall is no longer providing the protection and the marriage is vulnerable.

~ Maggie

Copyright 2013 by Tammy Rentsch

Cover Design by Lynda Alfano
Published by Juania Books LLC
www.juaniabooks.com

All rights reserved.
No part of this book may be reproduced, scanned or distributed in any printed, mechanical, photocopying or electronic form including information storage and retrieval systems, without prior written permission from the author or publisher. The only exception is by a reviewer, who may quote short excerpts in a review.
Please do not participate in or encourage piracy of copyrighted materials in violation of the author's rights. Purchase only authorized editions.
Library of Congress Control Number 2015936232
ISBN 978-0-9818047-9-8

Printed in the United States of America
First printing 2015

Visit juaniabooks.com to follow author's blog and to contact her for speaking engagements.

Always Pray & Don't Give Up
Praying Scripture for Your Marriage

Tammy Rentsch

Unless otherwise noted, all Scripture quotations are taken from the HOLY BIBLE, NEW INTERNATIONAL VERSION. Copyright © 1973, 1978, 1984 International Bible Society.

Scripture marked AMP was taken from THE AMPLIFIED BIBLE, Old Testament copyright © 1965, 1987 by the Zondervan Corporation. The Amplified New Testament copyright © 1958, 1987 by The Lockman Foundation. Used by permission.

Scripture marked CEV was taken from the Contemporary English Version, public domain.

Scripture marked KJV was taken from the Holy Bible, King James Version. Copyright © by E. E. Gaddy and Associates, Inc., 1982. All rights reserved.

Scripture [marked MSG] taken from *THE MESSAGE*. Copyright © 1993, 1994, 1995, 1996, 2000, 2001, 2002. Used by permission of NavPress Publishing Group.

Scripture marked NASB was taken from the New American Standard Bible. Copyright © 1960, 1962, 1963, 1968, 1971, 1972, 1973, 1975, 1977 by the Lockman Foundation. Copyright © 1978, 1985 by Thomas Nelson, Inc. All Rights Reserved.

Scripture [marked NKJV] taken from the New King James Version. Copyright © 1982 by Thomas Nelson, Inc. Used by permission. All rights reserved.

The Scripture quotations [marked NRSV] contained herein are from the New Revised Standard Version Bible, copyright © 1989, Division of Christian Education of the National Council of Churches of Christ in the U.S.A. Used by permission. All rights reserved.

Verses marked TLB are taken from *The Living Bible*, copyright © 1971. Used by permission of Tyndale House Publishers, Inc., Wheaton, Illinois 60189. All rights reserved.

For Jesus
The author and perfecter of my faith
(Hebrews 12:2)

Editorial Reviews

Praying Scripture is the most powerful and effective way to pray for your marriage. It can be a daunting task to search out all the passages that apply, though. In this book, Tammy has done the hard work for us in compiling a beautiful arrangement of God's attributes along with verses to pray for myself, as a wife, and verses to pray over my husband and marriage. The Lord has used many of these passages to bear fruit in my own life and marriage.

Mariel Davenport, Author
Knowing God Through His Names
A Housewife Desperate for God

Tammy Rentsch is passionate about prayer. She prays faithfully and frequently. She is also committed to loving her spouse enough to pray for their marriage. Read this book and you will be equipped and encouraged to pray consistently and powerfully for your marriage with the Scriptures as your guide.

Dr. Brian D. Russell
Professor of Biblical Studies and
Dean of the School of Urban Ministries,
Asbury Theological Seminary

Contents

1. One September Morning   9

2. The Unexpected Happens   15

3. Do You Know Him?   24

4. Learning to Listen   28

5. Guide to Using Weekly Prayer Sheets   33

6. Weekly Prayer Sheets   43

7. Blank Prayer Sheets   223

     Suggested Reading   232

     Works Cited   235

     About Tammy   237

1

One September Morning

My journey of learning to pray Scripture for my marriage began one September morning in 1999 when I was spending my time alone with God. But this morning was different. God had put it on my heart that I was to stop teaching the women's Sunday school class at my church. My husband had turned 40 that year and our oldest son was entering middle school, and I felt God was telling me to quit teaching so that I would have more time and energy for my family. And this particular morning, God spoke very clearly to me saying, *Tammy, there is a battle going on; Satan is fighting to keep your husband in the darkness, he is fighting to pull you down in discouragement, and he is fighting to keep your kids from a close walk with Me. There's a big battle coming and the only thing that's going to win this battle is prayer. I'm going to teach you how to pray for your marriage through Moms In Touch.*[1] And one month later He did just that!

God Birthed this Prayer Ministry

It was on October 14, while in prayer at Moms In Touch, that God spoke to my heart. Another mom, Natalie Page, prayed, "Thank you for bringing me here to pray with other moms, Lord. For I pray at home for my children, but when praying alone I can become discouraged and want to give up. This has been so encouraging today to come and pray with other moms…" The Holy Spirit at that moment spoke very clearly and powerfully to my heart, *That's it; that's what's happening: wives are at home praying for their husbands and marriages, but praying alone they are becoming discouraged and wanting to give up. We need a "Wives in Touch"; i.e., we need to be bathing our husbands and marriages in prayer the way we are bathing our children and their schools!*[2]

---

[1] This is a prayer ministry through which I had been meeting weekly with other moms to pray Scripture for our children, their teachers, and their schools. For more information regarding this prayer ministry see www.MomsInPrayer.org. (Same vision – New Name. Formerly Moms In Touch.)

[2] All around me, I was seeing marriages and families falling apart and it was breaking my heart—when God spoke the above words of hope, encouragement, and instruction to me!

And thus it all began. Natalie and I prayed about it. I spoke to my husband about it and asked his permission. I asked him if it would be all right with him if I prayed for him and our marriage each week with Natalie in our home. I told him that I would not be praying anything personal but that we would be praying Scripture. He agreed and said that would be fine with him. I remember being very happy and thinking to myself, *Wow, bless your heart, you don't have any idea what you just said yes to!* For I believed my husband had basically just said, "Yes, Tammy, you can pray and ask God to open the floodgates of heaven and release tons of power down on my life and the life of our marriage each week!"

One month later on November 17, 1999 Natalie and I began to meet together for one hour a week to pray—to release God's power into our lives, our husbands, our marriages, and our homes. That morning I wrote in my journal, *My heart right now: I found myself saying yesterday, I'm angry at Satan, for this week I witnessed him tear another marriage apart, of a dear sister in Christ. I know the answer is not to be angry or to fear Satan but to fight Satan with the weapons God has given me of prayer and His Word! I am convinced that the key to holding a marriage together is 1) prayer and 2) obedience to God's Word, both working hand in hand. Oh dear Lord, I pray that You will make me a prayer warrior for Your glory; give my heart the desire and power to obey Your Word always.*

Praying Brought Changes

For the next five years I prayed Scripture for my marriage. When I first started, I remember thinking, *Wow; I think my husband's soul is going to be saved next week!* For I had already been praying for 13 years and now I was praying Scripture and praying in agreement with another believer. What can stand against that? Nothing! But in actuality, that's not what happened. What did happen was that God changed me!

Praying Scripture for myself and my family first changed me, and as I changed there was a ripple effect on our whole household. I more lived God's Word, daily, as I prayed Scripture for myself week after week with another believer and day after day in my quiet time with God. Little by little, slowly, gradually, and steadily, God's Word was changing me and molding me. My husband saw it. My kids saw it. What was happening on the inside was becoming more and more visible on the outside.

One of the biggest things praying Scripture did for me was to give me a more consistent, steady, level walk with God. I remember praying and asking God to help me with this. For I felt that my walk with Him was like a roller coaster: up on the mountaintop one day and down in the valley the next. But as I began to pray Scripture for myself each week, things began to change. When I felt there was a whole list of things that needed to be worked on in me, it was as though God was saying to me, *We are going to work on just this one thing this week.* It was refreshing to work on just one aspect of my life or character at a time. I felt I was making progress by the end of each week. Praying God's Word into my life was changing and growing me, little by little.

The Ministry Began to Grow

After a time, my friend Natalie moved about two hours away from where I lived. So I then started a *Praying Scripture for Your Marriage* prayer group at my church on Wednesday evenings during the Bible study hour. I opened it up to anyone who wanted to participate, and I soon had a group of four to five ladies with whom I was praying. We would stick to the guidelines of all praying and no talking. We had the sweetest time of fellowship together as we cried and prayed and rejoiced together week after week. We would all stay together for the praise, confession, and thanksgiving time. Then we broke up into groups of two or three for the time of intercession and praying for ourselves, our husbands, our marriages, and our homes. If we were not done praying by the time an hour was up, I, as the facilitator, would speak up and close our time by uniting our hearts together in prayer and summing up the remainder of the prayer sheet.

For five years, I always had another believer to unite my heart with and pray. I distinctly remember a time that Natalie and I were praying in her side yard, which overlooked a creek and some trees. I was crying as I prayed for my husband and my marriage and God said to my heart, *I am so well pleased that you are praying. There are angels encamped all around you and your family.* I could not see any angels with my physical eyes, but my heart of faith knew that they were there; and they were not angels like those we see in pictures or postcards, like babies with wings. I knew they were God's soldiers with mighty swords, fighting battles I could not fight!

I continued to share *Praying Scripture for Your Marriage* with others whom God put in my life, and it was exciting for me to see the things that happened in their lives. Again, just as with me, the changes occurred in the women's lives as they met and prayed. Specifically, I was seeing again and again that *Praying Scripture for Your Marriage* was teaching the women to pray Scripture about everything, for all areas of their lives. Many of the women had not previously been introduced to the idea of praying Scripture. Once they started praying Scripture for their marriage, they saw the power and fruit of it and their eyes were opened to the power of praying God's Word into all areas of their lives! I have come to realize that this is really the heart of this ministry. The big picture is that it teaches God's children to pray His Word. Any good thing that happens in people's marriages, as a result, is just icing on the cake!

God Continued to Grow the Ministry

One night my husband asked me what my dreams were for myself, and out of my mouth came, *I want to share Praying Scripture for Your Marriage with other churches.* I thought to myself, where did that thought just come from? Did those words really just come out of my mouth? The thought of it was both exciting and scary to me at the same time. The next morning, though, God confirmed the passion and desire to me when I was journaling, *God, do You want me to do this—share this with other churches?* Just then, I looked at the Scripture printed on the page of the journal; it was 1 Peter 4:10. I read the Scripture from my Living Bible, "God has given each of you some special abilities; be sure to use them to help each other, passing on to others God's many kinds of blessings." I knew God was saying yes to me, and so the journey began of sharing this ministry with other churches and doing a half-day workshop in which I would share my story and teach how to pray Scripture for one's own marriage.

I Saw Answers to Prayer

As I continued to pray, I saw things happen, answers to prayer unfold before my very eyes. My husband went through a hard time when he turned 40, and a season of going through what the world calls "mid-life crisis" lasted for about a year and a half. During that time, I just kept praying God's Word week after week, focusing on God being free to mold me into all He wanted me to be. I did my best to just pray and love my husband through that season. And one day I looked out the window and saw my husband running and playing and smiling with our dog, Hank, and I knew the battle was over. God had broken through and won what I called "the battle of Gettysburg" in our lives. Life was back to "normal" again in my husband, as well as in our marriage relationship. God had fought and won a major battle in our lives; not the whole war, but a major battle had been fought and won by God as I faithfully prayed week after week, as He had instructed me to.

I was praying specifically and I was seeing specific answers. For example, one week the Scripture I prayed was Romans 4:20–21, praying to be like Abraham and, against all hope, to have hope! While giving my husband a back rub after work one night that week, we were talking about our kids and I said some words of encouragement—for I was always the optimist in the relationship—and my husband said, "That's my wife, always hoping!" He never used the word *hope* in his vocabulary; that just wasn't a word he would normally use, but that day he did! It was huge to me; God infused hope into my spirit saying, *Tammy, I am hearing and answering all your prayers!*

My favorite example is this: one week I was praying that I would be a submissive wife, from the truth of Ephesians 5:22, "Wives, submit to your husbands as to the Lord."[3] Applying that Scripture to my life, I asked God to show me any area where I was not being submissive. He revealed to me that I was failing to be submissive in the area of intimacy. For when my husband wanted to be intimate, it was usually late at night and I was tired and exhausted. I realized that it had become "habit" for me to pull away whenever my husband would touch me. So this week, as the result of praying and with God's help, I was choosing instead to respond to my husband's every touch—in the bedroom and out—and not pull away as I had been doing. So that meant, for example, whenever my husband would come up behind me in the kitchen and put his arms around me, instead of continuing with what I was doing, I would stop what I was in the middle of and embrace him back! Well, it only took about two days of this, and my husband said lightheartedly as we sat on the front porch one evening, "All right, what's going on?!" I replied, "Do you really want to know?" He responded with a definite "Yes!" So I shared with him the Scripture truth I had prayed that week and the things God had revealed to me, causing me to respond differently toward him. With that, he got a big smile on his face and said with happiness and excitement in his voice, "What's the Scripture for next week?!"

One of the most powerful examples of answered prayer and God working specifically was when the Scripture to pray was Ephesians 4:29, "Do not let any unwholesome talk come out of your mouths, but only what is helpful for building others up according to their needs, that it may benefit those who listen." I had prayed the Scripture for myself, and Natalie was now praying the Scripture for me in agreement. While I was quiet and still, listening to Natalie pray for me, I heard the Holy Spirit say to me, *Sometimes the best way you can have words that are helpful and building up is to say nothing at all.* Wow, I knew that was straight from God to me!

It is powerful to me to pray with another believer, for it was when Natalie was praying for me that God showed my heart the truth. It happened while I was quiet, not talking, and focused on Him. For when praying by myself, I am usually doing all the talking, and rarely am I quiet and still long enough to listen to what God may be trying to tell me. I am working on this area, though, and making much progress!

God Prepared Me

One day I was listening to Dr. David Jeremiah on the radio. He was preaching on the book of Jeremiah, and he said the book can be summed up by saying: God told Jeremiah to preach repentance to the people. God told Jeremiah in advance that the people would not repent, but Jeremiah was to go and preach to the people anyway.

---

[3] Scripture quotations are from the New International Version unless otherwise indicated.

The lesson for us is this: we are to obey God, and the result of our obedience is in His hands.

This said to me personally that my task was to love my husband with God's love, live the life before him, pray for him, and leave the results in God's hands. If there was fruit, when there was fruit, how much fruit there was, and so on, was all in God's hands, not mine!

2

The Unexpected Happens

My journey of learning to always pray and not give up began after five years of praying Scripture for my marriage. There are eighty-nine weekly prayer sheets and I had prayed through them two and a half times. My husband was now 45 years old. Both of our dads had died during this time. Our sons were now teenagers and walking down paths away from a close walk with God. I was praying with all my heart for my husband's salvation, for our marriage, and for our sons. Yet, one Saturday night in August 2004, my husband of 23 years, whom I dearly loved, announced that he had decided to divorce. One year later it would be revealed that he had committed adultery. He chose not to turn away from that relationship, and our marriage ended in divorce in December, 2006.

God is Faithful

At that time, I had a plate that could be written on with a dry-erase marker. I kept this special plate on the counter in our kitchen, and I would write a Scripture on it each week, whatever God was saying to my heart. Just hours prior to my husband announcing that he had decided to divorce, I had written Psalm 112:7. Personalizing the verse, I had written, "You will not fear bad news; you will be steadfast, trusting the Lord." My husband's news that day may have come as a surprise to me, but it did not come as a surprise to my God! God made Himself very real to me, very present with me, by giving me a specific, extremely applicable truth to hold onto. It was as though He was saying, *Tammy, I'm right here with you; you're not alone. Don't be afraid. I am aware of what is going on right now. I haven't abandoned you. I'm going to work this all out. Just trust Me!*

For years I had considered Psalm 119:92 to be my life verse:[4] "If your law had not been my delight, I would have perished in my affliction." For it is so true; if

---

[4] What is a life verse? "A 'life verse' is a verse or short passage from the Bible you claim as a rallying cry to guide and focus the current season in your life. It's a truth or a challenge straight from God's Word that rings true for you at this time." For more details see "Life Verse," http://media.willowcreek.org/wp-content/files_mf/life_verse.pdf, (April 24, 2014).

God's Word had not been my delight and my anchor, I do not believe I would have survived all that I have gone through, or at least I would not have handled it as well as I have. Yet over the course of the next few years, the Bible verse that would become most meaningful to me (i.e., my new life verse), would be a verse with a different focus. It would be a Scripture, not about me, but one about the goodness and faithfulness of my God! Deuteronomy 30:9 (MSG) reads, "God, your God, will outdo himself in making things go well for you...." It would take me a lifetime to give testimony to the truth of this.

God, My God, Outdid Himself in Making Things Go Well for Me

God now had me all to Himself, and the first thing He did was give me a rainbow right in the middle of my storm! I had always dreamed of living in a log cabin—specifically, one above a two car garage. Well, God put me in a log cabin apartment for one year! But this apartment was not just above a two car garage. It was above a *three* car garage, overlooking a pond and a stable with two horses! God always does immeasurably more than we could ever ask, dream or imagine (Ephesians 3:20)!

Though I was seeing God's goodness to me, in the year that I stayed in North Carolina, hoping our marriage was going to be put back together, I was slowly dying from a broken heart and depression. I never knew or thought that anyone could die from depression but I now believe you can and I almost did. But that was not in God's plan for me and He has the final say!

So, in September 2005, God brought me to Florida to be with family and to heal my broken heart. During this time He began to teach me about how much He loved me and He began to sink it deep into my heart that He had a good plan for my life (Jeremiah 29:11) and that I was not alone (Matthew 28:20). He put person after person and ministry after ministry in my life to rescue me and, eventually, to heal me.

First, He helped me through a dear, long-time friend, Kathi Joy, and a ministry she has founded called Welcome Home Outreach. It is a prayer-healing ministry that God used in my life to break down strongholds of lies I believed about myself and to break, through prayer, generational curses[5] on my family and marriage.

For me, Kathi coming and spending a week's time with me was a huge blessing and stepping stone in my life! Through her and her ministry, my eyes were

---

[5] What is a generational curse? In the words of the founder of Welcome Home Outreach, Kathi Joy, "A generational curse can be defined as any reoccurring problem or repeating negative cycle in a person's life." The Welcome Home Outreach ministry provides someone to walk with individuals who want to stop these negative cycles. To find out more information regarding this ministry you may contact them through the ministry's email address of: WelcomeHomeOutreach@yahoo.com.

opened to things that I did not see on my own. Our work together gave me a new perspective of myself and my value in Christ. Much healing began in my life that week!

☙❧

Secondly, God brought me to a ministry called Celebrate Recovery.[6] Kathi Joy put me in the car the first week I got to Florida and said, "Come on, we're going to Celebrate Recovery." I responded, *What's that?* She replied with a smile, "You'll see when you get there!" Celebrate Recovery became my lifeline for the first year of my healing. I attended CR every Friday night for four years. CR is a 12-step program that acknowledges Jesus as our "Higher Power." Their motto is that it is for anyone with a "hurt, habit, or hang-up." Thus, in my eyes, it is for everyone! For we all have hurts, habits, and hang-ups! At CR I came to understand the power of addictions and as a result I gleaned a glimpse of understanding regarding what had happened in my marriage and to my family. I learned that I have no control. I can't cause people I love to make what I think are right choices, and it's not my job or my place to try to. But God is in complete control, and I can trust Him. Most of all, at CR I was able to cry and pour out my pain week after week. I was allowed to cry as much as I needed to and as hard as I needed to. For at home it was too painful for my loved ones to watch. CR was a "safe place" for me to go and to pour out myself, my hurts, my fears, and my pains. No one there tries to "fix" you. They're just there to love you, whatever it is you are going through. Little by little, I got better and better, stronger and stronger, until God healed my broken heart as I cooperated with Him.

☙❧

My heart physically hurt for over two years, and in that time I would wake up crying every morning. But I would spend time with God and He would give me words of comfort, hope, and encouragement through songs that He would put in my heart each day. I would receive comfort and strength as I crawled up in His lap (figuratively speaking) and cried. He would wrap His arms of love around me and hold me until I was ready to get up and face the day. Many a morning I would start my day by listening to the song "Me and God" by Josh Turner. Sometimes I would dance to the song in the living room of my little apartment, and other times I would just sit curled up on my couch and cry as I listened to the words of this song that was so special to me. Then I would go off to work and make it through the day! Also, I made it a habit to put a sticky note on my computer at work with the words of truth that God had given me in the morning to hold onto for the day. Sometimes it was words of Scripture; sometimes it was the words of the song that God had given me that morning. Other times it may have been words He impressed on my heart or words of encouragement someone had spoken to me.

---

[6] For more information regarding this ministry see www.celebraterecovery.com.

These are the things that got me through the day. For there was a long, exhausting, real battle going on in my mind. I was in a severe depression. Satan was doing his best to destroy me and my faith in my God. But God was with me, protecting me, sustaining me, healing me, helping me through each and every day.

❦

God put many other ministries and people in my life to help me through this season as well. My sister, Cere, and her family took me into their home for ten months, until I was strong enough to move into an apartment on my own. My sister nursed me back to good health by getting me up every morning at nine and feeding me a healthy breakfast of oatmeal with raisins, walnuts, cinnamon (and I confess a spoonful of brown sugar too). I don't remember it now, but she tells me that I wouldn't finish my meal unless she was sitting down and eating with me. That's how bad I was. My sister would also take me everywhere she went: to the grocery store, to the park with her daughter, in the car to pick her daughter up from school, to her Premier Designs jewelry shows, and so on, just to get me out of the house every day. Often at night, my brother-in-law would make a big batch of popcorn and we would all watch movies together. This may all seem very simple and ordinary, but to me it was life-giving! It was best for me not to be alone at that time. And as a result, the life was coming back into me day by day, literally, as I continued to stay alive and keep going. I believe that when my sister gets to heaven she will have a beautiful jewel in her crown—her reward for what she did for me! I am forever grateful to her and her family!

❦

God also gave me a Stephen Minister.[7] This is a wonderful ministry where a person who has been trained by the church walks by your side and helps you through your hard time. I went once a week to the home of Miss Lillian, an 80-year-old retired missionary. She would sit and listen to me talk about my week. She would let me cry. Then she would offer words of wisdom, encouragement, and truth. She would praise me for my progress, which I did not see on my own. Then the biggest and most precious thing she would do for me was, to pray for me. There is something very powerful about *hearing* someone pray for you! This, too, helped me keep going. When the time was right and a sufficient amount of healing had occurred, Miss Lillian released me from her care so she could minister to the next person in need of her love and support. I am eternally grateful for the time and love she invested in me!

❦

Last but not least, God gave me a "Life Coach." In my eyes, Deborah was and still is like my own personal cheerleader! She sees my progress that I don't see on my own. During our sessions together, she points out my progress or victories and

---

[7] For more information regarding this ministry see www.stephenministries.org.

celebrates them with me. She cheers me on to keep moving forward and be all that I can be. In Deborah's own words,

> Life coaching is a way of uncovering who you are, your values, what you want for your life and how you're going to get there. Whether it be a life transition, career, business, prosperity or relationships, life coaching shines a light on things your might not have looked at before and then you are able to make better choices on living every area of your life in truth and with aliveness. I believe coaching promotes awareness…and once the awareness door is cracked…what's possible for you from that place?[8]

We live 1200 miles apart, so our life coaching sessions were held over the phone. It was for a homework assignment from my life coach that I made my first dreamboard in November 2006. My dreamboard was an assignment to help me look forward and not back. It was my dreams, passions, desires, and God's words of truth to me on poster board. I had words of songs and Scriptures, as well as words and pictures cut out of magazines, all on my dreamboard. My dreamboard helped me look forward and persevere. It helped me believe what was true instead of what I was feeling. It made God tangible to me. It showed me my progress. My dreamboard literally saved my life! I truly believe that.

Specifically, for any of you who have ever struggled with depression, you know that it hits you even harder at the holidays. I remember one night in 2007, during the Christmas season, when I woke up in the middle of the night feeling alone, sad, and hurting. So I got up and stood in front of my dreamboard at three o'clock in the morning and with tears streaming down my face, I said out loud, *Satan, I put you under my feet! God, You tell me You have plans for me, plans to prosper me and not to harm me, plans for a hope and a future. You tell me I matter to You. I am important to You. You love me. You will never throw me away. I have a bright future. The best is yet to come. This is going to end well for me because I'm a daughter of the King!* I stood there with tears streaming down my face as I pressed my dreamboard against my chest, as my way of crying out to God, asking Him to supernaturally sink the words of my dreamboard down into my heart. Then I was able to go back to bed and sleep in peace knowing I was going to be all right and make it through. It was extremely important for me to get my eyes off my pain and onto my God in order to make it through, and my dreamboard helped me do just that!

૱

Another gift that was put in my life when I first came to Florida was the book

---

[8] For more information regarding lifecoaching with Doborah see www.lifecoach-deborah.com.

Beauty by the Book: *Seeing Yourself as God Sees You* by Nancy Stafford.[9] On the first page I wrote the words, *This book was put in my hands in September 2005. It has transformed my life!* For it was through reading this book that I came to learn that I was beautiful just because God made me and there is no one else in the whole world like me. I give this book away to my hostesses at all my Premier Designs jewelry shows because I want them to know that they are beautiful too. Actually, I just gave another one of these special books away today to my new neighbor and wrote a note inside; it's a note I would want to write to every woman. It says, *May this book bless, help, and heal you as much as it did me. May you know and believe you are beautiful just because God made you and there's no one else in the whole world like you!*

That leads me to the next blessing that was brought into my life: Premier Designs.[10] It was through my sister, Cere, that I was introduced to Premier Designs while living with her those first ten months in Florida. It was through going to her jewelry shows and going to the Premier monthly trainings that I began to fall in love with the company: its philosophy, purpose, and objectives, and its people. So by November 2005, I too had become a Premier "jewelry lady," as we like to call ourselves. When I arrived in Florida, God said to my heart one day that He wanted me to learn to just enjoy being alive and enjoy being a woman. It was through Premier that I learned to enjoy being a woman. And it was through Premier's founder, Andy Horner, a precious man in his eighties, that I learned that I am special. I have value and worth. I am somebody. As I started believing these truths on the inside, it started shining on the outside. God transformed me; I blossomed. It was as though I had been this closed flower all my life and now He was breathing His truths into me about who I am, and I was opening up like a beautiful flower, blossoming into all God had created me to be!

God took care of me physically as well. On my first dreamboard, I had pictures of fruits and vegetables and a woman sleeping peacefully. God was telling me to eat right, get rest, and take good care of myself—for when you are in a depression, you are not doing a good job at those things. One day, through my friend Gretchen, I learned about a product called Juice Plus.[11] She explained to me that Juice Plus is simply 17 fruits, vegetables, and grains in a capsule! It was affordable, and since I had worked for a chiropractor many years previously who taught me a lot about nutrition, it made a lot of sense to me. For I thought, *I'm trying to eat healthier, but I know I'm not eating enough fruits and vegetables.* So I started taking Juice Plus

---

[9] For more information regarding this speaker, actress, and author see www.nancystafford.com.
[10] For more information regarding this direct sales jewelry company see www.premierdesigns.com.
[11] For more information regarding the Juice Plus product and the company behind it see www.juiceplus.com.

in 2005 and going to Juice Plus events where I would hear doctors speak on the difference that good nutrition makes. Today, at the age of 53, I feel better and stronger than I ever have. I am in the midst of a journey of learning to take better and better care of myself!

And for the grand finale of God outdoing Himself in making things go well for me— something I never dreamed of! In April 2010 I went with my mom on a line dancing cruise to the Panama Canal. Wow! I ask you, what could be grander or more fun than that? Nothing!

These Six Years of Singleness Were a Gift to Me

It was a season of God taking me from "broken to beautiful and blessed," or in the words of a plaque on my wall, "Just when the caterpillar thought the world had ended, it became a butterfly." That was me! Being single was my one-on-one time with God, Him having me all to Himself! It was not always an easy time, but it was a necessary time. It was my time of healing. It was a time of learning to let go of my picture for my life and letting God paint His. It was my time of learning to enjoy being alive and enjoy being a woman. It was my time of learning to have fun. It was a time with family and friends that I otherwise would not have had. It was a time of making new friends and forming new relationships. It was a time of rest and restoration, a time of preparation for what was to come. It was a special time, an anointed time, a time filled with hand-picked blessings from my God!

You Can Pray to God about Anything

On one of my early dreamboards, I had the words, "Smile, laugh, have fun!" For that is what God was telling me He wanted me to do. But I really didn't know how to have fun. I am more of a task-oriented, diligent, organized, check-the-boxes-off-my-to-do-list type of person. So having fun just didn't come naturally to me. But one day I found myself saying, *God, I really don't know how to have fun. Please teach me!* That's when I told my now-grown sons, *See, you can pray to God about anything!* And as ever, God answered my prayer. He sent me my friend Amy, who introduced me to beginner ballroom dance lessons!

Ever since I moved to Florida in 2005, I had this overwhelming desire to dance. First I took line dancing lessons with my sister on Wednesday afternoons at the local community center. My sister doesn't really like to dance, but she just did it because she loves me! Now about four years later, I was living on my own in an apartment, working full-time and going to school full-time. Life was good but I was exhausted, or as my friend Amy cheerfully put it, "All work and no play makes Tammy a boring girl!" And one day Amy told me she had signed up to take beginner ballroom dance lessons. I asked her to sign me up too. (I had to ask her three times, actually—she couldn't believe that I really wanted to do this!) I thought it sounded like fun and good exercise. Dance was that and so much more!

Dancing became another vehicle used to help save my life; it kept me out of depression. For, yes, four years had gone by and I was working hard at healing, but I would still dip into depression on and off, especially over the holidays. Dancing gave me something to look forward to every single week. When I was on the dance floor, I was not thinking about the pain of the past. I was not worried about my sons or scared about my future. I was just happy and in the moment. I was smiling, laughing, and having fun! On the dance floor, I became known by many as "the girl with the big smile"! Wow, when God turns things around in our lives, He turns them around completely! Little did those people know that only a few years prior I had almost died from a broken heart and from depression, but now I was being described as the girl with the big smile!

An Unexpected Surprise

I now know, realize, and believe that the reason I had such a strong desire to dance was because that is how God was going to bring me to meet the man I would soon marry (Genesis 2:18, 22). I met my husband, Allan, in February 2009 on the dance floor. He swept me off my feet by being kind, being a gentleman, and treating me like a lady. After dating for 15 months, Allan Rentsch and I married on January 22, 2011. God has given me a man who, in his own words, walks by my side and holds my hand while I reach for the next rung in this ladder that I am climbing. Once again, God outdid Himself in making things go well for me!

And God continues to outdo Himself to this day. In October 2011 while attending a Juice Plus national conference in Nashville, Tennessee, I had the unexpected surprise and blessing of seeing Josh Turner (yes, the same "Me and God" song Josh Turner) perform at the Grand Ole Opry! I didn't realize it at the time, but God later showed me that that was Him, shouting to me from heaven, "I LOVE YOU!"

Always Pray and Don't Give Up (Luke 18:1)

You might not realize it right now, but God Himself wants you, too, to see and know that He is shouting to you from heaven, "I LOVE YOU!" He has unexpected, good surprises and hand-picked blessings in store for you and your future. Just keep going and don't give up!

Always pray, because God hears and answers prayer!

And don't give up:

- Don't give up on God!
- Don't give up on His plan!
- Don't give up on His goodness!
- And don't give up on His Love!

Because His Love is going to work everything out!

3

Do You Know Him?

I would like to pause for a moment and ask you a very personal but very important question. Do you know this God, of Deuteronomy chapter 30, who outdoes Himself in making things go well for His children who love Him and obey His commandments? Or, put another way, do you know Jesus, the calmer of the storm that we read about in the Gospel of Mark chapter four? Below you will find a sermon I wrote for my preaching class at Asbury Theological Seminary. For me, it says it all. As you read, consider where you think you fit into this story.

Jesus Is the Answer to Your Storm

Have you ever gone white water rafting? Have you ever fallen out of the boat when you went white water rafting? Well, it's a frightening experience! About ten years ago, my family and I went white water rafting in North Carolina. It was beautiful—the clean, crisp water, the mountains all around us. One minute we were having a great time going down the river and the next minute my then 15 year old son, as well as my brother and his wife were all in the water, literally holding on for dear life! I am happy to say that, one by one, they were all pulled back into the safety of the raft by the guide! This is the closest I have ever come to experiencing fear while on the water; and it is just a glimpse of what the disciples must have experienced in the account recorded in Mark 4:35-41.

> [35] That day when evening came, he said to his disciples, "Let us go over to the other side." [36] Leaving the crowd behind, they took him along, just as he was, in the boat. There were also other boats with him. [37] A furious squall came up, and the waves broke over the boat, so that it was nearly swamped. [38] Jesus was in the stern, sleeping on a cushion. The disciples woke him and said to him, "Teacher, don't you care if we drown?"
>
> [39] He got up, rebuked the wind and said to the waves, "Quiet! Be still!" Then the wind died down and it was completely calm. [40] He said to his disciples, "Why are you so afraid? Do you still have

no faith?"
⁴¹ They were terrified and asked each other, "Who is this? Even the wind and the waves obey him!"

This incident occurred fairly early in Jesus' ministry. In the previous chapters, Jesus has called the twelve disciples. He has been healing the sick, driving out demons and teaching with authority in the towns and synagogues. On this particular day, Jesus had been teaching the crowd that had gathered. He taught while in a boat a short distance from shore where the crowd was gathered. He taught them in parables that day and when evening came, Jesus said to his disciples, "Let us go over to the other side." This is where our story for today picks up.

From what we read here, it seems that the storm came up suddenly and unexpectantly. And the storm came upon the disciples when they were both with Jesus and simply following His instructions to them, i.e., "Let us go over to the other side." They were being obedient to His request; they were doing His will and yet they find themselves in a storm, and not just any storm, but a severe storm. So severe that the disciples were fearing for their lives! So what did they do? They went to Jesus, who was sleeping, and woke Him up and cried out to Him for help!

It's true that sometimes we experience storms in our lives as the result of our sin and disobedience. But, it is also true that just like the disciples, we too can be doing our best to be listening to and following Jesus' voice and instructions to us and yet find ourselves in a severe, unexpected storm. When this happens in our lives, may we follow the disciples' example to us and know and remember that Jesus is with us in this storm and cry out to Him for help. For, Jesus is the answer to our storm!

I wondered if it might have been hard for the disciples to awaken Jesus. For we never want to awake a sleeping person. But in this instance, I doubt that it was difficult for them; for they were fearing for their lives. So they were going to wake Jesus up! But, I think about many Christians and how people often say, "I don't want to pray about that; it's too small. I don't want to *bother God* about something so small and unimportant." But you know, I have two children, a son 24 and one 22. They are both grown and live on their own, 600 miles from me. And I've received phone calls from my one son saying, "Mom, do I have to thaw my steak before I can cook it on the grill, or can I grill it frozen?" or some other cute, little cooking question. Then I've received a phone call from my other son, and just recently so, saying "Mom, I need you to pray for me. I'm not doing so well. My friend's roommate just shot and killed himself last night." Now, was I glad to receive both phone calls? Yes! Was one happy and light-hearted and the other heart-wrenching? Yes! But out of all the people in the world that my sons could have called, am I glad they chose to call me? Yes! Was I glad just to hear their voices? Yes! So, if I, a human parent, feel this way, how much more does our Heavenly Father feel this way? Go to him about everything, the big storms and the little storms in your life. He wants to hear from you!

Now, what was the result of the disciples going to Jesus? Jesus got up and confronted the storm, with just three simple words! Verse 39a says, "He got up, rebuked the wind and said to the waves, 'Quiet! Be still!'" and it was so! Verse 39b goes on to say, "Then the wind died down and it was completely calm." This reminds me of Genesis chapter one, when we read "And God said, 'Let there be light'…and it was so…'Let there be water under the sky'… and it was so… 'Let the land produce vegetation'… and it was so." We need to know that when God speaks, things happen! It's that simple!

How do you deal with the storms in your life? Do you panic or get fearful? Do you try to take control? Why not go to Jesus and let him handle it for you? Pray and ask Jesus to confront the storms in your life and He will do it; things will happen! My personal experience is that He will either calm the storm or, while the storm still rages around you, He will calm you so that you can make it through the storm. Either way, Jesus is the answer to your storm!

There is something very interesting in this passage that I never saw before. Look at this with me. Verse 36 states, "Leaving the crowd behind, they took him along, just as he was, in the boat. There were also other boats with him." The New Living Translation says, "…other boats followed," and The Message says, "…other boats came along." There were other boats out on the water when the storm came and when Jesus calmed the storm. Wow! So, the result of the disciples going to Jesus for help did not just affect them, but it affected everyone else on the water too, i.e., the other boats. They all saw and experienced the miracle! One could say that there was a rippling effect of blessings and good, as the result of the disciples going to Jesus for help. I love that! It is so encouraging to me. For I believe the same is true for us today! When we go to Jesus and ask Him to confront the storms in our lives and He acts, it will not just affect us but it will affect all those around us! So, keep praying! Keep talking to Jesus! Keep going to Him, asking Him to confront your storms, asking Him to do a miracle! Know that people are watching. They will see and experience the effects of God working in your life. My friend, know that God is doing something much bigger than you know or see or realize! Most of all, remember Jesus is the answer to your storm!

We cannot leave this passage of Scripture without addressing verses 40-41 where, we read, Jesus confronts the disciples' fear and lack of faith: "He said to his disciples, 'Why are you so afraid? Do you still have no faith?'" Ouch, this is hard to read. But, the Scripture does not tell us, we don't know, what tone of voice was Jesus using when He spoke these words? Was He stern and harsh or was He gentle and compassionate? Like, I so want you to have faith in Me! But what Scripture does tell us in the previous chapters is that the disciples have been witnessing miracle after miracle as Jesus has been healing the sick and driving out demons. So, in essence, He seems to be saying, even after all you have seen, "do you still have no faith?" Verse 41 gives us some encouragement that the disciples are herein beginning to understand who Jesus is, that He is indeed the Son of God. For we read, "They were terrified and asked each other, 'Who is this? Even the wind and the waves obey him!'" They are growing here in their faith and understanding of Jesus' supernatural power and authority.

Where are you in your faith today? Do you know and remember that Jesus is with you when storms come? Do you go to Him, asking Him to confront your storms? Or do you even know this Jesus that I've been talking about today? This "calmer of the storm." Maybe you can't relate to this story that I've been talking about. Maybe you relate more to my opening story than to this one. Are you in turbulent waters, hanging on for dear life to anything you can find, trying to keep your head above water just to survive in this thing called life? Do you need the guide, the Savior of the world, to powerfully yet lovingly grab hold of you and pull you safely into the boat of salvation in Him? He has the power and authority to save you and forgive your sins. He has the love for you to do it. Two thousand years ago, He laid His life down for you on the cross. He is just waiting for you to ask Him to do it! All you have to do is say three simple words. "Jesus, save me!" And it will be so! Jesus is the answer to your storm!

4

Learning to Listen

Storms will come. Part of learning to let Jesus be the answer to the storms in our lives is to learn to listen for His voice, seeking His direction, His encouragement, His strength, and His words of hope for us found in the truth of His Word. For many, this is a struggle—to read the Bible and receive a word of truth for the day that will truly make a difference. That is why I would like to pause, once again, and share with you something I learned many years ago that transformed my time spent with God and, ultimately, my whole life. Since then, I have seen it do the same for countless others, as I have shared it along the way. This three-point Bible study method of studying God's Word was first taught to me at Bible Study Fellowship (BSF).[12] My time with God became most alive and vibrant when I learned this way of studying His Word. It is so powerful and wonderful! Once I was taught this way of studying the Bible, I could not wait to get up in the morning to read my Bible! I couldn't wait to see what God was going to say to me! I believe this was the beginning of my learning to listen for His voice.

I , here and now, share this three-point Bible study method with you, in the hopes that it will bless you in some way as well. Below you will find my, once handwritten, notes that I took while sitting in a Bible Study Fellowship class—being taught this very special way of studying God's Word. Feel free to read the below instructions and make them own, i.e., tweak them to fit your personality and style and any time-frame constraints that may be in your life right now. Have fun with this! Enjoy getting to know your Heavenly Father better and better as you spend unrushed, focused time with Him.

---

[12] BSF is an international, interdenominational Bible study. For more details regarding Bible Study Fellowship see www.bsfinternational.org.

Three-Point Bible Study Method

Preparation

- You will need a pen, paper (notebook/journal), your Bible…
- You will need *time*…as Anne Graham Lotz taught us at her *Just Give Me Jesus* Women's Conference: Carve out the time to spend with God each day. Keep it consistently, as you keep an appointment with a doctor.
- Pray before you begin…

  Ask God to give you a teachable, moldable heart.

  Ask God to give you understanding of His Word through the power of His Holy Spirit.

  And ask Him to help you understand what He wants to say to you, *personally today*, through His Word.
- Now, read the passage of Scripture (usually a subsection of one chapter).

Step 1 (overview)

Answer the following questions:

    Who?

    What?

    Where?

    When?

Then write a short summary sentence.

Step 2 (digging for details)

Look for the truths in the passage of Scripture:

    Sin (to confess)

    Promise (to cling to)

    Action (to follow or not to follow)

Command (to obey or not to do)

Example (to follow or not to follow)

Then write a "truth statement" (regarding whichever truth is standing out to you/tugging at your heart).

Step 3 (application)

Change your "truth statement" into a question that *cannot* be answered with a yes or no, but demands an action to be taken. (Begin your question with a word like *how*, *who*, *when*, or *why*.) Now respond with prayerful, immediate obedience in answering the application question.

Example of Three-Point Bible Study Method

Prayer:

Heavenly Father, please help me, through the power of Your Holy Spirit today, to understand Your Word and what You personally want to say to me through it. Open my eyes and heart to things I would not see or understand on my own, and help me believe and act on what You tell me. I love You, Lord.

Step 1 (overview)

Read Matthew 4:18–20:
[18] "As Jesus was walking beside the Sea of Galilee, he saw two brothers, Simon called Peter and his brother Andrew. They were casting a net into the lake, for they were fishermen. [19] 'Come, follow me,' Jesus said, 'and I will make you fishers of men.' [20] At once they left their nets and followed him."

Who? Jesus and two brothers, Simon called Peter and his brother Andrew.

What? Jesus was walking by the sea and the two brothers were at work fishing.

Where? Beside the Sea of Galilee.

When? Since they were fishing, it could have been early morning, but the text does not give us information regarding the time of day. By the context of the Scripture, this was at the beginning of Jesus' ministry.

Summary sentence: As Jesus was walking by, He called two brothers to follow Him and become fishers of men!

Step 2 (digging for details)

Sin to confess: No sin to confess is seen in this passage.

Promise to cling to: If I follow Jesus, He can make me into a fisher of men. Jesus sees me when I am working and doing my normal, everyday tasks. He sees all I can become in Him and for Him.

Action: Take the time to go for a walk; you never know what may happen on that walk! Spend time with my siblings, working side by side with them. Do my work with the anticipation of Jesus showing up!

Command to obey: Come and follow Jesus.

Example to follow: Be like Jesus and take the time to stop what I am doing and spend time with people as they show up in my life today. Be like Peter and Andrew and immediately respond to Jesus when He speaks to me, even if it means leaving what is familiar to me and even if I may be afraid. It will be worth it!

Truth statement that is standing out to me the most: Take the time to stop what I am doing and spend time with people today.

Step 3 (application)

Possible application questions: Lord, what do You want me to stop doing so I can spend more time with people? Who do You want me to spend more time with right now? Who is right in front of me that I am failing to see, who needs Your love and a touch from You?

Note: Many times God's Holy Spirit will speak the answer as I am writing the question. I believe this happens so often because I am still and quiet and focused on Him; i.e., I am giving God the time and opportunity to speak to my heart. However, if I do not get an immediate answer to my application question, I simply write out a prayer regarding it. For example, I may write: *Lord, please help me slow down today and have eyes to see the person You want me to spend some time with for Your glory. Please bless our time together with Your love. Thank You, Lord.* Then I go about my day and sure enough, after spending time reading the Bible, underlining it, journaling about it, and praying about it, it is in the forefront of my mind throughout the day and He does it! God answers my prayer, showing me who He wants me to spend time with that day. I may get an unexpected phone call from a friend or a knock at the door. It will just happen, without much effort on my part, but now my job is to respond and stop what I am doing to spend time with that person!

5

Guide to Using Weekly Prayer Sheets

The Purpose of this Prayer Ministry

This ministry is designed for wives to meet together, for one hour a week, to pray and release God's power into our lives, our husbands, our marriages, and our homes.

- It is *not* a time of gossip, complaining, or grumbling, but rather a concentrated time of praying God's Word.
- It is a time of *no* "talking" (that we may honor God and our husbands, our families), but rather a time of *all* praying; for praying is where the power is!
- It is *not* a time of praying, "Lord, change my husband," but rather a time of praying, "Lord, *bless my husband*!"

I journaled the following thought on October 14, 1999: *Lord, may my husband become all the husband You want him to be, by me first becoming all the wife You want me to be! It begins by letting You change me, Lord.*

Note: I cannot stress enough how important it is to adhere to the above bullet point statements. They are exactly what was spoken to my heart by God's Holy Spirit, and not my *own* thoughts. Simply but earnestly said, these are not polite suggestions. They are instructions to follow, keep and adhere to week after week as you pray for yourself, your husband, your marriage and your home. Follow God's guidelines for praying for your marriage and be greatly blessed and amazed at what He will do!

What it Means to Pray Scripture

Praying Scripture is simply praying God's Word back to Him. It is personalizing and applying the truth of God's Word to your life and the lives of others. Some examples would be:

- Proverbs 21:9 says, "Better to live on the corner of the roof than share a house with a quarrelsome wife." Now personalized, I would pray, *Lord, help me to not be a quarrelsome wife, for Your Word says it is better to live on the corner*

of the roof than to share a house with a quarrelsome wife.
- Psalms 56:3 says, "When I am afraid, I will trust in you." Personalizing this for my husband, I would pray, *Lord, when my husband is afraid, may he trust in You.*

How to Conduct the Prayer Time

The prayer sheets are designed to be used as wives meet together in person to pray for one hour a week. However, they are a tool for you to use as the Lord leads you. For example, as an option, you might pray over the phone or pray through more than one sheet a week. You might pray with one other believer or meet with a small group of ladies in your home or at your church. Men may meet together to pray for their wives, themselves, their marriages and their homes or like my friend Gretchen and her husband do, couples may use the prayer sheets to pray through together. Whatever works for you!

Getting Started:

- Pray and ask God to show you who He wants you to pray with. If no one is put on your heart or in your path right away, begin praying the Scriptures on your own, rather than wait.
- For some, praying out loud with others may be something new, outside of your comfort zone. That is what is so beautiful about praying Scripture. All you have to do is pray exactly what is written there for you. It is the perfect place to start, and over time, you will become more comfortable with praying outloud.
- It is good to have your Bible open in front of you when praying through the prayer sheets. I suggest this for two reasons. First, that way you can pray the Scriptures from your favorite translation. Second, it is good to see the Scripture you are praying in its context. (Often, something in the surrounding passage will give you new insight or add to something you may want to pray.)
- When praying in a group, all stay together while praying through the praise, confession, and thanksgiving sections; then break into groups of two or three for the intercession time. Assign one person to be the facilitator (this can be the same person every week or you can switch it up and take turns); after an hour the facilitator will close the prayer time, thus honoring everyone's time.
- Note: You may find that God gives you additional Scriptures to pray. For this reason, blank prayer sheets are provided at the end of this book for you to fill in, as you see fit.

Personally, I pray every Wednesday morning with my friend Maggie. We live 600 miles apart, so we pray over the phone. We start our time together at 6:45 a.m. and end promptly at 8:00 a.m. We allow the first 15 minutes for sharing about our week. We adhere to the "purpose" and do not talk about our husbands; this is our "girl time" together, talking about ourselves and how we are doing. After 15 minutes, I, as the facilitator, turn our focus to our prayer time.

When praying through the intercession portion of the sheet, I first pray the Scripture for myself; then Maggie prays it for me. Next, Maggie prays the Scripture for herself; then I pray it for her in agreement. Then we move on and pray for our husbands in the same fashion until we have completed the entire prayer sheet (or until our hour is up, whichever comes first).

As noted earlier, if the hour is up before we have made it through the entire prayer sheet; I close our time in prayer by uniting our hearts together and praying whatever Scriptures are left to be prayed. For example, for Week 1 I would say, *Lord, Maggie and I unite our hearts together and we pray that You would bless our homes by making them a place where justice is lived out. For Your Word says in Proverbs 17:15 that "acquitting the guilty and condemning the innocent—the* LORD *detests them both." Lord, please help us to put Your Word into practice as it says in Luke 6:46–49, and by Your Spirit, Lord Almighty, bless this prayer ministry. We praise You that You are the Victor, Lord!"*

For the remainder of the week, in my time alone with God each morning, I pray the Scriptures again for myself, my husband, my marriage, and my home. This is very short and to the point and takes just a few minutes; but it keeps the Scriptures alive in me and gives the Holy Spirit opportunity to work and to open my eyes to how my prayers are, indeed, being answered.

When I have prayed through all eighty-nine prayer sheets, I start over with Week 1. That is because my life and walk with God are now in a different place, almost two years later; and God's Word is alive and active (Hebrews 4:12) and will minister to me in a new way.

Important - a word of wisdom regarding sharing answers to prayer! Know that you are going to be excited about answers to prayer that you will be seeing. For you *will* have answers to prayer, because you will be praying Scripture and praying in agreement with another believer. And God hears and answers prayer! Yet, you need to know that it is very important that answers to prayer *not* be shared at the beginning of your time together. Rather, I have learned that it is best and most effective for them to be *prayed* during the "thanksgiving" portion of your prayer time. This is because, *when praying*, the Holy Spirit will guide and choose your words, making sure they are not too personal, thus honoring your husband and family.

Be Encouraged regarding the power of praying for yourself and others! I want to share with you a very special passage in the Bible that gives us a powerful example of the power of praying for ourselves and the power of praying for others. It is the story of a young woman named Hannah. She is a woman of great faith and also of great pain. For you see she had been barren for years and desperately desired a child. The Bible tells us that Hannah, in her sadness and distress, cried out to the Lord for a son, and He heard her cry for a child and He gave her a son [Samuel]. 1 Samuel 1:10-11, & 20 (NRSV) says,

> [10] She [Hannah] was deeply distressed and prayed to the LORD, and wept bitterly. [11] She made this vow: "O LORD of hosts, if only you will look on the misery of your servant, and remember me, and not forget your servant, but will give to your servant a male child, then I will set him before you as a nazirite until the day of his death. He shall drink neither wine nor intoxicants, no razor shall touch his head." …[20] In due time Hannah conceived and bore a son. She named him Samuel, for she said, "I have asked him of the LORD."

This story reveals that God is a God who can and will perform miracles! He is a God who cares about the barren, the hurting, the downcast. He is a God who hears and answers prayer! All this in and of itself is powerful, wonderful and encouraging, but that's not the end of the story—there's more! When reading on into chapter two of 1 Samuel we find that God not only gave Hannah a son that she had so longed for, but He gave her so much more! 1 Samuel 2:21 tells us that Hannah went on to have even more children: three sons and two daughters, to be exact! And why was this? Yes, first and foremost, it was the goodness of God, but when looking closely at the text, we find that the gift of Hannah having more children was the *direct result of intercessory prayer.* [Hannah had not prayed and asked God for more children but someone else had interceded and prayed God's blessings for Hannah and her husband Elkanah!] The text specifically tells us that Eli, the priest, saw Hannah and her husband Elkanah come to the temple to worship each year and *he prayed on their behalf!* Eli had seen Hannah's faithfulness to give Samuel [the son God had given her] back to God [as she had promised—see 1 Samuel 10-11, above] and Eli asked the Lord to bless Hannah and her husband Elkanah with children. 1 Samuel 2:18-21 (NRSV) reads:

> [18] Samuel was ministering before the LORD, a boy wearing a linen ephod. [19] His mother used to make for him a little robe and take it to him each year, when she went up with her husband to offer the yearly sacrifice. [20] Then Eli would bless Elkanah and his wife, and say, "May the LORD repay you with children by this woman for the gift that she made to the LORD"; and then they would return to their home. [21] And the LORD took note of Hannah; she conceived and bore three sons and two daughters. And the boy Samuel grew up in the presence of the LORD.

Wow! God took note of Hannah and blessed her beyond anything she had asked for! And all because someone had prayed! Know that the same is true for you and me today. As you pray Scripture for yourself, your husband, your marriage and your home, I believe:

1) God will hear and answer the cries of your heart!
2) He will do miracles!
3) He will give you more than you ask for!
4) He will bless abundantly those you are interceding in prayer for!

And for those times when the answers to prayer may seem a long time in coming, I pray for you that you may you not lose heart; but, may the Lord keep you strong in prayer until His purpose has been fulfilled in your life and the lives of those you are praying for.[13]

How the Prayer Sheets Were Put Together

The very day that God's Holy Spirit birthed this ministry in my heart, when I came home from my prayer time at Moms In Touch, God flooded my heart and mind with His Word. I sat down at my dining room table and wrote as quickly as I could to keep up with the Holy Spirit. God was bringing Scriptures to my mind: Scriptures I had memorized, Scriptures on index cards that I had been praying for myself and my family, and Scriptures I had recently read. I wrote the Scriptures on pieces of notebook paper—Scriptures to pray for the wife, Scriptures to pray for the husband, Scriptures to pray for the marriage, Scriptures to pray for the home—and put them in a folder. I knew in my heart that God was sovereignly bringing them to my mind in the order in which He wanted them to be prayed. Thus each week when I sat down to put a new prayer sheet together, I simply went to the very next Scripture in line. I did *not* think to myself, what do I need to pray for myself this week or what do I want to pray for my husband this week, for I did not want my "flesh" to get in the way of God's work. Every week I stood in great awe of God's amazing love, power, and sovereignty as I watched His prayer sheet for the week unfold before my very eyes, many times with tears in my eyes as well. What a mighty God we serve!

The Power of Praying Scripture

1) Hearts, attitudes, actions, and thinking are transformed.
2) God's Word is prayed and not our own selfish wants.
3) God's power is unleashed to work in people's lives:

---

[13] Stormie Omartian, *The Power of Praying for Your Adult Children: Book of Prayers* (Eugene: Harvest House Publishers, 2009), 21.

Jeremiah 23:29 says, "'Is not my word like fire,' declares the LORD, 'and like a hammer that breaks a rock in pieces?'"

Hebrews 4:12 states, "For the word of God is living and active. Sharper than any double-edged sword, it penetrates even to dividing soul and spirit, joints and marrow; it judges the thoughts and attitudes of the heart."

4) God's desires and purposes are accomplished:
Isaiah 55:10–11 reads, "'As the rain and the snow come down from heaven, and do not return to it without watering the earth and making it bud and flourish, so that it yields seed for the sower and bread for the eater, so is my word that goes out from my mouth: It will not return to me empty, but will accomplish what I desire and achieve the purpose for which I sent it.'"

The Power of Praying Together

1) We pray in one accord with others.
2) True, sweet, intimate fellowship occurs.
3) Abundant encouragement is received.
4) God brings victory over discouragement and the temptation to give up.
5) Battles are won as we devote concentrated time to specific, fervent prayer of God's Word.
6) Our hearts are strengthened as we focus on praising God for who He is, His character, His attributes.

Words journaled in November 2000: *I journaled this [the entry following] in October 1999 in anticipation of God doing this, and it is now November 2000 and I have indeed lived and experienced this. I praise You and thank You, Heavenly Father...*

Thoughts journaled on October 15, 1999 (which still ring true today)

- Moms In Touch is a great and powerful ministry where I pray Scripture for my children, their teachers, and their school.

- But how much more do I need to first be bathing my husband and marriage in prayer (God's order of priorities, Genesis 2).

- For we women were first created to be helpers to our husbands; then came giving birth (I am a wife first, then a mom).

- What better, more powerful way to be a helper to my husband than to pray for him?!

- This is the greatest blessing I can give to my children as well, i.e., being devoted to God, His priorities and ways—by praying and unleashing God's power to strengthen our marriage and bless their dad and mold me into the wife God wants me to be.

God's Divine Order for the Family

<u>Colossians 3:18–21</u>

>[18] Wives, submit to your husbands, as is fitting in the Lord.

>[19] Husbands, love your wives and do not be harsh with them.

>[20] Children, obey your parents in everything, for this pleases the Lord.

>[21] Fathers, do not embitter your children, or they will become discouraged.

<u>Colossians 3:18–21</u> (TLB)

>[18] You wives, submit yourselves to your husbands, for that is what the Lord has planned for you. [19] And you husbands must be loving and kind to your wives and not bitter against them nor harsh.

>[20] You children must always obey your fathers and mothers, for that pleases the Lord. [21] Fathers, don't scold your children so much that they become discouraged and quit trying.

<u>Colossians 3:18–21</u> (The Message)

>[18] Wives, understand and support your husbands by submitting to them in ways that honor the Master.

>[19] Husbands, go all out in love for your wives. Don't take advantage of them.

>[20] Children, do what your parents tell you. This delights the Master no end.

>[21] Parents, don't come down too hard on your children or you'll crush their spirits.

God's Word on Marriage

Genesis 2:24

²⁴ For this reason a man will leave his father and mother and be united to his wife, and they will become one flesh.

Mark 10:2–9

² Some Pharisees came and tested him by asking, "Is it lawful for a man to divorce his wife?"

³ "What did Moses command you?" he replied.

⁴ They said, "Moses permitted a man to write a certificate of divorce and send her away."

⁵ "It was because your hearts were hard that Moses wrote you this law," Jesus replied. ⁶ "But at the beginning of creation God 'made them male and female.' (Gen. 1:27) ⁷ 'For this reason a man will leave his father and mother and be united to his wife, ⁸ and the two will become one flesh.' (Gen. 2:24) So they are no longer two, but one flesh. ⁹ Therefore what God has joined together, let no one separate."

1 Corinthians 7:10–16

¹⁰ To the married I give this command (not I, but the Lord): A wife must not separate from her husband. ¹¹ But if she does, she must remain unmarried or else be reconciled to her husband. And a husband must not divorce his wife.

¹² To the rest I say this (I, not the Lord): If any brother has a wife who is not a believer and she is willing to live with him, he must not divorce her. ¹³ And if a woman has a husband who is not a believer and he is willing to live with her, she must not divorce him. ¹⁴ For the unbelieving husband has been sanctified through his wife, and the unbelieving wife has been sanctified through her believing husband. Otherwise your children would be unclean, but as it is, they are holy.

¹⁵ But if the unbeliever leaves, let him do so. A believing man or woman is not bound in such circumstances; God has called us to live in peace. ¹⁶ How do you know, wife, whether you will save your husband? Or, how do you know, husband, whether you will save your wife?

God's Word of Instruction and Encouragement to Those Who are Married to Unbelievers

1 Peter 3:1–6

Wives, in the same way be submissive to your husbands so that, if any of them do not believe the word, they may be won over without words by the behavior of their wives, ² when they see the purity and reverence of your lives. ³ Your beauty should not come from outward adornment, such as braided hair and the wearing of gold jewelry and fine clothes. ⁴ Instead, it should be that of your inner self, the unfading beauty of a gentle and quiet spirit, which is of great worth in God's sight. ⁵ For this is the way the holy women of the past who put their hope in God used to make themselves beautiful. They were submissive to their own husbands, ⁶ like Sarah, who obeyed Abraham and called him her master. You are her daughters if you do what is right and do not give way to fear.

6

Weekly Prayer Sheets

Meeting together to pray and release
God's power into our lives, our husbands,
our marriages, our homes…

Week 1

- ❤ **Praise**[14] God is our <u>Victor</u>: "One who defeats or vanquishes an adversary; the winner in a fight, battle, or war."[15]
  - o Deuteronomy 20:3-4 "...Today you are going into battle against your enemies. Do not be fainthearted or afraid; do not be terrified or give way to panic before them. For the LORD your God is the one who goes with you to fight for you against your enemies to give you victory."[16]
  - o Joshua 21:43-45 "So the LORD gave Israel all the land he had sworn to give their forefathers...The LORD gave them rest on every side...Not one of all the LORD's good promises to the house of Israel failed; every one was fulfilled."
  - o Psalm 44:1-8 "...With your hand you drove out the nations and planted our fathers...It was not by their sword that they won the land...it was your right hand, your arm, and the light of your face, for you loved them. You are my King and my God, who decrees victories for Jacob. Through you we push back our enemies...I do not trust in my bow, my sword does not bring me victory; but you give us victory over our enemies...In God we make our boast all day long..."
  - o Psalm 118:13-17 "I was pushed back and about to fall, but the LORD helped me...[I] will proclaim what the LORD has done."
  - o Proverbs 21:30-31 "...Victory rests with the LORD."
  - o 1 Corinthians 15:51-58 There is victory over death through Jesus; therefore, may we stand firm. "...Always give yourselves fully to the work of the Lord, because you know that your labor in the Lord is not in vain."
- ❤ **Confession**   Psalm 86:5
- ❤ **Thanksgiving**   1) We thank You that You are forgiving and good, Lord.
  2) We thank You that You are bringing people to pray for their marriages.
  3) I thank You for Sunday's sermon guiding, encouraging, and teaching more about my role as a submissive wife. (Insert an example from your own life.)

---

[14] The *Praying Scripture for Your Marriage* prayer sheets follow the Moms In Touch format of praise, confession, thanksgiving, intercession. Please note that the "attributes of praise," their corresponding definitions (unless otherwise noted) and the Scripture references, were taken directly from the 1997 *Moms in Touch International Leader's Guide and Personal Quiet Time*, p.4.1-4.6. As previously noted, all other Scriptures [i.e., those regarding confession, thanksgiving, the wife, the husband, the marriage, the home, application, and this prayer ministry] are my unique compilation. For details see, "How the Prayer Sheets Were Put Together," page 37.

[15] "Victor." Def. 1. William Morris, ed., *The American Heritage Dictionary of the English Language*, New College Edition (Boston: Houghton Mifflin Company, 1976), 1428.

[16] Scripture quotations are from the New International Version unless otherwise indicated.

          4) We thank You for answered prayer, and that You fight battles that we cannot.
          5) _____

- ♥ **Lord, bless my husband by giving him a <u>wife</u> who…**
  - trusts You and chooses to hide beneath the shadow of Your wings until this storm passes...
  - Psalm 57:1-3 (TLB) May we cry to the God of heaven who does such wonders for us. Thank You that You will send down help from heaven to save us (this marriage) because of Your love and Your faithfulness.[17]
- ♥ **Lord, bless our <u>husbands</u>**   Salvation (if applicable): 2 Timothy 2:25-26 (TLB)
  - 1 Chronicles 29:19 (personalized) Lord, give them the whole-hearted devotion to keep Your commands, requirements, and decrees, and give them the desire and ability/power to do everything You ask them to do.
- ♥ **Lord, bless our <u>marriages</u>**
  - Give life to dead marriages, Lord, we pray!
  - Romans 4:17-21 God gives life to the dead...may we be fully persuaded that You have power to do as You have promised.
  - vv. 18-20 (paraphrased and personalized) Against all hope, may we hope in You, Lord...without weakening in our faith and when the facts seem to say our marriage is dead or this is impossible for You to do; may we not waver in unbelief regarding Your promises, Lord, but may we be strengthened in our faith and may we give You the glory (for bringing dead marriages to life).
- ♥ **Lord, bless our <u>home</u>**
  - May our home be a place where justice is lived out, for Proverbs 17:15 says, "Acquitting the guilty and condemning the innocent—the LORD detests them both."
- ♥ **<u>Application</u>**
  - Luke 6:46-49 Lord, help us to put Your Word into practice.
- ♥ **Lord, bless this <u>prayer ministry</u>**
  - Zechariah 4:6b "'Not by might, nor by power, but by my Spirit,' says the LORD Almighty." (Thought: By Your Spirit, Lord, give people the desire to make prayer a priority and their marriage a priority. Do as You will, Lord! It's all You, Lord!)
- ♥ **<u>Praise</u>**   You are our Victor, Lord![18]

---

[17] When Scripture has been personalized or paraphrased, it is not in quotation marks.
[18] The *Praying Scripture for Your Marriage* prayer sheets *end* with praise. I made this modification after listening to a message by Dr. David Jeremiah, in which he pointed out that the Lord's Prayer (see Matthew 6:9-13, NAS) both begins *and* ends with praise. (There is such power and hope received in praising God for who He is!)

Week 2

- ♥ **Praise** God is our <u>Hope</u>: "To be confident; trust. To look forward to with confidence of fulfillment; expect with desire."[19]
    - o Isaiah 40:28-31 (NIV) "…[God] will not grow tired or weary…those who hope in the LORD will renew their strength…" (NASB) "…Those who wait for the LORD will gain new strength…"
    - o Jeremiah 29:11-13 "For I know the plans I have for you,' declares the LORD…'plans to give you hope…'" (I do not need to fret, but rest in the fact that God knows His plan for me. I am to call upon Him, pray, listen to Him, and seek Him with all my heart.)
    - o Lamentations 3:21-25 Call to mind the truths of God's Word and have hope: "…The LORD is good to those whose hope is in him…"
    - o Romans 15:4, 13 We have God's written Word to teach us, so that through the endurance taught in the Scriptures and the encouragement they provide we might have hope…"May the God of hope fill you with all joy and peace as you trust in him…"
    - o Hebrews 6:17-20 Jesus is our anchor of hope for our soul, <u>firm and secure</u>!
    - o 1 Peter 1:3 Jesus is our <u>living hope</u>!

- ♥ <u>**Confession**</u> Psalm 103:8-19
- ♥ <u>**Thanksgiving**</u>
    1) We thank You so, Lord, for the truth and power and encouragement of Your Word.
    2) We thank You for the power of prayer.
    3) We thank You that You love us each one, and that You are always faithful to Your Word.
    4) _____ [20]

- ♥ **Lord, bless my husband by giving him a <u>wife</u> who …**
    - o holds her tongue!

---

[19] "Hope." Def. 2. William Morris, *The American Heritage Dictionary of the English Language*, New College Edition. (Boston: Houghton Mifflin Company, 1976), 634.

[20] This blank line is here for you so that you can record your own thanksgivings, thanking God for who He is and what He is doing in your life, as well as in your marriage and family. Since this prayer ministry is based on a time of *no talking but all praying*, this is where you can record and share the answers to prayer you are seeing, all the while honoring your husband and family by *not* sharing anything too personal that they would not want shared with others. Some examples may be: after praying Week 1's prayer sheet, you might pray here, "Lord, thank you that I had more hope in my heart this past week after focusing on Scriptures revealing that You are the Victor" or you might pray, "Lord, thank you that there has been more peace in our home as the truth of Proverbs 17:15 was prayed for our home and family last week."

- o Proverbs 10:19 "When words are many, sin is not absent, but he who holds his tongue is wise." (NIV) "When there are many words transgression is unavoidable. But he who restrains his lips is wise." (NASB)

♥ **Lord, bless our <u>husbands</u>**   Salvation (if applicable): Acts 26:18 (TLB)
  - o John 8:31-32 That they will hold to God's teaching/to His Word…and thus know the truth, and the truth will set them free (free from worry, discouragement, deceit of the enemy, etc.).

♥ **Lord, bless our <u>marriages</u>**   Psalm 31:19-24 (TLB) Know/trust God's truth…
  - o (v. 19) God has great blessings stored up for those who trust and reverence Him.
  - o (v. 20) Hide and shelter our marriages from conspiracies of the enemy.
  - o (v. 21) May God's never-failing love protect our marriages like a wall of a fort!
  - o (v. 22) God will never desert us or our marriages.
  - o (v. 23) God protects those loyal to Him.
  - o (v. 24) Depend on God!

♥ **Lord, bless our <u>homes</u>**
  - o Proverbs 17:19 May we not quarrel and/or build up walls, for "He who loves a quarrel, loves sin; and he who builds a high gate invites destruction."

♥ **<u>Application</u>**
  - o Luke 6:46-49 Lord, help us to put Your Word into practice.

♥ **Lord, bless this <u>prayer ministry</u>**
  - o 1 Chronicles 4:10 fourfold prayer of blessing:
    - o Bless this ministry indeed
    - o Enlarge its territory
    - o Empower this ministry; may Your hand be with it
    - o Keep this ministry free from sin…from bringing pain or harm upon itself or others.

♥ **<u>Praise</u>**   You are our Hope, Lord!

Week 3

- ♥ **Praise** God is <u>supreme</u>: Highest in rank, power, authority; superior, highest in degree; utmost.
  - o Deuteronomy 10:14-17 "To the LORD your God belong the heavens…the earth and everything in it…Circumcise your hearts therefore, and do not be stiff necked any longer…"
  - o Psalm 95:3-7 "For the LORD is the great God, the King above all gods. In his hand are the depths of the earth…let us bow down in worship…for he is our God and we are the people of his pasture, the flock under his care."
  - o Isaiah 44:6-8 "This is what the LORD says…I am the first and I am the last, apart from me there is no God…"
  - o Acts 17:24-28 "The God who made the world and everything in it is the Lord of heaven and earth…"

- ♥ **Confession**   Psalm 51:4-12 (see TLB and NIV)
- ♥ **Thanksgiving**   1) We thank You, Lord, that You are in complete control and thus we do not need to worry or fret about anything.
  2) We thank You that You love us dearly, more than we can comprehend (Romans 8:38-39).
  3) We thank You for the gift of being Your children.
  4) _____
  _____

- ♥ Lord, bless my husband by giving him a <u>wife</u> who…
  - o trusts in God to sustain and strengthen her…
  - o Psalm 89:21 "…My hand will sustain him; surely my arm will strengthen him."
- ♥ Lord, bless our <u>husbands</u>   Salvation (if applicable): 2 Corinthians 4:3-6
  - o James 4:7-8 That they will submit themselves to God, resist the devil, and he will flee from them. That they will come near to God and He will come near to them. That they will wash their hands of sin, that their hearts will be purified, that they will not be double-minded, we pray.

- ♥ Lord, bless our <u>marriages</u>
  - o Colossians 3:23 Lord, help us to work at our marriages with all our hearts as working for You, Lord, and not for men.

- ♥ Lord, bless our <u>homes</u>
  - o Deuteronomy 7:25-26 May no "detestable thing" be brought into our homes. Lord, clean up our hearts (and thus our homes); remove from us idols and covetousness, we pray.

- ♥ **Application**
    - o Luke 6:46-49 Lord, help us to put Your Word into practice, we pray.
- ♥ **Lord, bless this prayer ministry**
    - o Psalm 91:4b May Your faithfulness protect this ministry and be its shield, we pray.
- ♥ **Praise**   We praise You, Lord, that You are supreme!

Week 4

- ❤ **Praise**   God is <u>sovereign</u>: Holding the position of ruler, royal, reigning; independent of all others; above or superior to all others; controls everything, can do anything.
    - o   1 Chronicles 29:10-13   "…You are the ruler of all things. In your hands are strength and power…"
    - o   Job 42:2 "I know that you can do all things; no plan of yours can be thwarted."
    - o   Psalm 33:11 "The plans of the LORD stand firm forever, the purposes of his heart through all generations."
    - o   Matthew 10:29-31   "…Even the very hairs of your head are all numbered. So don't be afraid…"
    - o   Romans 8:28   "…In all things God works for the good of those who love him, who have been called according to his purpose."
- ❤ <u>**Confession**</u>   Psalm 32:1-5
- ❤ <u>**Thanksgiving**</u>   1) Oh, how we thank You, Lord, that You "control everything and can do anything."
    2) We thank You for all You are doing in our lives and the life of our marriages.
    3) We thank You that You are strong and mighty and gentle, patient and persevering with us.
    4) _____
    _____

- ❤ Lord, bless my husband by giving him a <u>wife</u> who…
    - o   is still, trusting God's Word…
    - o   Exodus 14:14 "The LORD will fight for you; you need only to be still." (My thoughts: The power of prayer: it stills, quiets, and calms our hearts.)
- ❤ Lord, bless our <u>husbands</u>   Salvation (if applicable): 2 Corinthians 10:4-5
    - o   Psalm 25:4-5 Show (<u>husband's name</u>) Your ways, O Lord, teach him Your paths; guide him in Your truth and teach him; for You are God my Savior; may (<u>husband's name</u>) put his hope in You all day long, we pray.
- ❤ Lord, bless our <u>marriages</u>
    - o   Hebrews 13:5-6 Help us, Lord, to keep our lives free from the love of money, being content with what we have because You have said, never will You leave us or forsake us. Help us to say with confidence, the Lord is our helper, we will not be afraid. What can man do to us?
- ❤ Lord, bless our <u>homes</u>

- o Proverbs 16:24 May our homes be filled with pleasant words, for they are like a honeycomb, sweet to the soul and healing to the bones.

♥ **Application**
- o Luke 6:46-49 May we put God's Word into practice!
- o Psalm 119:11 May we hide Your Word in our hearts that we might not sin against You. (Memorize one scripture this week.)

♥ **Lord, bless this prayer ministry**
- o Matthew 9:38 Lord, we pray and ask You to raise up prayer warriors for the life of marriages.

♥ **Praise**   We praise You, Lord, that You are sovereign!

Week 5

- ♥ **Praise**   God is <u>omnipotent</u>: All powerful; having unlimited power or authority; almighty.
  - o 2 Chronicles 32:7-8   "Be strong and courageous. Do not be afraid or discouraged…for there is a greater power with us…the LORD…"
  - o Psalm 147:3-11   The Lord has power to heal the broken hearted; great is our Lord and mighty in power.
  - o Isaiah 40:28-31   "…The LORD is the everlasting God, the Creator…He gives strength to the weary…"
  - o Jeremiah 32:17   "Ah, sovereign LORD, you have made the heavens and the earth by your great power…Nothing is too hard for you."
  - o Matthew 19:26   "…With God all things are possible"!
  - o Ephesians 1:19-20a (TLB)   "I pray that you will begin to understand how incredibly great his power is to help those who believe him. It is that same mighty power that raised Christ from the dead"

- ♥ **Confession**   Isaiah 55:6-12a

- ♥ **Thanksgiving**   1) Oh, thank You, Lord, that all things are possible with You and nothing is too hard for You.
  2) Thank You that You persevere in working with our hearts to make us more like Jesus.
  3) Thank You that You are always there for us to turn to.
  4) _____
  _____

- ♥ **Lord, bless my husband by giving him a <u>wife</u> who…**
  - o reminds herself of God's faithfulness and thus has hope…
  - o Lamentations 3:21-25   "This I call to mind and therefore I have hope: because of the LORD's great love we are not consumed, for his compassions never fail. They are new every morning; great is your faithfulness. I say to myself, 'The LORD is my portion; therefore I will wait for him.' The LORD is good to those whose hope is in him, to the one who seeks him."

- ♥ **Lord, bless our <u>husbands</u>**   Salvation (if applicable): 2 Peter 3:8-9
  - o Proverbs 15:16-17   May Your Holy Spirit lovingly speak Your truth to our husbands' hearts, Lord, that "better is a little with the fear of the LORD than great wealth with turmoil. Better a meal of vegetables where there is love than a fattened calf with hatred." May their hearts be filled with a fear of the Lord and God's love.

- **Lord, bless our <u>marriages</u>**   Give us singleness of heart in our marriages, Lord.
    - Jeremiah 32:39 "I [God] will give them singleness of heart and action, so that they will always fear me for their own good and the good of their children after them."

- **Lord, bless our <u>homes</u>**   Thank You, Lord, that…
    - Jeremiah 29:11-13 You know the plans You have for [<u>your family's name</u>]—plans to prosper us and not to harm us, plans to give us hope and a future. Lord, may You draw each one of us in our family to call upon You and come and pray to You, and thank You that You will listen. May each one in our family seek You. For Your Word says, "You will seek me and find me when you seek me with all your heart."

- **<u>Application</u>**
    - Luke 6:46-49 May we live Your Word, Lord, put Your Word into practice.
    - Luke 18:1 May we keep praying and not give up!
    - Psalm 119:11 May we memorize Your Word that we might not sin against you.

- **Lord, bless this <u>prayer ministry</u>**
    - Romans 12:2b May God's good, pleasing, and perfect will be done.

- **<u>Praise</u>**   We praise You, Lord, that You are omnipotent—all-powerful!

Week 6

- ♥ <u>Praise</u>   God is <u>omniscient</u>: Having infinite knowledge; knowing all things.
  - o Psalm 139:1-6, 13-14 God knit us together in our mother's womb; He knows us and is familiar with all our ways because He made us/He is our Creator.
  - o Matthew 6:8 "…Your Father knows what you need before you ask him."
  - o John 6:64-65 "…Jesus had known from the beginning which of them did not believe and who would betray him…"
  - o Romans 11:33-36 "Oh, the depth of the riches of the wisdom and knowledge of God!…"
  - o Hebrews 4:12-13 Nothing in all creation (including our thoughts and attitudes of the heart) is hidden from God's sight.

- ♥ <u>Confession</u>   1 John 1:8-9

- ♥ <u>Thanksgiving</u>   1) We thank You, Lord, that You love us so very much, more than we can fully understand, I believe, and You just want us to love You back/really love You, Lord. (It's that simple; I make it too hard sometimes.)
  2) Thank You that when we are too weak to carry on, You carry us through, Lord.
  3) Thank You for the gift of our husbands, Lord; they are especially hand-picked from You to us.
  4) _____
  _____

- ♥ Lord, bless my husband by giving him a <u>wife</u> who…
  - o always prays and doesn't give up…
  - o Luke 18:1 "…Jesus told His disciples a parable to show them that they should always pray and not give up."

- ♥ Lord, bless our <u>husbands</u>   Salvation (if applicable): Ezekiel 36:25-27
  - o Proverbs 15:18 that they will be patient men who calm quarrels, for Your Word says, "A hot-tempered man stirs up dissension, but a patient man calms a quarrel."
  - o Patient: "1) Capable of bearing affliction with calmness. 2) Tolerant; understanding. 3) Persevering; constant. 4) Capable of bearing delay and waiting for the right moment."[21]

---

[21] "Patient." Def. 1, 2, 3, 4. William Morris, *The American Heritage Dictionary of the English Language*, New College Edition. (Boston: Houghton Mifflin Company, 1976), 961.

- ♥ **Lord, bless our <u>marriages</u>**
    - o Jeremiah 31:4a build up our marriages, we pray (rebuilding our marriages on Your foundation/following the truth of Your ways, Lord, when need be, where we have done it our way instead of Your way, Lord/e.g. God's divine order for the family). May we remember that nothing is too difficult for You, Lord. (Jeremiah 32:17) (NASB)

- ♥ **Lord, bless our <u>homes</u>**
    - o Psalm 119:105 May Your Word be a lamp unto our feet and a light unto our path in our homes, we pray. The Living Bible words it this way: "Your words are a flashlight to light the path ahead of me, and keep me from stumbling." O Lord, may we as a family spend time in Your Word daily so that we may see what You want us to see and so that we may not stumble and get hurt.

- ♥ **<u>Application</u>**
    - o May we apply what we pray—that our husbands are a hand-picked gift from God to us. May we treat them that way; may our body language, attitude, tone of voice, etc., display respect…display a thankful heart/that they truly are a gift from God to us.

- ♥ **Lord, bless this <u>prayer ministry</u>**
    - o Zechariah 4:6b "'Not by might, nor by power, but by my Spirit,' says the LORD Almighty." (Thought: By Your Spirit, Lord, give people the desire to make prayer a priority and their marriage a priority. Do as You will, Lord! It's all You, Lord!)

- ♥ **<u>Praise</u>** We praise You, Lord, that You are omniscient—all-knowing!

Week 7

- ♥ **Praise**   God is <u>omnipresent</u>: Present at all places, at all times.
    - o Psalm 46:1-7 (NIV)   "God is our refuge and strength, an ever present help in trouble." (NASB) "...a very present help in trouble..."
    - o Psalm 139:5-18   "...Where can I go from your Spirit? Where can I flee from your presence?... If I rise on the wings of the dawn, if I settle on the far side of the sea, even there your hand will guide me, your right hand will hold me fast..."
    - o Isaiah 66:1-2   "This is what the LORD says: 'Heaven is my throne, and the earth is my footstool...Has not my hand made all these things...This is the one I esteem: he who is humble and contrite in spirit, and trembles at my word.'"
    - o 2 Timothy 4:16-18   "...The Lord stood at my side and gave me strength...The Lord will rescue me from every evil attack and will bring me safely to his heavenly kingdom. To him be the glory forever and ever. Amen."
    - o Hebrews 13:5-6 (TLB)   "...For God has said, 'I will never, *never* fail you nor forsake you.' That is why we can say without any doubt or fear 'The Lord is my Helper and I am not afraid of anything that mere man can do to me.'"

- ♥ <u>**Confession**</u>   1 John 2:1-2

- ♥ <u>**Thanksgiving**</u>   1) Thank You that You are always with every single one of us, Lord, and thus we do not need to be afraid; You are our helper.
    2) Thank You for your faithfulness and love.
    3) Thank You for the power of Your Word and Your Holy Spirit working in our lives.
    4) _____

- ♥ **Lord, bless my husband by giving him a <u>wife</u> who...**
    - o trusts the Lord and makes Him her hope and confidence...
    - o Jeremiah 17:7-8 (TLB)   "Blessed is the man who trusts in the Lord and has made the Lord his hope and confidence. He is like a tree planted along a river bank, with its roots reaching deep into the water—a tree not bothered by the heat nor worried by long months of drought. Its leaves stay green and it goes right on producing all its luscious fruit."

- ♥ **Lord, bless our <u>husbands</u>**   Salvation (if applicable): Isaiah 55:10-11
    - o Proverbs 15:23   That they will have a timely, apt reply, for "a man finds joy in giving an apt reply—and how good is a timely word!"

- ♥ **Lord, bless our <u>marriages</u>**

- Deuteronomy 33:26-29 Lord, hold our marriages with Your everlasting arms and drive out our enemies, the enemies against our marriage trying to destroy our marriage…for example, the enemy of Satan and our own stubborn flesh, our pride, pushing for our own way, selfishness, weariness, discouragement, despair, hopelessness, wrong priorities, disobedience to Your Word and Your ways, Lord, unforgiveness in our hearts, etc.

♥ **Lord, bless our <u>homes</u>** May the Sabbath be honored in our homes…
- Exodus 23:12 May it be a day of rest and refreshment; may we honor You, Lord, by honoring/obeying Your Word: "Remember the Sabbath day by keeping it holy." (Exodus 20:8)

♥ <u>**Application**</u>
- Luke 6:46-49 Lord, may we come to You and put Your Word into practice…dig down deep. (Personalized for me) Lord, I pray that I will come to You moment by moment each day seeking You and Your ways for my life, seeking how You want me to respond to my husband, respond to each situation of the day and as a result may I be a blessing, his encourager and #1 cheerleader. May I stand by his side through the hard times (for You stand at my side and give me strength: 2 Timothy 4:17).

♥ **Lord, bless this <u>prayer ministry</u>**
- 1 Chronicles 4:10 fourfold prayer of blessing:
    - Bless this ministry indeed
    - Enlarge its territory
    - Empower this ministry; may Your hand be with it
    - Keep this ministry free from sin…from bringing pain or harm upon itself or others

♥ <u>**Praise**</u>   We praise You, Lord, that You are omnipresent—"present at all places, at all times"!

Week 8

- ♥ **Praise**   God is <u>immutable</u>: Never changing or varying; unchangeable.
    - o 1 Samuel 15:29 "He who is the Glory of Israel does not lie or change his mind; for he is not a man, that he should change his mind."
    - o Psalm 100:5 "For the LORD is good and his love endures forever; his faithfulness continues through all generations."
    - o Psalm 102:25-27 "…But you [God] remain the same, and your years will never end."
    - o Psalm 119:89, 152 "Your Word, O LORD, is eternal; it stands firm in the heavens…you established them [your statutes] to last forever."
    - o Hebrews 6:17-19a "Because God wanted to make the unchanging nature of his purpose very clear to the heirs of what was promised, he confirmed it with an oath…"
    - o James 1:17 "Every good and perfect gift is from above, coming down from the Father of the heavenly lights, who does not change like shifting shadows."

- ♥ <u>**Confession**</u>   Psalm 86:5

- ♥ <u>**Thanksgiving**</u>   1) We thank You, Father, that You alone have the power to heal the brokenhearted and to set things right. You have the power to rebuild and repair and restore relationships.
    2) We thank You that You are perfect in faithfulness (Isaiah 25:1).
    3) We thank You that You never give up on us or Your purpose in our lives. We can trust You: You are good, always.
    4) _____
    _____

- ♥ Lord, bless my husband by giving him a <u>wife</u> who…
    - o has an undivided heart toward You and a heart that is teachable, walks in Your truth…
    - o Psalm 86:11 "Teach me your way, O LORD, and I will walk in your truth; give me an undivided heart, that I may fear your name."

- ♥ Lord, bless our <u>husbands</u>   Salvation (if applicable): Ephesians 1:17-18
    - o Proverbs 16:6 May they fear the Lord and avoid evil, for Your Word says, "Through love and faithfulness sin is atoned for; through the fear of the LORD a man avoids evil."

- ♥ Lord, bless our <u>marriages</u>

- Psalm 71:20-21 Lord, restore and build up our marriages we pray...restoring honor and comforting us once again, through it all...Your Word says, "Though you have made me see troubles, many and bitter, <u>you will</u> restore my life again; from the depths of the earth <u>you will</u> again bring me up. <u>You will</u> increase my honor and comfort me once again." (emphasis added)

♥ **Lord, bless our <u>homes</u>**
- John 16:33 We pray for Your <u>peace</u> in our homes, Lord; Your word says, "I [Jesus] have told you these things, so that in me you may have peace. In this world you will have trouble. But take heart! I have overcome the world."

♥ **<u>Application</u>**
- Psalm 119:11 Memorize one scripture this week: "I have hidden your word in my heart that I might not sin against you." May we choose to do this, Lord. There is power in memorizing Your Word!
- Lesson I learned from the book *A Woman After God's Own Heart* by Elizabeth George... The better follower I am, the better leader my husband will be...[22] Lord, help us to not just think about and/or not just pray about being a better follower of our husbands, but help us this week and always to live it out.

♥ **Lord, bless this <u>prayer ministry</u>**
- Psalm 91:4b May Your faithfulness protect this ministry; be its shield...from any schemes, hindrance, obstacles, etc., of the enemy, we pray.

♥ **<u>Praise</u>** We praise You, Lord, that You are immutable—never changing!

---

[22] Elizabeth George, *A Woman After God's Own Heart* (Eugene: Harvest House Publishers, 1997), 60-62.

Week 9

- ♥ **Praise** God is <u>faithful</u>: Constant, loyal, reliable, steadfast, unwavering, devoted, true, dependable.
  - o Psalm 146:5-10 "Blessed is he whose help is the God of Jacob, whose hope is in the LORD his God, the Maker of heaven and earth, the sea, and everything in them—the LORD, who remains faithful forever…"
  - o Isaiah 25:1 "O LORD, you are my God; I will exalt you and praise your name, for in perfect faithfulness you have done marvelous things, things planned long ago." (My thoughts: One definition of perfect is "complete; thorough" …therefore, this verse says to my heart: God is perfect in faithfulness, i.e., He is completely and thoroughly faithful!)
  - o 1 Corinthians 10:13 God is faithful to provide a way out when tempted.
  - o 1 John 1:9 God is faithful to forgive when we come to Him and confess our sin.
  - o Deuteronomy 7:9 "Know therefore that the LORD your God is God; he is the faithful God, keeping his covenant of love to a thousand generations of those who love him and keep his commands."

- ♥ **Confession**   Romans 5:20b
- ♥ **Thanksgiving**   1) O precious Heavenly Father, we so thank You for Your goodness and faithfulness, Your love, hope, and strength that You shower upon us as we look to You.
  2) We thank You for Your amazing grace.
  3) We thank You that You are real and right by our side every moment of every day.
  4) We thank You for the lives and marriages You are touching through this prayer ministry of Yours, Lord.
  5) _____
  _____

- ♥ Lord, bless my husband by giving him a <u>wife</u> who…
  - o devotes herself to prayer, being watchful and thankful…
  - o Colossians 4:2 (NIV) "Devote yourselves to prayer, being watchful and thankful."
  - o Colossians 4:2 (TLB) "Don't be weary in prayer; keep at it; watch for God's answers and remember to be thankful when they come."

- ♥ Lord, bless our <u>husbands</u>   Salvation (if applicable): Jeremiah 32:40
  - o Proverbs 16:7 May our husbands' ways be pleasing to You Lord, that even their enemies will live at peace with them.

- ♥ Lord, bless our <u>marriages</u>
    - o Psalm 94:17-19 Lord, may You help us that our marriages will not die…when we (our marriages) are slipping, thank You that You support us (our marriages)… when we are anxious, console us and bring joy to our souls, we pray and thank You, Lord.

- ♥ Lord, bless our <u>homes</u>
    - o Colossians 1:18b (NASB) that He Himself (Christ Jesus) might come to have first place in everything (in our attitudes, our actions, our activities).

- ♥ <u>Application</u>
    - o Psalm 119:11 May we continue to memorize Your Word weekly, helping us to hide Your Word in our hearts that we might not sin against You.
    - o Further applications from lessons I learned from the book *A Woman After God's Own Heart* by Elizabeth George …As wives, may we each day ask ourselves:
        - o Was I a blessing or a burden to my husband today?!
        - o Was I a help or a hindrance to my husband today?!
        - o Did I fit into my husband's plans today or did I fight for my own way?![23]

        This is a good checklist for me, regarding being a submissive wife.

        O Lord, grow us in leaps and bounds in this area, we pray, that You may be greatly glorified in our marriages.

- ♥ Lord, bless this <u>prayer ministry</u>
    - o Matthew 9:38 O Lord, we pray and ask You to send out prayer warriors unto the harvest of hurting, struggling marriages!

- ♥ <u>Praise</u>   We so praise You, Lord, that You are ever faithful!

---

[23] Ibid.

Week 10

- ♥ **Praise** God is <u>holy</u>: Spiritually perfect or pure; sinless; deserving awe, reverence, adoration.
    - o 1 Samuel 2:2 "There is no one holy like the Lord; there is no one besides you; there is no Rock like our God."
    - o Psalm 99:5 "Exalt the Lord our God and worship at his footstool; he is holy."
    - o Isaiah 57:15-19 "For this is what the high and lofty One says—he who lives forever, whose name is holy: 'I live in a high and holy place, but also with him who is contrite and lowly in spirit, to revive the spirit of the lowly and to revive the heart of the contrite...'"
    - o Luke 1:49-55 "For the Mighty One has done great things for me—holy is his name. His mercy extends to those who fear him..."
    - o 1 Peter 1:15-16 "But just as he who called you is holy, so be holy in all you do; for it is written: 'Be holy, because I am holy.'"
    - o Revelation 15:3-4 "...For you alone are holy. All nations will come and worship before you, for your righteous acts have been revealed."

- ♥ **Confession**   Psalm 139:23-24 and 1 John 1:8-9
- ♥ **Thanksgiving**   1) Thank You, God, that You are a forgiving God.
2) Thank You that You love us, each one, dearly.
3) Thank You for the gift of today, and that You have great plans and eternal purposes for each day.
4) Thank You that You heal, You give hope, You strengthen, encourage, comfort, provide...we are so blessed!
5) _____
_____

- ♥ Lord, bless my husband by giving him a <u>wife</u> who...
    - o does not lose heart when the Lord rebukes her...
    - o Hebrews 12:4-11 "...Endure hardship as discipline"; help us to "submit to the Father of our spirits and live...God disciplines us for our good, that we may share in his holiness. No discipline seems pleasant at the time, but painful. Later on, however, it produces a harvest of righteousness and peace for those who have been trained by it."

- ♥ **Lord, bless our <u>husbands</u>**   Salvation (if applicable): Luke 24:45
    - o Psalm 86:11 Teach (<u>husband's name</u>) Your way, O Lord, and may he walk in Your truth; give (<u>husband's name</u>) an undivided heart, that he may fear Your name.

- ♥ **Lord, bless our <u>marriages</u>**
    - o Psalm 146:9b (NASB) Lord, thwart the way of the wicked, we pray, and protect our marriages by Your faithfulness …
    - o Psalm 91:4b (NASB) "His faithfulness is a shield and bulwark."
    - o Bulwark: "1) A wall or wall-like structure raised as a defensive fortification; rampart. 2) Anything serving as a principal defense against attack or encroachment."[24] (My summary thought: anything used to protect or defend.)
- ♥ **Lord, bless our <u>homes</u>**
    - o 1 Corinthians 14:33 "For God is not a God of disorder but of peace…" Analogy/Application: Lord, we pray for orderliness in our homes, that our homes will be a place of order and thus peace, not chaos.
- ♥ **<u>Application</u>**
    - o Luke 6:46–49 May we come to You, Lord, and put Your Word into practice. (Live God's Word.)
    - o Psalm 119:11 May we hide Your Word in our hearts that we might not sin against You. (Memorize God's Word.)
    - o 1 John 3:18 says, "Dear children, let us not love with words or tongue but with actions and in truth." May we love with action this week by taking the action of writing our husbands a note telling them how much we appreciate them. (O Lord, help us to appreciate our husbands and not take them for granted.) This is just one suggestion of how to put love into action. Pray and follow God's leading in your life regarding this. God will faithfully reveal to you what will make your husband feel loved and respected, as you seek God's face.
- ♥ **Lord, bless this <u>prayer ministry</u>**
    - o Romans 12:2b Lord, we pray for your good, pleasing, and perfect will to be done in the life of this ministry.
- ♥ **<u>Praise</u>** Lord, we praise You that You are holy!

---

[24] "Bulwark." Def. 1, 2. William Morris, *The American Heritage Dictionary of the English Language*, New College Edition. (Boston: Houghton Mifflin Company, 1976), 175.

Week 11

- ❤ **Praise**   God is <u>just</u>:   Right or fair, impartial, upright, lawful, correct, true, righteous.
  - o Deuteronomy 32:4 "He is the Rock, his works are perfect, and all his ways are just. A faithful God who does no wrong, upright and just is he."
  - o Psalm 9:7-10 "The Lord reigns forever; he has established his throne for judgment. He will judge the world in righteousness…Those who know your name will trust in you, for you, Lord, have never forsaken those who seek you."
  - o Psalm 89:14-17a "Righteousness and justice are the foundation of your throne; love and faithfulness go before you…"
  - o Psalm 119:137-138 "…The statutes you have laid down are righteous; they are fully trustworthy."
  - o Psalm 145:17-20 "The Lord is righteous in all his ways and loving toward all he has made…"
  - o Isaiah 30:15-18 "…Yet the Lord longs to be gracious to you; he rises to show you compassion. For the Lord is a God of justice. Blessed are all who wait for him."

- ❤ **Confession**   Psalm 32:3-5 and 1 John 2:1-2

- ❤ **Thanksgiving**   1) O Heavenly Father, thank You for the gift of life You have given us.
  2) Thank You for the gift of being Your child, belonging to You now and forever.
  3) Thank You that "great are your purposes and mighty are your deeds" (Jeremiah 32:19a).
  4) Thank You that we are so blessed as we put our hope and our confidence in You, Lord (Jeremiah 17:7).
  5) _____
  _____

- ❤ Lord, bless my husband by giving him a <u>wife</u> who…
  - o fears You and puts her hope in You…
  - o Psalm 147:11 "The Lord delights in those who fear him, who put their hope in his unfailing love."

- ❤ Lord, bless our <u>husbands</u>   Salvation (if applicable): Psalm 18:16-17
  - o Proverbs 16:13 May they be honest and speak the truth, for "kings take pleasure in honest lips; they value a man who speaks the truth."

- ❤ Lord, bless our <u>marriages</u>

- o John 1:16 God's blessing upon our marriages, we pray, for "from the fullness of his grace we have all received one blessing after another."

♥ **Lord, bless our <u>homes</u>**
- o Psalm 31:19-20 (personalized and paraphrased) O Lord, shower Your goodness upon our homes/our families as we fear You. You are our refuge and our shelter. Fill our homes up with You and Your presence, that our homes will be a refuge to our families from the harshness of the world, we pray.

♥ **<u>Application</u>**
- o Luke 6:46-49 May we live Your Word!
- o Psalm 119:11 May we memorize Your Word!
- o 1 John 3:18 May we love with action and in truth this week, and always, by looking for our husbands' strengths and by choosing to focus on their strengths. May we make the deliberate choice to not focus on their weaknesses and on those things that irritate us; but, instead, may we remember Your Word, Lord, of Matthew 7:3 and may we focus on taking care of the plank in our own eye and then the speck will fade away!

♥ **Lord, bless this <u>prayer ministry</u>**
- o Zechariah 4:6b Bless, protect, and grow it, Lord: not by might, nor by power, but by Your Spirit, Lord Almighty.

♥ **<u>Praise</u>** We praise You, Lord Almighty, that You are just!

Week 12

- ♥ **Praise**　God is <u>wise</u>:　From root to know or to see; but wisdom goes past knowledge to understanding and action; having keen perception, discernment, power of judging rightly; always making right choices.
    - o 1 Chronicles 28:9-10　"…The LORD searches every heart and understands every motive behind the thoughts…"
    - o Proverbs 3:19-20　"By wisdom the LORD laid the earth's foundations, by understanding he set the heavens in place; by his knowledge the deeps were divided, and the clouds let drop the dew."
    - o Isaiah 28:29　"All this also comes from the LORD Almighty, wonderful in counsel and magnificent in wisdom."
    - o Daniel 2:20-22　"Praise be to the name of God forever and ever; wisdom and power are his…"
    - o Romans 11:33-36　"Oh, the depths of the riches of the wisdom and knowledge of God!…"
    - o James 3:17-18　"But the wisdom that comes from heaven is first of all pure; then peace-loving, considerate, submissive, full of mercy and good fruit, impartial and sincere. Peace makers who sow in peace raise a harvest of righteousness."

- ♥ **Confession**　　Psalm 103:8-19
- ♥ **Thanksgiving**　　1) O Heavenly Father, thank You for Your goodness to us all.
    2) Thank You that You are all wise, perfect in faithfulness, all powerful, You always do what is right; You are the most precious comforter and encourager.
    3) Thank You for Your love, for Your <u>unfailing</u> love.
    4) _____

    _____

- ♥ Lord, bless my husband by giving him a <u>wife</u> who…
    - o is not quarrelsome…
    - o Proverbs 25:24　"Better to live on a corner of the roof than share a house with a quarrelsome wife." (see also Proverbs 21:9, 19 and Proverbs 27:15-16)

- ♥ **Lord, bless our <u>husbands</u>**　　Salvation (if applicable): John 6:64-65
    - o Proverbs 16:32　Bless them and mold them into men who are patient and control their temper, for Your Word says, "Better a patient man than a warrior, a man who controls his temper than one who takes a city."

- ♥ Lord, bless our <u>marriages</u>
    - o Proverbs 18:10 "The name of the LORD is a strong tower; the righteous run to it and are safe." Personalized: Lord, we run to You with our marriages; in the name of Jesus we pray that You will make our marriages strong in You and keep them safe from the enemy, who would love to destroy them, and keep them safe from the enemies of pride, stubbornness, business, discouragement, wrong priorities, unforgiveness, bitterness, etc.

- ♥ Lord, bless our <u>homes</u>
    - o Nehemiah 8:10b to be filled with laughter/joy in our hearts…may the joy of the Lord be our strength.

- ♥ <u>Application</u>
    - o Luke 6:46-49 May we live Your Word!
    - o Psalm 119:11 May we memorize Your Word!
    - o 1 John 3:18 May we love with action and in truth by doing something special for our husband this week, just for him! Examples may be:
        - o Make his favorite dinner or dessert.
        - o Bring him his lunch or a dessert at his job site or at school if possible.
        - o Surprise him with a candlelight dinner one night…even if your budget calls for hot dogs!
        - o Give him a back rub.
        - o Write him a note.
        - o Greet him at the door with a hug and a kiss and a smile!
        - o Tell him you missed him today!
        - o Pray and let God give you the idea that will best bless your husband.

- ♥ Lord, bless this <u>prayer ministry</u>
    - o 1 Chronicles 4:10 fourfold prayer of blessing:
        - o Bless this ministry indeed
        - o Enlarge its territory
        - o Empower this ministry; may Your hand be with it
        - o Keep this ministry free from sin…free from bringing pain or harm upon itself or others

- ♥ <u>Praise</u>   We praise You, Lord, that You are wise!

Week 13

- **Praise**   God is <u>eternal</u>:   Without beginning or end; existing through all time; everlasting.
    - Exodus 15:18 "The LORD will reign forever and ever."
    - Deuteronomy 33:27 "The eternal God is your refuge, and underneath are the everlasting arms..." Refuge: "1) Protection or shelter, as from danger or hardship. 2) Anything to which one may turn for help, relief, or escape."[25]
    - Psalm 90:1-2 "...Before the mountains were born or you brought forth the earth and the world, from everlasting to everlasting you are God."
    - Isaiah 26:3-4 (TLB) "He will keep in perfect peace all those who trust in him, whose thoughts turn often to the Lord! Trust in the Lord God always, for in the Lord Jehovah is your everlasting strength."
    - Jeremiah 31:3 "...I [the LORD] have loved you with an everlasting love..."
    - Romans 1:20 "For since the creation of the world God's invisible qualities—his eternal power and divine nature—have been clearly seen, being understood from what has been made, so that men are without excuse."

- **<u>Confession</u>**   Psalm 51:4-12

- **<u>Thanksgiving</u>**   1) We thank You for You, Lord, for who You are and for the gift of being Your children.
    2) Thank You for Your goodness, Your love, Your forgiveness, Your power, Your patience.
    3) Thank You for the gift of this day, and that You have great purposes for this day (Jeremiah 32:19a).
    4) Thank You that You care about every detail of our lives (1 Peter 5:7, TLB) and (Matthew 10:30, NIV).
    5) _____

    _____

- **Lord, bless my husband by giving him a <u>wife</u> who...**
    - is submissive...
    - Ephesians 5:22-24 "Wives, submit to your husbands as to the Lord..."
    - 1 Peter 3:1-2   Lord, may we submit, honor, and respect our husbands in our hearts, actions, and attitudes.

- **Lord, bless our <u>husbands</u>**   Salvation (if applicable): Romans 1:20

---

[25] "Refuge." Def. 1, 3. Ibid., 1094.

- o Proverbs 18:12 May they be humble, for Your Word says, "Before his downfall a man's heart is proud, but humility comes before honor."

♥ **Lord, bless our marriages**
- o Proverbs 18:13 May we be good listeners to one another as husband and wife, for Your Word says, "He who answers before listening—that is his folly and his shame."

♥ **Lord, bless our homes**
- o to be filled with love…
- o Romans 5:5 (NASB) "Hope does not disappoint, because the love of God has been poured out within our hearts through the Holy Spirit who was given to us."
- o 1 Corinthians 13:2b (NIV) "If I have a faith that can move mountains, but have not love, I am nothing."
- o 1 Corinthians 16:14 (NIV) "Do everything in love."

♥ **Application**
- o Luke 6:46-49 May we live Your Word!
- o Psalm 119:11 May we memorize Your Word!
- o May we remember/think upon the details of our marriage vows and live them out this week and always!

♥ **Lord, bless this prayer ministry**
- o Psalm 91:4b May Your faithfulness be its shield and rampart, Lord, we pray.

♥ **Praise** We praise You, Lord, that You are eternal!

Week 14

- ♥ **Praise**   God is the <u>Creator</u>: The One who brought the universe and all matter of life in it into existence.
    - o Genesis 1:1-2 "In the beginning God created the heavens and the earth..."
    - o Psalm 95:3-7 "...Let us kneel before the LORD our Maker, for he is our God and we are the people of his pasture, the flock under his care."
    - o Jeremiah 32:17 "Ah, Sovereign LORD, you have made the heavens and the earth by your great power and outstretched arm. Nothing is too hard for you."
    - o Acts 17:24-28 "The God who made the world and everything in it is the Lord of heaven and earth...he himself gives all men life and breath and everything else..."

- ♥ **Confession**   Psalm 32:1-5

- ♥ **Thanksgiving**   1) Thank You, Lord, for creating us, giving us life, saving our souls, and making us whole.
    2) Thank You for all the hard times You have seen us through: all the times You carried us, comforted us, encouraged us, cheered us on...would not let us give up.
    3) We thank You that no matter what life holds, we are Yours, You love us, and nothing can ever change those truths...what a wonderful thing.
    4) Thank You that You are always there.
    5) _____
    _____

- ♥ **Lord, bless my husband by giving him a <u>wife</u> who**...
    - o has a quiet and gentle spirit...
    - o 1 Peter 3:3-4 "...the unfading beauty of a gentle and quiet spirit..." (peace in the midst of the storm; Holy Spirit, be my thermostat; keep me on an even keel).

- ♥ **Lord, bless our <u>husbands</u>**   Salvation (if applicable): Matthew 18:12-14
    - o Psalm 18:1-3 May this be our husbands' heart, we pray: "I love you O LORD, my strength. The LORD is my rock, my fortress and my deliverer; my God is my rock, in whom I take refuge. He is my shield and the horn of my salvation, my stronghold. I call to the LORD, who is worthy of praise, and I am saved from my enemies."

- ♥ **Lord, bless our <u>marriages</u>**

- o Proverbs 18:24b May we (myself and my spouse) know and remember that "there is a friend who sticks closer than a brother"—Jesus.
- o Friend: "1) One with whom one is allied in a struggle or cause; a comrade. 2) One who supports, sympathizes with..."[26]
- o May we remember that You, Lord Jesus, are our help and supporter; with You this marriage can stand and be wonderful (my thoughts) and help us to be a friend to each other as husband and wife, Lord, we pray.

♥ **Lord, bless our <u>homes</u>**
- o Psalm 139:23-24 Fill our homes with right attitudes, we pray: "Search me, O God, and know my heart; test me and know my anxious thoughts. See if there is any offensive way in me, and lead me in the way everlasting."

♥ **<u>Application</u>**
- o Luke 6:46-49 May we live Your Word!
- o Psalm 119:11 May we memorize Your Word!
- o 1 John 3:18 May we love with action and truth by:
  - o <u>Appreciating</u>
  - o <u>Admiring</u>
  - o <u>Accepting</u> and
  - o <u>Adapting to</u> our husbands[27]

♥ **Lord, bless this <u>prayer ministry</u>**
- o Matthew 9:38 We pray and ask You, Lord, to send out workers; call wives to pray for their husbands and marriages, raise up prayer warriors, we pray.

♥ **<u>Praise</u>** We praise You, Lord, that You are our Creator!

---

[26] "Friend." Def. 4, 5. Ibid., 527.
[27] I first learned this principle of the 4 A's [appreciate, admire, accept, adapt to your husband] while attending a women's weekly small-group Bible study, in 2001. The Bible study leader's words struck a cord with me, so much so, that I decided to implement them into the "application" section of the prayer sheets.

Always Pray & Don't Give Up (Luke 18:1)

Week 15

- ♥ **Praise**   God is <u>good</u>:   Virtuous, excellent; upright; God is essentially, absolutely, and consummately good.
  - o Psalm 25:8 "Good and upright is the LORD, therefore he instructs sinners in his ways."
  - o Psalm 34:8-10 "Taste and see that the LORD is good…those who seek the LORD lack no good thing."
  - o Psalm 86:5 "You are forgiving and good, O LORD, abounding in love to all who call to you."
  - o Psalm 119:68 "You are good, and what you do is good; teach me your decrees."
  - o Psalm 136:1 "Give thanks to the LORD, for he is good. His love endures forever."
  - o Psalm 145:8-9 "…The LORD is good to all; he has compassion on all he has made."

- ♥ **Confession**   Isaiah 55:6-11

- ♥ **Thanksgiving**
  1) We thank You, Lord, for Your goodness bestowed upon all of our lives.
  2) We thank You for Your faithfulness to Your Word.
  3) We thank You that You are the Master rebuilder, repairer, restorer and the Master "untangler" of our tangled-up lives.
  4) We thank You that You are so very patient, forgiving, and persevering in our lives. You are so good to us all.
  5) _____
  _____

- ♥ Lord, bless my husband by giving him a <u>wife</u> who…
  - o does not look at a speck in his eye when there is a plank in her own…
  - o Matthew 7:3-5 "Why do you look at the speck of sawdust in your brother's eye and pay no attention to the plank in your own eye?..."

- ♥ Lord, bless our <u>husbands</u>   Salvation (if applicable): 2 Timothy 2:24-26
  - o Psalm 139:10 that Your hand will guide them, may Your right hand hold them fast (see vv. 5-10).

- ♥ Lord, bless our <u>marriages</u>
  - o Psalm 1:3 May our marriages be like a tree planted by streams of water, which yields its fruit in season and whose leaf does not wither (see vv. 1-3).

- ♥ Lord, bless our <u>homes</u>

- o Isaiah 32:17-18 May our homes be peaceful dwelling places, secure homes, undisturbed places of rest.

♥ **Application**
- o Psalm 119:11 May we memorize Your Word!
- o May we:
    - o Think only Truth: Philippians 4:8 and Joshua 1:8
    - o Live only Truth: Luke 6:46-49 and Joshua 1:8
    - o Think only about today (thus not worrying about tomorrow): Matthew 6:33-34
    - o Delight in correction: Proverbs 3:11-12

  In my heart this is a lifelong assignment God has given me as His child.

♥ Lord, bless this <u>prayer ministry</u>
- o Romans 12:2b God's good, pleasing, and perfect will be done.

♥ **Praise**   We praise You, Lord, that You are good!

Week 16

- ♥ **Praise** God is <u>Jehovah</u>: The Self Existent One, I Am. The true eternal God, the one who is, used 6519 times in the Old Testament translated LORD or Lord God.
  - o Exodus 3:13-15 God gave himself the name "I Am"…"to be remembered from generation to generation."
  - o 1 Chronicles 16:23-29 "…For great is the LORD and most worthy of praise; he is to be feared above all gods…Ascribe to the LORD the glory due his name…"
  - o Psalm 102:27 "But you remain the same, and your years will never end."
  - o Psalm 105:1-8 "Give thanks to the LORD, call on his name…Remember the wonders he has done…He is the LORD our God…"
  - o Jeremiah 16:19-21 "O LORD, my strength and my fortress, my refuge in time of distress…I will teach them my power and might. Then they will know that my name is the LORD."
  - o John 8:58 "'I tell you the truth,' Jesus answered, 'before Abraham was born, I am!'"

- ♥ <u>Confession</u>   1 John 1:8-9

- ♥ <u>Thanksgiving</u>
  1) We thank You, Heavenly Father, that You love us so much more than we can comprehend, I believe.
  2) We thank You for Your constant goodness and grace to us.
  3) Thank You that You are our Father, our Good Shepherd, our help, our hope, our strength, our joy, our friend all at the same time.
  4) Thank You, Lord, for the opportunities You are giving to share this prayer ministry with others and for how You so powerfully, lovingly, and sovereignly work in all our lives. You are good always. You are always here for us.
  5) _____

  _____

- ♥ Lord, bless my husband by giving him a <u>wife</u> who…
  - o builds him up…
  - o Ephesians 4:29 "Do not let any unwholesome talk come out of your mouths, but only what is helpful for building others up according to their needs, that it may benefit those who listen."

- ♥ Lord, bless our <u>husbands</u>   Salvation (if applicable): Acts 26:18 (see TLB)

- o Psalm 20:1-2 "May the LORD answer you when you are in distress; may the name of the God of Jacob protect you. May he send you help from the sanctuary and grant you support from Zion."

♥ **Lord, bless our <u>marriages</u>**
- o Psalm 40:11-14 (personalized for our marriages) Do not withhold Your mercy from us, O Lord; may Your love and truth always protect us/our marriage. For troubles without number surround us (business, discouragement, wrong priorities), our sins have overtaken us and we cannot see. They are more than the hairs of my head, and my heart fails within me. Be pleased, O Lord, to save our marriage; O Lord, come quickly to help us. May all who seek to take the life of our marriage be put to shame and confusion; may all who desire the ruin of this marriage (seen and unseen) be turned to disgrace.

♥ **Lord, bless our <u>homes</u>**
- o Ephesians 4:29 May our homes be a place of encouragement, building up, gracious speech...

♥ **<u>Application</u>**
- o Luke 6:46-49 May we live Your Word!
- o Psalm 119:11 May we memorize Your Word!
- o Genesis 2:18 "The LORD God said, 'It is not good for the man to be alone. I will make a helper suitable for him.'" May we live out being a helper to our husbands. May we pray and ask God to show us each day how we can specifically be a helper to our husbands that day!

♥ **Lord, bless this <u>prayer ministry</u>**
- o Zechariah 4:6b "'Not by might, nor by power, but by my Spirit,' says the LORD Almighty"... Your will by Your Spirit for this ministry, we pray, and Lord we pray also that by Your Spirit...give people the desire to make prayer a priority and their marriage a priority...for Your glory, Lord!

♥ **<u>Praise</u>** We praise You, Lord, that You are Jehovah!

Week 17

- ♥ <u>Praise</u>   God is <u>Jehovah Tsidkenu</u>: The Lord Our Righteousness
  - o Jeremiah 23:5-6 "…This is the name by which he will be called: The LORD Our Righteousness."
  - o Ezekiel 36:25-27 "…I will cleanse you from all your impurities and from all your idols. I will give you a new heart…"
  - o Romans 3:21-26 "But now a righteousness from God, apart from the law, has been made known…"
  - o Romans 5:17-19 "…receive God's abundant provision of grace…the gift…Jesus Christ…"
  - o 2 Corinthians 5:21 "God made him who had no sin to be sin for us, so that in him we might become the righteousness of God."
  - o 1 John 1:7-9 "…If we confess our sins, he is faithful and just and will forgive us our sins and purify us from all unrighteousness."

- ♥ <u>Confession</u>   1 John 2:1-2

- ♥ <u>Thanksgiving</u>   1) Thank You for Your abundant provision of grace in our lives, Heavenly Father; thank You for Jesus; thank You for the gift of being Your child.
  2) Thank You that You have Your perfect, good plan for each of us, Lord.
  3) Thank You that You are the answer to all things!
  4) Thank You for loving us so, simply because we are Yours!
  5) _____
  _____

- ♥ Lord, bless my husband by giving him a <u>wife</u> who…
  - o is patient and gentle…
  - o Proverbs 25:15 (NIV) "Through patience a ruler can be persuaded, and a gentle tongue can break a bone."
  - o Proverbs 25:15 (MSG) "Patient persistence pierces through indifference; gentle speech breaks down rigid defenses."

- ♥ Lord, bless our <u>husbands</u>   Salvation (if applicable): 2 Corinthians 4:3-6
  - o Psalm 32:8-9 Lord, may You instruct (husband's name) and teach him in the way he should go; counsel (husband's name) and watch over him. May (husband's name) not be like the horse or the mule, which have no understanding but must be controlled by bit and bridle or they will not come to You. For (v. 10) "Many are the woes of the wicked, but the LORD's unfailing love surrounds the man who trusts in him."

- ♥ Lord, bless our <u>marriages</u>
  - o Psalm 18:16-19 (personalized for our marriages) Reach down from on high and take hold of our marriages, Lord. Draw them up out of deep waters. Rescue our marriages from our powerful enemy, from our foes (Satan, fatigue, despair, discouragement, business, pride, stubbornness, wrong priorities, unforgiveness, disrespect, hard hearts, unwillingness to do things God's way, etc.), who are too strong for us. They confront us in the day of our disaster, but You, Lord, are our support…rescue our marriages because You delight in us.

- ♥ Lord, bless our <u>homes</u>
  - o Psalm 141:9-10 We pray protection from the evil one and his schemes/deceit: Keep us from the snares they have laid for us, from the traps set by evildoers. Let the wicked fall into their own nets, while we pass by in safety.

- ♥ <u>Application</u>
  - o Luke 6:46-49 May we live Your Word!
  - o Psalm 119:11 May we memorize Your Word!
  - o Philippians 2:3-4 May we study our husband…what are his likes, dislikes, interests…may we line ourselves up with him. For Your Word says, "Do nothing out of selfish ambition or vain conceit, but in humility consider others better than yourselves. Each of you should look not only to your own interest, but also to the interest of others."

- ♥ Lord, bless this <u>prayer ministry</u>
  - o 1 Chronicles 4:10 fourfold prayer of blessing:
    - o Bless this ministry
    - o Enlarge its territory
    - o Empower this ministry; may Your hand be with it
    - o Keep this ministry free from sin…free from bringing pain or harm upon itself or others

- ♥ **<u>Praise</u>** We praise You, Lord, that You are our Righteousness!

Week 18

- ♥ **Praise** God is <u>Jehovah McKaddesh</u>: The Lord Who Sanctifies—Sanctified means set apart for holy use. It is the Holy Spirit who empowers us to live holy lives.
  - o Exodus 31:12-13 "...Say to the Israelites, 'You must observe my Sabbaths. This will be a sign between me and you for the generations to come, so you may know that I am the LORD, who makes you holy.'"
  - o Leviticus 20:8 "Keep my decrees and follow them. I am the LORD, who makes you holy."
  - o Ephesians 4:11-16 "...Speaking the truth in love, we will in all things grow up into him who is the Head, that is, Christ..."
  - o Philippians 1:6 (NIV) "...being confident of this, that he who began a good work in you will carry it on to completion until the day of Christ Jesus." (TLB) "And I am sure that God who began the good work within you will keep right on helping you grow in his grace until his task within you is finally finished on that day when Jesus Christ returns."
  - o 1 Thessalonians 5:23-24 (NIV) "May God himself, the God of peace, sanctify you through and through. May your whole spirit, soul and body be kept blameless at the coming of our Lord Jesus Christ. The one who calls you is faithful and he will do it." (TLB) "May the God of peace himself make you entirely pure and devoted to God; and may your spirit and soul and body be kept strong and blameless until that day when our Lord Jesus Christ comes back again. God, who called you to become his child will do all this for you, just as he promised."
  - o 1 Peter 2:9 "...a people belonging to God...declare the praises of him who called you out of darkness into his wonderful light."

- ♥ **Confession**   Psalm 86:5
- ♥ **Thanksgiving**   1) Thank You for the gift of being Your children, being called out of the darkness into Your wonderful light.
  2) Thank You for pouring into our hearts a love for You, Lord, and for Your Word; thank You for how You and Your Word have carried us through all things and always will, for You are faithful.
  3) Thank You for all that You will do!
  4) Thank You for all the things You are doing that we can't see!
  5) _____
  _____

- ♥ **Lord, bless my husband by giving him a <u>wife</u> who...**

- is submissive even when he may be unreasonable…
- 1 Peter 2:18 (NASB) (Applying this verse to our marriages, our role as a wife) "Servants, be submissive to your masters with all respect, not only to those who are good and gentle, but also to those who are unreasonable."
- 1 Peter 2:18 (NIV) "Slaves, submit yourselves to your masters with all respect, not only to those who are good and considerate, but also to those who are harsh."

♥ **Lord, bless our <u>husbands</u>**   Salvation (if applicable): 2 Corinthians 10:4-5
  - Psalm 20:7 May they put their trust in You, Lord, and not in their own strength, etc., for Your Word says, "Some trust in chariots and some in horses, but we trust in the name of the LORD our God." (v. 8) "They are brought to their knees and fall, but we rise up and stand firm."

♥ **Lord, bless our <u>marriages</u>**
  - Jeremiah 20:11a May we remember and thus have hope…the Lord is with us like a mighty warrior fighting for our marriages, fighting so that our enemy will not prevail.

♥ **Lord, bless our <u>homes</u>**
  - May they be a place of truthfulness:
    - John 8:32 know the truth
    - John 14:6 Jesus is the truth
    - Zechariah 8:16 speak the truth to each other
    - Ephesians 4:15 speak the truth in love

♥ **<u>Application</u>**
  - Psalm 119:11 May we memorize Your Word!
  - Luke 6:46-49 May we come to You, Lord, and put Your Word into practice (live it!)…dig down deep that we will stand through the storms of life!

♥ **Lord, bless this <u>prayer ministry</u>**
  - Psalm 91:4b May Your faithfulness protect this ministry; be its shield…from any schemes, hindrances, or obstacles of the enemy, we pray.

♥ **<u>Praise</u>** We praise You, Lord, that You are the Lord Who Sanctifies!

Week 19

♥ **Praise**   God is <u>Jehovah Shalom</u>:   The Lord Our Peace—Since we have been justified through faith, we have peace with God through our LORD Jesus Christ. (Romans 5:1)

- Judges 6:22-24a "…The LORD said to him, 'Peace! Do not be afraid'…The LORD is Peace."
- Isaiah 9:6 "For to us a child is born, to us a son is given, and the government will be on his shoulders. And he will be called Wonderful, Counselor, Mighty God, Everlasting Father, Prince of Peace."
- Isaiah 26:3-4 (NIV) "You will keep in perfect peace him whose mind is steadfast, because he trusts in you. Trust in the LORD forever, for the LORD, the LORD, is the Rock eternal." (TLB) "He will keep in perfect [My thoughts: complete, thorough] peace all those who trust in him, whose thoughts turn often to the Lord! Trust in the Lord God always, for in the Lord Jehovah is your everlasting strength."
- John 14:25-27 "…Peace I leave with you; my peace I give you. I do not give to you as the world gives. Do not let your hearts be troubled and do not be afraid." (see also John 16:33)
- Ephesians 2:11-18 "…But now in Christ Jesus you who once were far away have been brought near through the blood of Christ. For he himself is our peace…"
- Colossians 1:15-20 "…For God was pleased to have all his fullness dwell in him, and through him to reconcile to himself all things…by making peace through his blood, shed on the cross."

♥ **Confession**   Romans 5:20b

♥ **Thanksgiving**   1) Thank You for Your grace shown to us through Jesus.
2) Thank You that we can have peace in the midst of the storms of life because we have You!
3) Thank You that as Your children, we can never lose Your love, Your presence, or our worth in You!
4) Thank You for the gift of each day, Lord, and for all that You are doing in people's lives and the lives of marriages everywhere!
5) _____

♥ **Lord, bless my husband by giving him a <u>wife</u> who…**

- is submissive to him, for it is Your plan for us, Lord…
- Colossians 3:18 (TLB) "You wives, submit yourselves to your husbands, for that is what the Lord has planned for you."

- o Colossians 3:18 (NIV) "Wives, submit to your husbands, as is fitting in the Lord."
- o "Submission: an attitude of the will; more than obedience. Resting, leaning, trusting, abandoning yourself to the LORD. Void of stubbornness." (The Woman's Study Bible) (NKJV)

♥ **Lord, bless our <u>husbands</u>**   Salvation (if applicable): 2 Peter 3:8-9
- o Matthew 6:33-34 May they seek first God's kingdom and his righteousness, and all these things will be given to them as well. Therefore may they not worry about tomorrow, for tomorrow will worry about itself (see also vv. 25-32).

♥ **Lord, bless our <u>marriages</u>**
- o Psalm 3:3a O Lord, be a shield around us/around our marriages, we pray. (O Lord, shield our marriages from the world's ways, false hopes and/or expectations, the tinsel of the world, discouragement, despair, wrong priorities, deception from the evil one/our adversary/Satan, business, laziness, lack of hope, unforgiveness, pride, stubbornness, etc.)

♥ **Lord, bless our <u>homes</u>**
- o May they be a place of comfort, where all can be themselves, and not a place of perfectionism or materialism. May children and/or spouses not feel that things or schedules, routines, and checklists, etc., are more important than their hearts.
- o Psalm 59:9, 17 Protect our homes, Lord; fill them with Your love.
- o Psalm 139:1-3, 23-24 You are familiar with all our ways, Lord...search our hearts, Lord, and show us any offensive ways in us.
- o Isaiah 32:17-18 Work in our hearts through the power of Your Holy Spirit, that our homes will be peaceful dwelling places.

♥ <u>**Application**</u>
- o Psalm 119:11 May we memorize Your Word!
- o Luke 6:46-49 May we live Your Word!

♥ **Lord, bless this <u>prayer ministry</u>**
- o Matthew 9:35-38 Lord, there are so many hurting marriages; marriages in need of Your healing touch. We pray and ask You, Lord of the harvest, to send out workers into the harvest field. May the truth of Your gospel save souls and save marriages, we pray!

♥ <u>**Praise**</u> We praise You, Lord, that You are our Peace!

Week 20

- ♥ **Praise**   God is <u>Jehovah Shammah</u>:   The Lord Is There—This name promises His presence...
    - o Deuteronomy 31:1-8 "...Be strong and courageous. Do not be afraid or terrified because of them, for the LORD your God goes with you; he will never leave you nor forsake you." (My thoughts: He will never give up on you or leave you or desert you or abandon you or your situation) "...The LORD himself goes before you and will be with you; he will never leave you nor forsake you. Do not be afraid; do not be discouraged." (Thought: We never need to be afraid or discouraged because the truth is that God goes before us and is with us!)
    - o Matthew 28:16-20 "...When they saw [Jesus], they worshiped him; but some doubted. Then Jesus came to them and said, 'All authority in heaven and on earth has been given to me. Therefore go and make disciples...teaching them to obey everything I have commanded you. And surely I am with you always, to the very end of the age.'" (Thought: When we are struggling with doubt, Jesus does not condemn us or get angry or frustrated with us, but instead He lovingly encourages us and directs us with truth...and it's because of Jesus' authority that we can go and do...)
    - o 1 Corinthians 3:16 "Don't you know that you yourselves are God's temple and that God's Spirit lives in you?" (Thought: God is not only with me, but as His child, His Holy Spirit indwells me.)
    - o Exodus 33:14-17 "The LORD replied, 'My Presence will go with you, and I will give you rest...'"
    - o Psalm 139:1-10 "...You hem me in behind and before; you have laid your hand upon me...Where can I go from your Spirit?..."
- ♥ **Confession**   Psalm 139:23-24 and then 1 John 1:8-9
- ♥ **Thanksgiving**   1) Oh, thank You, Lord, that You are so good; You are in such complete control; You take such good, wonderful care of us all.
    2) Thank You, Lord, that You alone can comfort and encourage like no person can.
    3) Thank You that You are so very, very faithful, Lord.
    4) Thank You that You alone have the authority and power to forgive completely and perfectly, and You simply desire us to know You intimately, love You dearly/deeply, trust You completely, and live for You cheerfully/willingly.
    5) _____

    _____

- ♥ Lord, bless my husband by giving him a <u>wife</u> who...

- o has a gentle answer and weighs her answers...
- o Proverbs 15:1 "a gentle answer turns away wrath, but a harsh word stirs up anger."
- o Proverbs 15:28 "the heart of the righteous weighs its answers, but the mouth of the wicked gushes evil."

♥ **Lord, bless our <u>husbands</u>**   Salvation (if applicable): Ezekiel 36:25-27
- o Psalm 143:8-10 Show them the way they should go, rescue them from their enemies, teach them to do Your will, lead them on level ground: Let the morning bring (<u>husband's name</u>) word of Your unfailing love, may he put his trust in You. Show (<u>husband's name</u>) the way he should go, to You may he lift up his soul. Rescue (<u>husband's name</u>) from his enemies, O Lord, may he hide himself in You. Teach (<u>husband's name</u>) to do Your will, for You are his God. May Your good Spirit lead him on level ground.

♥ **Lord, bless our <u>marriages</u>**
- o 1 Peter 4:19 (NIV) Whenever we/our marriages suffer according to God's will, may we commit ourselves/our marriage to You, our faithful Creator, and may we continue to do good.
- o 1 Peter 4:19 (TLB) So if our marriage is suffering according to God's will, may we keep on doing what is right and trust ourselves/our marriage to the God who made us, for He will never fail us.

♥ **Lord, bless our <u>homes</u>**
- o Ezekiel 36:25-27 Cleanse our homes/our families/our hearts from all our impurities and from all our idols...give us hearts that obey You and Your ways, by the power of Your Holy Spirit working in us, we pray.

♥ **<u>Application</u>**
- o Psalm 119:11 May we memorize Your Word!
- o Luke 6:46-49 May we live Your Word!
- o Luke 18:1 May we always pray and not give up!

♥ **Lord, bless this <u>prayer ministry</u>**
- o Titus 3:1-2 O Lord, we so pray, please keep this ministry pure from the sin of gossip, complaining, and grumbling. May this ministry ever honor You, Lord, honor our husbands and our homes/families, we pray. Your Word says, "Remind the people to be subject to rulers and authorities, to be obedient, to be ready to do whatever is good, to slander no one, to be peaceable and considerate, and to show true humility toward all men."

♥ **<u>Praise</u>**   We praise You, Lord, that You are there!

Week 21

♥ **Praise**   God is <u>Jehovah Rapha</u>:   The Lord Heals—He heals our bodies, but more importantly, He heals and restores our spirit and soul.

- o Exodus 15:22-26 "...For three days they traveled in the desert without finding water. When they came to Marah, they could not drink its water because it was bitter...So the people grumbled against Moses, saying, 'What are we to drink?' Then Moses cried out to the LORD, and the LORD showed him a piece of wood. He threw it into the water, and the water became sweet...'If you listen carefully to the LORD your God and do what is right in his eyes, if you pay attention to his commands and keep his decrees, I will not bring on you any of the diseases I brought on the Egyptians, for I am the LORD who heals you.'"
- o Duet. 32:39 "...There is no god besides me. I put to death and I bring to life, I have wounded and I will heal, and no one can deliver out of my hand."
- o Psalm 103:1-4 "Praise the LORD, O my soul; all my inmost being, praise his holy name. Praise the LORD, O my soul, and forget not all his benefits—who forgives all your sins and heals all your diseases, who redeems your life from the pit and crowns you with love and compassion."
- o Psalm 147: 3-6 "He heals the brokenhearted and binds up their wounds. He determined the number of stars and calls them each by name. Great is our LORD and mighty in power, his understanding has no limit. The LORD sustains the humble but casts the wicked to the ground."
- o Isaiah 53:4-5 "Surely he took up our infirmities and carried our sorrows...he was pierced for our transgressions, he was crushed for our iniquities; the punishment that brought us peace was upon him, and by his wounds we are healed."
- o Matthew 8:16-17 "When evening came, many who were demon-possessed were brought to him, and [Jesus] drove out the spirits with a word and healed all the sick. This was to fulfill what was spoken through the prophet Isaiah: 'He took up our infirmities and carried our diseases.'"

♥ **Confession**   Psalm 32:3-5 and 1 John 2:1-2

♥ **Thanksgiving**
1) Thank You, Lord, that You can change bitter (attitudes and situations) to sweet.
2) Thank You that You can heal (broken hearts and broken lives) with a word.
3) Thank You for being so very good, Lord!
4) Thank You that Your unfailing love for Your children will not be shaken. You have compassion on us. (Isaiah 54:10)
5) _____

- ♥ Lord, bless my husband by giving him a <u>wife</u> who…
    - o stands firm in doing it God's way and gives herself fully to the work of the Lord…
    - o 1 Corinthians 15:58 "Therefore [since we have victory, even over death, through Jesus, v. 57], my dear brothers, stand firm. Let nothing move you. Always give yourselves fully to the work of the Lord, because you know that your labor in the Lord is not in vain."
- ♥ Lord, bless our <u>husbands</u>   Salvation (if applicable): Isaiah 55:10–11
    - o Proverbs 19:11 Lord, give them wisdom and patience to overlook an offense. Your Word says, "A man's wisdom gives him patience; it is to his glory to overlook an offense." (NIV) "A wise man restrains his anger and overlooks insults. This is to his credit." (TLB)
- ♥ Lord, bless our <u>marriages</u>
    - o Amos 3:3 O Lord, teach us and give us the desire and enable us/empower us to walk together in our marriage. Your Word says, "Do two walk together unless they have agreed to do so?"
- ♥ Lord, bless our <u>homes</u>
    - o May Your Word, honoring and obeying it, be the foundation of our homes/families, we pray…
    - o Deuteronomy 6:17–18a "Be sure to keep the commands of the LORD your God…Do what is right and good in the LORD's sight, so that it may go well with you."
    - o John 14:21 "Whoever has my commands and obeys them, he is the one who loves me. He who loves me will be loved by my Father, and I too will love him and show myself to him."
    - o Psalm 119:105 (NIV) "Your word is a lamp to my feet and a light to my path." (TLB) "Your words are a flashlight to light the path ahead of me, and keep me from stumbling."
- ♥ <u>Application</u>
    - o Colossians 4:2 (NIV) "Devote yourselves to prayer, being watchful and thankful." (TLB) "Don't be weary in prayer, keep at it, watch for God's answers and remember to be thankful when they come."
- ♥ Lord, bless this <u>prayer ministry</u>
    - o Romans 12:2b God's good, pleasing, and perfect will be done, we pray.
- ♥ <u>Praise</u>   We praise You, Lord, that You are the Lord who heals!

Week 22

- ❤ **Praise** God is <u>Jehovah Jireh</u>: The Lord Will Provide—From the root word 'to see,' God would foresee our need of redemption. This name tells us God is willing and able to meet every need of His people.
  - o Genesis 22:8, 13-14 "Abraham answered, 'God himself will provide the lamb for the burnt offering, my son.'...Abraham looked up and there in a thicket he saw a ram caught by its horns...So Abraham called that place the LORD Will Provide..." (Thought/Application: May we too look up and see God's sovereign, perfect provision for our lives.)
  - o Acts 14:17 "...[God] has shown kindness by giving you rain from heaven and crops in their seasons; he provides you with plenty of food and fills your hearts with joy."
  - o Romans 8:32 "He who did not spare his own Son, but gave him up for us all—how will he not also, along with him, graciously give us all things?"
  - o 2 Corinthians 9:8 "And God is able to make all grace abound to you, so that in all things at all times, having all that you need, you will abound in every good work."
  - o Matthew 6:8b "Your Father knows what you need before you ask him."
  - o 1 Timothy 6:17 "Command those who are rich in this present world not to be arrogant nor to put their hope in wealth, which is so uncertain, but to put their hope in God, who richly provides us with everything for our enjoyment." (Thought: From these Scriptures we see that God provides perfectly, powerfully, plentifully, graciously, sacrificially, completely, foreknowingly, and richly; we are so loved, so blessed, so wonderfully taken care of by our loving, powerful, sovereign Heavenly Father. May we ever praise Him!)

- ❤ **Confession** Psalm 103:8-19

- ❤ **Thanksgiving**
  1) Thank You, Lord, for the wonderful gift of being Your children...wonderfully, perfectly taken care of by You, our gracious Heavenly Father.
  2) Thank You that we can trust You so very completely.
  3) Thank You that You love us, each one, so dearly.
  4) Thank You that You have a wonderful, perfect plan for each of us; a plan of blessing and hope, through Jesus in our lives!

- ❤ **Lord, bless my husband by giving him a <u>wife</u> who...**
  - o loves the Lord, listens to His voice, and holds fast to Him...thus chooses life...
  - o Deuteronomy 30:19-20 "...Now choose life...love the LORD your God, listen to his voice, and hold fast to him..."

- ♥ **Lord, bless our <u>husbands</u>**   Salvation (if applicable): Ephesians 1:17-18
  - o Hebrews 13:20-21 (personalized) May You, the God of peace...equip (<u>husband's name</u>) with everything good for doing Your will, and may You work in (<u>husband's name</u>) what is pleasing to You, through Jesus Christ, to whom be glory for ever and ever, Amen.

- ♥ **Lord, bless our <u>marriages</u>** (personalized and paraphrased)
  - o Psalm 90:17 May the favor of the Lord our God rest upon our marriages; establish the work of our hands for us—yes, establish the work of our hands.
  - o Establish: "1) To make firm or secure; fix in a stable condition. 2) To originate on a firm, lasting basis; to found. 3) To introduce as a permanent entity..."[28]
  - o Application: O Lord, may our marriages be firm and secure, grounded in You and the truth of Your Word, Lord, which is firm, lasting and permanent. (Psalm 119:89, 152)

- ♥ **Lord, bless our <u>homes</u>**
  - o Malachi 3:16 May our homes be a place where the Lord is feared and honored...for oh, the blessings...Your Word says: "Then those who feared the LORD talked with each other, and the LORD listened and heard. A scroll of remembrance was written in his presence concerning those who feared the LORD and honored his name."

- ♥ **<u>Application</u>**
  - o Genesis 2:18 "The LORD God said, 'It is not good for the man to be alone. I will make a helper suitable for him.'" (Thought/Application: It is a gift/privilege to be a wife. May I live out Your Word, Lord, and be a helper to my husband. May I see him as a hand-picked blessing from You, Lord, to me. May my attitude, actions, tone of voice, body language, how I spend my time, etc., be helpful to my husband. Mold me into what he needs! Make me a gift to him!)

- ♥ **Lord, bless this <u>prayer ministry</u>**
  - o Zechariah 4:6b "'Not by might nor by power, but by my Spirit,' says the LORD Almighty."
  - o By Your Spirit, Lord, may Your will be done in this ministry...by Your Spirit, may it touch the lives and marriages You have planned for it to touch, for Your glory, Lord!

- ♥ **<u>Praise</u>** We praise You, Lord, that You will provide!

---

[28] "Establish." Def. 1, 4, 6. William Morris, *The American Heritage Dictionary of the English Language*, New College Edition. (Boston: Houghton Mifflin Company, 1976), 448.

Week 23

- ♥ **Praise**   God is <u>Jehovah Raah</u>:   The Lord Our Shepherd—Raah is also translated "companion" or "friend."
  - o Psalm 23 "The LORD is my shepherd"…He provides for me all I need; He leads me, gives me rest, protects me, restores me, guides me for His glory; He is always with me, thus I do not need to fear; He disciplines me, comforts me, prepares the way for me and blesses me to overflowing.
  - o Isaiah 40:11   He tends, gathers, carries us close to His heart; He gently leads…
  - o Ezekiel 34:11-16 The Sovereign Lord Himself searches for and looks after His sheep…He rescues, gathers, tends, blesses, feeds richly…searches for the lost and brings back the strays, binds up the injured and strengthens the weak, humbles the prideful, shepherds with justice.
  - o Matthew 18:10-14 God leaves the ninety-nine to go and look for the one that has wandered off…He is not willing that any should be lost.
  - o John 10:11-12, 27-30 Jesus laid down his life for us; He does not abandon us…listen to His voice, know Him, follow Him; we cannot be snatched out of His hand.
  - o Revelation 7:17 "For the Lamb at the center of the throne will be their shepherd; he will lead them to springs of living water. And God will wipe away every tear from their eyes."
- ♥ **Confession**   Psalm 51:4-12
- ♥ **Thanksgiving**   1) Thank You for so wonderfully, tenderly taking care of us all.
  2) Thank You that You never abandon us or give up on us!
  3) Thank You that You are so patient and persevering with us!
- ♥ Lord, bless my husband by giving him a <u>wife</u> who…
  - o lets love guide her life…suffers patiently and is ready to forgive…
  - o Colossians 3:12-14 (TLB) May we be willing to suffer quietly and patiently and be gentle and ready to forgive, never holding a grudge. Remembering the Lord forgave us, so we must forgive others. Most of all may love guide our lives…for this leads to perfect harmony.
- ♥ Lord, bless our <u>husbands</u>   Salvation (if applicable): Jeremiah 32:40
  - o Psalm 90:17 May the favor of the Lord our God rest upon (<u>husband's name</u>), establish the work of his hands for him—yes, establish ("To make firm or secure; fix in a stable condition.")[29] the work of his hands.

---

[29] "Establish." Def. 1. Ibid.

- ♥ Lord, bless our <u>marriages</u>
  - o Jeremiah 29:11 Thank You, Lord, for this truth: For I know the plans I have for (husband's and my name), declares the Lord, plans to prosper them and not to harm them, plans to give them hope and a future. (Thought: All the while remembering the truth from v. 10 as well…i.e., though your marriage may be struggling, going through hard and painful times right now, God knows how long these hard times will last; only He knows the future… God knows all the good that will come as a result of going through these hard times; He knows the blessing He has planned for you. Oh, dear child of God, persevere holding on tightly to God and His ways. He is faithful (Isaiah 25:1). He will not let you down (Hebrews 13:5-6). He loves you with an everlasting love (Jeremiah 31:3). He refreshes the weary (Jeremiah 31:25). He sustains and strengthens (Psalm 89:21). Be greatly encouraged; Jesus is your hope, an anchor for your soul, firm and secure (Hebrews 6:18-19).

- ♥ Lord, bless our <u>homes</u>
  - o Deuteronomy 6:4-9 May our homes be a place where the truths of God's Word are passed down/taught to our children…from generation to generation: "Hear, O Israel: The LORD our God, the LORD is one. Love the LORD your God with all your heart and with all your soul and with all your strength. These commandments that I give you today are to be upon your hearts. Impress them on your children. Talk about them when you sit at home and when you walk along the road, when you lie down and when you get up. Tie them as symbols on your hands and bind them on your foreheads. Write them on the doorframes of your houses and on your gates."

- ♥ <u>Application</u>
  - o Lesson I learned from the book *A Woman After God's Own Heart* by Elizabeth George…The better follower I am, the better leader my husband will be.[30] Lord, help us to not just think about and/or not just pray about being a better follower of our husbands, but help us, this week and always, to live it out …teach us, enable us, and give us the heart's desire to do so, Lord.

- ♥ Lord, bless this <u>prayer ministry</u>
  - o 1 Chronicles 4:10 fourfold prayer of blessing…bless, enlarge, empower, keep from harm… this ministry, we pray.

- ♥ <u>Praise</u>   We praise You, Lord, that You are our Shepherd!

---

[30] Elizabeth George, *A Woman After God's Own Heart,* (Eugene, Oregon, Harvest House Publishers, 1997), 60-62.

Week 24

- ♥ **Praise**   God is <u>Jehovah Nissi</u>:   The Lord Our Banner—Nissi is also translated "ensign" or "standard" and represents His cause, His victory.
  - o Exodus 17:15-16a "Moses built an altar and called it The LORD is my Banner. He said, 'For hands were lifted up to the throne of the LORD.'"
  - o Psalm 20:5-8 "We will shout for joy when you are victorious and will lift up our banners in the name of our God…Some trust in chariots and some in horses, but we trust in the name of the LORD our God…"
  - o Psalm 60:4 "But for those who fear you, you have raised a banner to be unfurled against the bow."
  - o Song 2:4 "He has taken me to the banquet hall, and his banner over me is love."
  - o Isaiah 11:10 "In that day the Root of Jesse will stand as a banner for the peoples; the nations will rally to him, and his place of rest will be glorious."
  - o 1 Corinthians 15:56-58 "The sting of death is sin, and the power of sin is the law. But thanks be to God! He gives the victory through our Lord Jesus Christ. Therefore, my dear brothers, stand firm. Let nothing move you. Always give yourselves fully to the work of the Lord because you know that your labor in the Lord is not in vain."

- ♥ **Confession**   Psalm 32:1-5

- ♥ **Thanksgiving**   1) Thank You, Lord, that You are so very real and right here by our side always.
  2) Thank You that You keep loving us so, even when we can be so sinful and stubborn, etc.
  3) Thank You for Your sovereignty, patience, and perseverance in our lives.
  4) Thank You that You never make a mistake; You always do what is right. You are perfect in sovereignty, power, wisdom, and love!
  5)_____

- ♥ **Lord, bless my husband by giving him a <u>wife</u> who…**
  - o chooses to put on the right hat at the right time and wears only one hat at a time…thus giving our husbands our wholehearted attention (from the book *A Woman After God's Own Heart* by Elizabeth George)…
  - o Colossians 3:23 "Whatever you do, work at it with all your heart, as working for the Lord not for men."

- ♥ **Lord, bless our <u>husbands</u>**   Salvation (if applicable): Luke 24:45

- o 1 Thessalonians 5:22-24   May God Himself, the God of peace, sanctify <u>(husband's name)</u> through and through...The one who calls you is faithful and He will do it. (NIV) Lord, may <u>(husband's name)</u> keep away from every kind of evil. May the God of peace Himself make <u>(husband's name)</u> entirely pure and devoted to God; and may his spirit and soul and body be kept strong and blameless until that day when our Lord Jesus Christ comes back again. God who called you to become His child, will do all this for you, just as He promised. (TLB)

♥ **Lord, bless our <u>marriages</u>**
- o Zechariah 10:12   Strengthen our marriages in You, Lord, we pray. "I will strengthen them in the LORD and in his name they will walk,' declares the LORD." (see v. 11 also)

♥ **Lord, bless our <u>homes</u>**
- o Ephesians 4:32   May our homes be a place where forgiveness abounds, showing kindness and compassion to one another (forgiving ourselves as well, as Jesus does): "Be kind and compassionate to one another, forgiving each other, just as in Christ God forgave you." (See also Colossians 3:12-14.)

♥ <u>**Application**</u>
- o Further applications from lessons I learned from the book *A Woman After God's Own Heart* by Elizabeth George...
- o Each day this week, and evermore, may we as wives ask ourselves:
  - o Was I a blessing or a burden to my husband today?!
  - o Was I a help or a hindrance to my husband today?!
  - o Did I fit into my husband's plans today or did I fight for my own way?![31]
- o Do a work in our hearts/lives as wives, Lord, we pray. Make us a channel of blessing!

♥ **Lord, bless this <u>prayer ministry</u>**
- o Psalm 91:4b   "His faithfulness will be your shield and rampart." O Heavenly Father, may Your faithfulness continue to shield, protect, and defend this ministry, we pray. Ever for Your glory, Lord!

♥ <u>**Praise**</u>   We praise You, Lord, that You are our Banner!

---

[31] Ibid.

Week 25

- ♥ **Praise** God is <u>Jehovah Sabaoth</u>: The Lord of Hosts—Commander of all the armies of heaven
  - o Deuteronomy 20:1-4 (NASB) "WHEN you go out to battle against your enemies and see horses and chariots *and* people more numerous than you, do not be afraid of them; for the LORD your God, who brought you up from the land of Egypt, is with you...Do not be fainthearted. Do not be afraid, or panic, or tremble before them, for the LORD your God is the one who goes with you, to fight for you against your enemies, to save you."
  - o 1 Samuel 17:37-47 "...David said to the Philistine, 'You come against me with sword and spear and javelin, but I come against you in the name of the LORD Almighty, the God of the armies of Israel, whom you have defied...and the whole world will know that there is a God in Israel. All those gathered here will know that it is not by sword or spear that the LORD saves; for the battle is the LORD's, and he will give all of you into our hands.'"
  - o Nehemiah 9:5b-6 "...Stand up and praise the LORD your God, who is from everlasting to everlasting...You alone are the LORD...You give life to everything, and the multitudes of heaven worship you."
  - o Psalm 103:19-22 "The LORD has established his throne in heaven, and his kingdom rules over all....Praise the LORD, all his heavenly hosts, you his servants who do his will..."
  - o Zechariah 14:9 "The LORD will be king over the whole earth. On that day there will be one LORD, and his name the only name."
  - o Revelation 11:15 "...He will reign forever and ever."

- ♥ **Confession**   Isaiah 55:6-10

- ♥ **Thanksgiving**   1) Thank You that the battle belongs to you, Lord. Thank You for all the battles You have lovingly, powerfully, and faithfully fought on our behalf!
  2) Thank You that Your love is constant.
  3) Thank You for the lives You are touching with this ministry and the lives and marriages You will touch and the opportunities You are bringing to "expand its territories." You are blessing, Lord. (1 Chronicles 4:10)
  4) Thank You that You are sovereign—You are in complete control now and forever; thus we do not need to fear or fret or be fainthearted or afraid because we are Yours, we are safe in the palm of Your hand and nothing can change that. (John 10:27-30) Thank You that You go before us. (John 10:4)

- ♥ **Lord, bless my husband by giving him a <u>wife</u>**...
    - o whose plate is not too full...being so busy that I have no time or energy for him and he only gets my leftovers. (Ouch!...Thank You, Lord!) (This is yet another application/lesson I learned from the book *A Woman After God's Own Heart* by Elizabeth George)[32]
    - o Genesis 2:18 "The LORD God said, 'It is not good for the man to be alone. I will make a helper suitable for him.'"
- ♥ **Lord, bless our <u>husbands</u>**   Salvation (if applicable): Psalm 18:16-17
    - o Philippians 1:6 May we as wives be confident of the truth of God's Word and thus leave God's work in His hands...that He who began a good work in (husband's name) will carry it on to completion until the day of Christ Jesus. (NIV) And I am sure that God who began the good work within (husband's name) will keep right on helping him grow in His grace until His task within him is finally finished on that day when Jesus Christ returns. (TLB)
- ♥ **Lord, bless our <u>marriages</u>**
    - o Colossians 1:17 "He is before all things, and in him all things hold together." (Thought: O Lord, You hold this whole universe together, hold our marriages together, we pray!)
- ♥ **Lord, bless our <u>homes</u>**
    - o Romans 5:20b to be a place filled with God's grace toward each other...For God's Word says, "But where sin increased, grace increased all the more."
- ♥ **<u>Application</u>**
    - o 1 John 3:18 "Dear children, let us not love with words or tongue but with actions and in truth." May we love with action this week by taking the action of writing our husbands a note telling them how much we appreciate them. (O Lord, help us to appreciate our husbands and not take them for granted.) This is just one suggestion of how to put love into action. Pray and follow God's leading in your life regarding this. As you seek God's face, He will faithfully reveal to you what will make your husband feel loved, encouraged, appreciated, and respected.
- ♥ **Lord, bless this <u>prayer ministry</u>**
    - o Matthew 9:38 "Ask the Lord of the harvest, therefore, to send out workers into his harvest field."
- ♥ **<u>Praise</u>** We praise You, Lord, that You are the Lord of Hosts!

---

[32] Ibid., 222-224.

Week 26

- ♥ **Praise**   God is <u>El</u>:   The God of Power and Might
  - o Exodus 15:1-3, 11-13 "...The LORD is my strength and my song...I will praise him...The LORD is a warrior; the LORD is his name...Who is like you—majestic in holiness, awesome in glory, working wonders?...In your unfailing love you will lead the people you have redeemed. In your strength you will guide them to your holy dwelling."
  - o Deuteronomy 3:24 "O Sovereign LORD, you have begun to show to your servant your greatness and your strong hand. For what god is there in heaven or on earth who can do the deeds and mighty works you do?"
  - o 2 Chronicles 20:6-12 "...O LORD, God of our fathers, are you not the God who is in heaven? You rule over all the kingdoms of the nations. Power and might are in your hand, and no one can withstand you...O our God...we have no power to face this vast army that is attacking us. We do not know what to do, but our eyes are upon you."
  - o Psalm 18:1-3 "I love you, O LORD, my strength. The LORD is my rock, my fortress and my deliverer; my God is my rock, in whom I take refuge. He is my shield and the horn of my salvation, my stronghold. I call to the LORD, who is worthy of praise, and I am saved from my enemies."
  - o Psalm 89:5-8 "...God is greatly feared; he is more awesome than all who surround him...You are mighty, O LORD, and your faithfulness surrounds you."
  - o Isaiah 43:10-13 "'You are my witnesses,' declares the LORD, 'and my servant whom I have chosen, so that you may know and believe me and understand that I am he. Before me no god was formed, nor will there be one after me. I, even I, am the LORD, and apart from me there is no savior. I have revealed and saved and proclaimed...Yes, and from ancient days I am he. No one can deliver out of my hand. When I act, who can reverse it?'"

- ♥ **Confession**   1 John 1:8-9
- ♥ **Thanksgiving**   1) Thank You, Lord, that when we do not know what to do, all we really need to do is put our eyes on You!
  2) Thank You for the truth and encouragement of Your word!
  3) Thank You that You alone are God and only You can save souls and only You can save marriages...all is in Your loving, all knowing, all wise, all powerful, yet gentle and completely sovereign hands!

- ♥ **Lord, bless my husband by giving him a <u>wife</u> who...**
  - o has a smile in her heart when he comes home (and greets him at the door like he is "the king of the castle")...
  - o Proverbs 15:30a "A cheerful look brings joy to the heart."

- ♥ Lord, bless our <u>husbands</u>   Salvation (if applicable): John 6:64-65
  - o Colossians 2:6-7a that they will be rooted in Christ and keep growing in Him…"So then, just as you received Christ Jesus as Lord continue to live in him, rooted and built up in him, strengthened in the faith as you were taught." (NIV) "And now just as you trusted Christ to save you, trust him, too, for each day's problems; live in vital union with him. Let your roots grow down into him and draw up nourishment from him. See that you go on growing in the Lord and become strong and vigorous in the truth you were taught." (TLB)
- ♥ Lord, bless our <u>marriages</u>
  - o Colossians 3:17-21 With thankfulness, God's divine order to be lived out…"And whatever you do, whether in word or deed, do it all in the name of the Lord Jesus, giving thanks to God the Father through him. Wives, submit to your husbands, as is fitting in the Lord. Husbands, love your wives and do not be harsh with them. Children, obey your parents in everything, for this pleases the Lord. Fathers, do not embitter your children, or they will become discouraged." (NIV) "…Whatever you do or say, let it be as a representative of the Lord Jesus…Fathers, don't scold your children so much that they become discouraged and quit trying." (TLB)
- ♥ Lord, bless our <u>homes</u>
  - o Isaiah 26:3-4 Bring perfect peace, helping us to trust in You forever, our Rock eternal: "You will keep in perfect peace him whose mind is steadfast, because he trusts in you. Trust in the LORD forever, for the LORD, the LORD himself, is the Rock eternal." (NIV) "He will keep in perfect peace all those who trust in him, whose thoughts turn often to the Lord! Trust in the Lord God always, for in the Lord Jehovah is your everlasting strength." (TLB)
- ♥ <u>Application</u>
  - o 1 John 3:18 "Dear children, let us not love with words or tongue but with actions and in truth." May we love with action this week and evermore by choosing to focus on our husbands' strengths!
- ♥ Lord, bless this <u>prayer ministry</u>
  - o Titus 3:1-2 Keep this prayer ministry pure, Lord, from gossip, complaining and grumbling; may You, our husbands, and our families be honored: "Remind the people to be subject to rulers and authorities, to be obedient, to be ready to do whatever is good, to slander no one, to be peaceable and considerate, and to show true humility toward all men."

♥ <u>Praise</u> We praise You, Lord, that You are the God of Power and Might!

Week 27

- ❤ **Praise**   God is <u>Elohim</u>:   The Triune God, Creator
    - o Genesis 1:1-5 "In the beginning God created the heavens and the earth…and the Spirit of God was hovering…And God said…and there was…"
    - o Psalm 95:1-7a "…For the Lord is the great God, the great King above all gods. In his hand are the depths of the earth, and the mountain peaks belong to him. The sea is his, for he made it, and his hands formed the dry land. Come, let us bow down in worship, let us kneel before the Lord our Maker; for he is our God and we are the people of his pasture, the flock under his care."
    - o Psalm 146:5-6 "Blessed is he whose help is the God of Jacob, whose hope is in the Lord his God, the Maker of heaven and earth, the sea, and everything in them—the Lord, who remains faithful forever."
    - o Isaiah 40:25-29 "'To whom will you compare me? Or who is my equal?' says the Holy One. Lift your eyes and look to the heavens: Who created all these? He who brings out the starry host one by one, and calls them each by name. Because of his great power and mighty strength, not one of them is missing…"
    - o Isaiah 54:5 "For your Maker is your husband—the Lord Almighty is his name—the Holy One of Israel is your Redeemer; he is called the God of all the earth."
    - o Colossians 1:15-20 "…For by him all things were created: things in heaven and on earth, visible and invisible, whether thrones or powers or rulers or authorities; all things were created by him and for him. He is before all things, and in him all things hold together…"

- ❤ **Confession**   1 John 2:1-2

- ❤ **Thanksgiving**
    1) Thank You, Lord, that You are so very good.
    2) Thank You for Your sovereign, loving care of our lives.
    3) Thank You for the opportunities You have given to share this powerful prayer ministry of Yours with others, and thank You for the power of Your Holy Spirit working in people's lives everywhere.
    4) Thank You that You are always faithful to equip us to do the work/task You ask of us; You are so very, very faithful.
    5)_____

- ❤ **Lord, bless my husband by giving him a <u>wife</u> who…**
    - o is not prideful, but wise in accepting advice…
    - o Proverbs 13:10 (NIV) "Pride only breeds quarrels, but wisdom is found in those who take advice."

- o Proverbs 13:10 (TLB) "Pride leads to arguments; be humble, take advice and become wise."
- ♥ **Lord, bless our <u>husbands</u>**   Salvation (if applicable): Romans 1:20
  - o Colossians 2:7b to have a heart overflowing with thankfulness.
- ♥ **Lord, bless our <u>marriages</u>**
  - o for God to be the head of our marriages, to have all supremacy in our marriages...
  - o Colossians 1:18 "And [Jesus] is the head of the body, the church; he is the beginning and the firstborn from among the dead, so that in everything he might have the supremacy."
  - o 1 Corinthians 11:3 "Now I want you to realize that the head of every man is Christ, and head of the woman is man, and the head of Christ is God."
- ♥ **Lord, bless our <u>homes</u>**
  - o Jeremiah 31:3b–4a Build our families up and rebuild us, where necessary, on the foundation of the truth of Your Word: "I have loved you with an everlasting love; I have drawn you with loving-kindness. I will build you up again and you will be rebuilt."
- ♥ <u>**Application**</u>
  - o 1 John 3:18 "Dear children, let us not love with words or tongue but with actions and in truth." O Lord, may we not just say the words "I love you" to our husbands, but may our actions and attitudes display that we truly love them. ("Actions speak louder than words!")
- ♥ **Lord, bless this <u>prayer ministry</u>**
  - o Romans 12:2b God's good, pleasing, and perfect will be done.
- ♥ <u>**Praise**</u>   We praise You, Lord, that You are the Triune God, Creator!

Week 28

- ♥ **Praise**   God is <u>El Elyon</u>:   The God Most High
  - o Genesis 14:17-20 "…He blessed Abram, saying, 'Blessed be Abram by God Most High, Creator of heaven and earth. And blessed be God Most High, who delivered your enemies into your hand.' Then Abram gave him a tenth of everything."
  - o Psalm 7:17 "I will give thanks to the LORD because of his righteousness and will sing praise to the name of the LORD Most High."
  - o Psalm 47 "…Shout to God with cries of joy. How awesome is the LORD Most High, the great King over all the earth!…Sing praises to God, sing praises; sing praises to our King, sing praises. For God is the King of all the earth…God reigns over the nations; God is seated on his holy throne…the kings of the earth belong to God; he is greatly exalted."
  - o Psalm 92:1-5 "It is good to praise the LORD…O Most High, to proclaim your love in the morning and your faithfulness at night…I sing for joy at the works of your hands. How great are your works, O LORD, how profound your thoughts!"
  - o Psalm 97:9-12 "For you, O LORD, are the Most High over all the earth; you are exalted far above all gods. Let those who love the LORD hate evil, for he guards the lives of his faithful ones and delivers them from the hand of the wicked. Light is shed upon the righteous and joy on the upright in heart. Rejoice in the LORD, you who are righteous, and praise his holy name."
  - o Psalm 148 "Praise the LORD…Let them praise the name of the LORD, for he commanded and they were created. He set them in place forever and ever…young men and maidens, old men and children. Let them praise the name of the LORD, for his name alone is exalted; his splendor is above the earth and the heavens. He has raised up for his people a horn, [Horn here symbolizes strong one, that is, king.] the praise of all his saints, of Israel, the people close to his heart. Praise the LORD."

- ♥ **Confession**   Psalm 86:5

- ♥ **Thanksgiving**   1) Thank You, Lord, that You are so very good.
  2) Thank You for Your faithfulness and grace to us, Your children.
  3) We can never thank You enough for the gift of being Your children; what a gift, what a blessing.
  4) Thank You for who You are and what You've done and what You will do. We thank You and praise You evermore.
  5)_____

- ♥ Lord, bless my husband by giving him a <u>wife</u> who…
    - o does not worry but prays with thanksgiving…
    - o Philippians 4:6-7 (NIV) "Do not be anxious about anything, but in everything, by prayer and petition, with thanksgiving, present your requests to God. And the peace of God, which transcends all understanding, will guard your hearts and your minds in Christ Jesus." (CEV) "Don't worry about anything, but pray about everything. With thankful hearts offer up your prayers and requests to God. Then, because you belong to Christ Jesus, God will bless you with peace that no one can completely understand. And this peace will control the way you think and feel."
- ♥ Lord, bless our <u>husbands</u>   Salvation (if applicable): Matthew 18:12-14
    - o Colossians 1:9-12 that they will walk in a manner worthy of God, bear fruit, grow, be strengthened to persevere and be patient, give thanks with joy.
- ♥ Lord, bless our <u>marriages</u>
    - o Protection from divorce…
    - o Psalm 91:4b "His [God Most High, vv. 1-2] faithfulness will be your shield and rampart." O God Most High, shield, protect, and defend our marriages, we pray.
    - o Psalm 31:21b (TLB) "[The Lord's] never-failing love protects me like the walls of a fort!" O Lord, put a wall like a fort around our marriages, we pray!
- ♥ Lord, bless our <u>homes</u>
    - o John 1:16 God's blessings upon our homes/our families: "From the fullness of his grace we have all received one blessing after another."
- ♥ <u>Application</u>
    - o May we remember/think upon the details of our marriage vows and live them out this week and evermore!
- ♥ Lord, bless this <u>prayer ministry</u>
    - o Zechariah 4:6b "'Not by might nor by power, but by my Spirit,' says the LORD Almighty." By the working of Your Holy Spirit, do what You will in and through this prayer ministry of Yours, Lord Almighty, ever for Your glory, Lord!
- ♥ **<u>Praise</u>** We praise You, Lord, that You are the God Most High!

Week 29

- ❤ **Praise**   God is <u>El Shaddai</u>:   The Almighty, All-Sufficient God
  - o Genesis 17:1 "When Abram was ninety-nine years old, the LORD appeared to him and said, 'I am God Almighty, walk before me and be blameless.'"
  - o 1 Chronicles 29:11-13   "...You are the ruler of all things. In your hands are strength and power..."
  - o 2 Corinthians 12:9 (AMP) "But He said to me, My grace (My favor and loving-kindness and mercy) is enough for you [sufficient against any danger and enables you to bear the trouble manfully]; for *My* strength *and* power are made perfect (fulfilled and completed) *and show themselves most effective* in [your] weakness. Therefore, I will all the more gladly glory in my weaknesses *and* infirmities, that the strength *and* power of Christ (the Messiah) may rest (yes, may pitch a tent over and dwell) upon me!"
  - o Ephesians 1:19-21 (TLB)   "I pray that you will begin to understand how incredibly great his power is to help those who believe him. It is that same mighty power that raised Christ from the dead and seated him in the place of honor at God's right hand in heaven, far, far above any other king or ruler or dictator or leader. Yes, his honor is far more glorious than that of anyone else either in this world or in the world to come."
  - o Hebrews 1:2-3 (NIV) "...sustaining all things by his powerful word..." (AMP) "...upholding *and* maintaining *and* guiding *and* propelling the universe by His mighty word of power..."
  - o Revelation 1:8 (AMP) "I am the Alpha and the Omega, *the Beginning and the End*, says the Lord God, He Who is and Who was and Who is to come, the Almighty (the Ruler of all)."

- ❤ **Confession**   Romans 5:20b

- ❤ **Thanksgiving**   1) Thank You, Lord, that You are the Ruler of all and we can rest in that.
  2) Thank You that You are so very good, always.
  3) Thank You that You are always faithfully working in our lives, watching over us, taking such special, attentive care of us all.
  4) Lord, thank You that when there doesn't seem to be a way, You make a way...Isaiah 43:16, 18-19.

- ❤ **Lord, bless my husband by giving him a <u>wife</u> who...**
  - o rejoices in the Lord always and is gentle...
  - o Philippians 4:4-5 (NIV) "Rejoice in the Lord always. I will say it again: Rejoice! Let your gentleness be evident to all. The Lord is near."

- ♥ Lord, bless our **husbands**   Salvation (if applicable): 2 Timothy 2:25-26
  - Philippians 4:4-5 (TLB) "Always be full of joy in the Lord I say it again, rejoice! Let everyone see that you are unselfish and considerate in all you do. Remember that the Lord is coming soon."
  - Galatians 5:22-23a that they will have God's love, joy, peace, patience, kindness, goodness and self-control.

- ♥ Lord, bless our **marriages**
  - to be filled with God's love...
  - Romans 5:5 God pours His love into our hearts by the Holy Spirit.
  - 1 Corinthians 13:2b "If I have a faith that can move mountains, but have not love, I am nothing."
  - 1 Corinthians 16:14 "Do everything in love."

- ♥ Lord, bless our **homes**
  - May they be a place where Your Word is honored and respected in the heart and obeyed...
  - James 1:22 (NIV) "Do not merely listen to the word, and so deceive yourselves. Do what it says."
  - James 1:22 (TLB) "And remember, it is a message to obey, not just to listen to. So don't fool yourselves." (See through v. 25.)
  - James 1:22 (AMP) "But be doers of the Word [obey the message], and not merely listeners to it, betraying yourselves [into deception by reasoning contrary to the Truth]."

- ♥ **Application**
  - May we choose to appreciate, admire, accept and adapt to our husbands.[33]

- ♥ Lord, bless this **prayer ministry**
  - Psalm 91:4b May Your faithfulness shield, protect, and defend this ministry, Lord, we pray.

♥ Praise We praise You, Lord, that You are the Almighty, All Sufficient God!

---

[33] I first learned this principle of the 4 A's [appreciate, admire, accept, adapt to your husband] while attending a women's weekly small-group Bible study, in 2001. The Bible study leader's words struck a cord with me, so much so, that I decided to implement them into the "application" section of the prayer sheets.

Week 30

- ♥ **Praise** God is <u>El Olam</u>: The Everlasting God
  - Genesis 21:33 "Abraham...called upon the name of the L<small>ORD</small>, the Eternal God."
  - Psalm 90:1-4 "...Before the mountains were born or you brought forth the earth and the world, from everlasting to everlasting you are God...a thousand years in your sight are like a day that has just gone by, or like a watch in the night."
  - Psalm 102:11-12 (NASB) "My days are like a lengthened shadow; And I wither away like grass. But Thou, O L<small>ORD</small>, dost abide forever; And Thy name to all generations."
  - Psalm 136 (NASB) "GIVE thanks to the L<small>ORD</small>, for He is good; For His lovingkindness is everlasting...Who remembered us in our low estate... And has rescued us from our adversaries...Who gives food to all flesh...Give thanks to the God of heaven, For His lovingkindess is everlasting."
  - Hebrews 13:8 (AMP) "Jesus Christ (the Messiah) is [always] the same, yesterday, today, [yes] and forever (to the ages)."
  - Revelation 1:17-18 "When I saw him, I fell at his feet as though dead. Then he placed his right hand on me and said: 'Do not be afraid. I am the First and the Last. I am the Living One; I was dead, and behold I am alive for ever and ever! And I hold the keys of death and Hades.'"

- ♥ **Confession**   Psalm 139:23-24 and then 1 John 1:8-9

- ♥ **Thanksgiving**   1) Thank You, Lord, that You are always thinking about us and watching everything that concerns us. (1 Peter 5:7, TLB)
  2) Thank You that Your lovingkindness endures forever. (Psalm 136)
  3) Thank You, Lord, that as Your children we will never be forgotten by You. You have wiped out our transgressions...for You have redeemed us. (See Isaiah 44:21-22.)
  4) Thank You, Lord, that You are sovereign. We can trust You. You are always there.
  5)_____

- ♥ **Lord, bless my husband by giving him a <u>wife</u> who**...
  - thinks upon what is true...
  - Philippians 4:8 (NIV) "...Whatever is true, whatever is noble, whatever is right, whatever is pure, whatever is lovely, whatever is admirable—if anything is excellent or praiseworthy—think about such things."

- o Philippians 4:8 (TLB) "…Fix your thoughts on what is true and good and right. Think about things that are pure and lovely, and dwell on the fine, good things in others. Think about all you can praise God for and be glad about."

♥ **Lord, bless our <u>husbands</u>**   Salvation (if applicable): Acts 26:18 (see TLB)
  - o Titus 2:6-8 to be good examples, show integrity.

♥ **Lord, bless our <u>marriages</u>**
  - o 2 Timothy 2:24-25 (NASB) Applying this Scripture to our marriages, may we not be quarrelsome, but be kind, teachable, patient when wronged, and with gentleness correct those in opposition.

♥ **Lord, bless our <u>homes</u>**
  - o Proverbs 15:8 (NIV) that they will be a place where prayer abounds: "The LORD detests the sacrifice of the wicked, but the prayer of the upright pleases him."
  - o Proverbs 15:8 (NASB) "The sacrifice of the wicked is an abomination to the LORD, But the prayer of the upright is His delight."

♥ **<u>Application</u>**
  - o May we:
    - o Think only Truth: Philippians 4:8 and Joshua 1:8
    - o Live only Truth: Luke 6:46-49 and Joshua 1:8
    - o Think only about today (thus not worrying about tomorrow): Matthew 6:33-34
    - o Delight in correction: Proverbs 3:11-12
  - o In my heart this is a lifelong assignment God has given me as His child.

♥ **Lord, bless this <u>prayer ministry</u>**
  - o Matthew 9:38 We pray and ask you, Lord, to send out workers; call wives to pray for their husbands and marriages; raise up prayer warriors, we pray.

♥ **<u>Praise</u>** We praise You, Lord, that You are the Everlasting God!

Week 31

- ♥ **Praise**   God is <u>Adonai</u>:   The Lord and Master
  - Deuteronomy 10:17 "For the LORD your God is God of gods and LORD of lords, the great God, mighty and awesome, who shows no partiality and accepts no bribes."
  - Psalm 16:1-2 (AMP) "Keep and protect me, O God, for in You I have found refuge, and in You do I put my trust and hide myself. I say to the Lord You are my Lord I have no good beside *or* beyond You."
  - Isaiah 45:22 "Turn to me and be saved, all you ends of the earth; for I am God, and there is no other."
  - Romans 14:9-12 "…It is written; 'As surely as I live,' says the Lord 'every knee will bow before me; every tongue will confess to God.' So then, each of us will give an account of himself to God."
  - 1 Corinthians 6:19-20 (AMP) "Do you not know that your body is the temple (the very sanctuary) of the Holy Spirit Who lives within you, Whom you have received [as a Gift] from God? You are not your own. You were bought with a price [purchased with a preciousness and paid for, made His own]. So then, honor God *and* bring glory to Him in your body."
  - Revelation 5:9-10 "…You are worthy to take the scroll and to open its seals, because you were slain, and with your blood you purchased men for God from every tribe and language and people and nation…"

- ♥ **Confession**   Psalm 32:3-5 and then 1 John 2:1-2
- ♥ **Thanksgiving**   1) Thank You for the precious gift of Jesus and the forgiveness offered to us through Him.
    2) Thank You that You love us all so very, very much, Lord.
    3) Thank You that "because [Jesus] lives I can face tomorrow…because I know He holds the future…life is worth the living just because He lives!" (Truths of a precious song)[34]
    4) Thank You, Lord, that You carry us and sustain us and rescue us. (Truths from Isaiah 46:3-4)
    5)_____

- ♥ **Lord, bless my husband by giving him a <u>wife</u> who…**
  - is compassionate and gracious, slow to anger and abounding in lovingkindness (make me more like You, Lord)…

---

[34] Bill and Gloria Gaither. *Because He Lives*. © 1974 by Spring House Productions, Gaither Music Group.

- o Psalm 103:8 (NASB) "The LORD is compassionate and gracious, Slow to anger and abounding in lovingkindness."
- o Psalm 103:8 (TLB) "He is merciful and tender toward those who don't deserve it; he is slow to get angry and full of kindness and love."

♥ **Lord, bless our <u>husbands</u>**   Salvation (if applicable): 2 Corinthians 4:3-6
- o Colossians 3:12-14 (TLB) May they be forgiving, gentle, and not be concerned about making a good impression: "Since you have been chosen by God who has given you this new kind of life, and because of his deep love and concern for you, you should practice tenderhearted mercy and kindness to others. Don't worry about making a good impression on them but be ready to suffer quietly and patiently. Be gentle and ready to forgive; never hold grudges. Remember, the Lord forgave you, so you must forgive others. Most of all, let love guide your life, for then the whole church will stay together in perfect harmony."

♥ **Lord, bless our <u>marriages</u>**
- o Psalm 103:8 (NASB) that we will be compassionate to one another, show God's grace to each other, be slow to anger and abounding in lovingkindness (toward one another as husband and wife).

♥ **Lord, bless our <u>homes</u>**
- o Proverbs 15:9 May our family pursue righteousness: "The LORD detests the way of the wicked, but he loves those who pursue righteousness."

♥ **<u>Application</u>**
- o Genesis 2:18 May we live out being a helper to our husbands. (Pray and ask God to show you each day how you can specifically be a helper to your husband that day!) "The LORD God said, 'It is not good for the man to be alone. I will make a helper suitable for him.'"

♥ **Lord, bless this <u>prayer ministry</u>**
- o Titus 3:1-2 Keep this prayer ministry pure, Lord, from gossip, complaining, and grumbling; may You, our husbands, and our families be honored. Your Word says, "Remind the people to be subject to rulers and authorities, to be obedient, to be ready to do whatever is good, to slander no one, to be peaceable and considerate, and to show true humility toward all men."

♥ **<u>Praise</u>** We praise You, Lord, that You are the Lord and Master!

Week 32

- ♥ **Praise**   God is our <u>Father</u>
    - o Deuteronomy 1:29-31   God goes before us, to fight for us…He carries us through the hard times; through the battles, as a father carries a son. (Thought: God knows the battles that lie ahead, before we know of them. He knows how to fight them; He has the power to fight them; we, His children, just need to rest in His care for us.)
    - o Psalm 68:4-6 "Sing to God, sing praise to his name…his name is the LORD…A father to the fatherless, a defender of widows…God sets the lonely in families, he leads forth the prisoners with singing; but the rebellious live in a sun-scorched land." (Thought: God is eternal, our defender, compassionate, our leader, our joy.)
    - o Matthew 6:9-13 (AMP)   "Pray, therefore, like this: Our Father Who is in heaven, hallowed (kept holy) be Your name…"
    - o John 10:27-30 "My sheep listen to my voice; I know them, and they follow me. I give them eternal life, and they shall never perish; no one can snatch them out of my hand. My Father, who has given them to me, is greater than all; no one can snatch them out of my Father's hand. I and the Father are one."
    - o John 14:6-11 "Jesus answered, 'I am the way and the truth and the life. No one comes to the Father except through me…'"
    - o 1 John 3:1-3 (AMP) "See what [an incredible] quality of love the Father has given (shown, bestowed on) us, that we should [be permitted to] be named *and* called *and* counted the children of God! And so we are! The reason that the world does not know (recognize, acknowledge) us is that it does not know (recognize, acknowledge) Him…"
- ♥ **Confession**   Psalm 103:8-19
- ♥ **Thanksgiving**   1) Thank You, Lord, for the gift of today and for the gift of being Your children.
2) Thank You that You love us all so very, very much, Lord.
3) Thank You that You are all we need; You supply all we need; You take care of us perfectly, compassionately, and completely.
4) Thank You, Lord, that You carry us through the hard times. Thank You that You are ever there for us, Lord.
5)_____
- ♥ **Lord, bless my husband by giving him a <u>wife</u> who…**
    - o has the heart attitude and lives out…that her body is not her own, but a gift from herself and the Lord, to her husband…

- o 1 Corinthians 7:4a "The wife's body does not belong to her alone but also to her husband."
- ♥ **Lord, bless our <u>husbands</u>**   Salvation (if applicable): 2 Corinthians 10:4-5
  - o Ephesians 4:29 "Do not let any unwholesome talk come out of your mouths, but only what is helpful for building others up according to their needs, that it may benefit those who listen."
- ♥ **Lord, bless our <u>marriages</u>**
  - o that we will not grow weary in doing good but will remember that we will reap a harvest if we do not give up…
  - o Galatians 6:9 (NIV) "Let us not become weary in doing good, for at the proper time we will reap a harvest if we do not give up."
  - o Galatians 6:9 (NASB) "And let us not lose heart in doing good, for in due time we shall reap if we do not grow weary."
  - o Galatians 6:9 (TLB) "And let us not get tired of doing what is right, for after a while we will reap a harvest of blessing if we don't get discouraged and give up."
- ♥ **Lord, bless our <u>homes</u>**
  - o to be filled with peace and quiet, not strife, for…
  - o Proverbs 17:1 "Better a dry crust with peace and quiet than a house full of feasting, with strife."
- ♥ **<u>Application</u>**
  - o Philippians 2:3-4 Study your husband…what are his interests, his dreams, etc.?! Line yourself up with him…"Do nothing out of selfish ambition or vain conceit, but in humility consider others better than yourselves. Each of you should look not only to your own interests, but also to the interest of others."
- ♥ **Lord, bless this <u>prayer ministry</u>**
  - o Ephesians 3:20-21 May You do immeasurably more than we could ask or imagine, Lord, through the power of Your Holy Spirit, throughout the generations, we pray: "Now to him who is able to do immeasurably more than all we ask or imagine, according to his power that is at work within us, to him be glory in the church and in Christ Jesus throughout all generations, for ever and ever! Amen."
- ♥ **<u>Praise</u>** We praise You, Lord, that You are our Father!

Week 33

- ♥ **Praise** God is <u>supreme</u>: Highest in rank, power, authority; superior, highest in degree; utmost.
  - o Deuteronomy 10:14-18 "...Circumcise your hearts, therefore, and do not be stiff-necked any longer. For the LORD your God is God of gods and LORD of lords, the great God, mighty and awesome, who shows no partiality and accepts no bribes..."
  - o Job 11:7-9 "Can you fathom the mysteries of God? Can you probe the limits of the Almighty?..."
  - o Psalm 95:1-9 "...For the LORD is the great God, the great King above all gods. In his hand are the depths of the earth, and the mountain peaks belong to him. The sea is his, for he made it, and his hands formed the dry land. Come, let us bow down in worship, let us kneel before the LORD our Maker; for he is our God and we are the people of his pasture, the flock under his care..."
  - o Acts 17:24-28 "The God who made the world and everything in it is the Lord of heaven and earth and does not live in temples built by hands. And he is not served by human hands, as if he needed anything, because he himself gives all men life and breath and everything else..."
  - o Colossians 1:15-20 "...He is before all things, and in him all things hold together. And he is the head of the body, the church; he is the beginning and the firstborn from among the dead, so that in everything he might have the supremacy..."
  - o Jude 24-25 (AMP) "Now to Him Who is able to keep you without stumbling *or* slipping *or* falling, and to present [you] unblemished (blameless and faultless) before the presence of His glory in triumphant joy *and* exultation [with unspeakable, ecstatic delight]—To the one only God, our Savior through Jesus Christ our Lord be glory (splendor), majesty, might *and* dominion, and power *and* authority, before all time and now and forever (unto all the ages of eternity). Amen (so be it)."

- ♥ **Confession**   Psalm 51:4-12
- ♥ **Thanksgiving** 1) We thank You, Lord, for You—for all that You are and forevermore will be. You are constant; Your love and loyalty are constant. You are ever faithful to Your plans and purposes in our lives.

   2) Thank You, Lord, that we can trust Your heart...as the words of a song go..."When you don't understand. When you don't see His plan. When you can't trace His hand. Trust His heart."[35]

---

[35] Babbie Mason. *Trust His Heart.* © 2006 by Spring Hill Music Group, Manufactured by EMI Christian Music G.

- ♥ Lord, bless my husband by giving him a <u>wife</u> who…
    - o does not complain to others but goes to God…
    - o Psalm 55:16-18 (NASB) (personalized and paraphrased) May we not complain to man, but call upon God; go to Him with our complaints (root: hurts and fears) that we will then receive God's peace in the midst of the battles all around us.
- ♥ Lord, bless our <u>husbands</u>   Salvation (if applicable): 2 Peter 3:8-9
    - o Ephesians 4:26-27 (TLB) May they not hold on to their anger: "If you are angry, don't sin by nursing your grudge. Don't let the sun go down with you still angry—get over it quickly; for when you are angry you give a mighty foothold to the devil."
- ♥ Lord, bless our <u>marriages</u>
    - o Stand with us to strengthen us in our marriages…
    - o 2 Timothy 4:17a (NIV) "But the Lord stood at my side and gave me strength."
    - o 2 Timothy 4:17a (NASB) "But the Lord stood with me, and strengthened me."
    - o 2 Timothy 4:17a (AMP) "But the Lord stood by me and strengthened me."
- ♥ Lord, bless our <u>homes</u>
    - o May our families promote love, for…
    - o Proverbs 17:9 (NIV) "He who covers over an offense promotes love, but whoever repeats the matter separates close friends."
    - o Proverbs 17:9 (TLB) "Love forgets mistakes; nagging about them parts the best of friends."
    - o Proverbs 17:9 (AMP) "He who covers *and* forgives an offense seeks love, but he who repeats *or* harps on a matter separates even close friends."
    - o Proverbs 17:9 (NASB) "He who covers a transgression seeks love, But he who repeats a matter separates intimate friends."
- ♥ <u>Application</u>
    - o 1 Corinthians 7:4a Lord ever give me an attitude of the heart and may I ever live out that my body is not my own but rather a gift from myself and You, Lord, to my husband: "The wife's body does not belong to her alone but also to her husband."
- ♥ Lord, bless this <u>prayer ministry</u>
    - o Romans 12:2b God's good, pleasing, and perfect will be done in and through this ministry.
- ♥ **<u>Praise</u>**   We praise You, Lord, that You are supreme!

Week 34

- ♥ **Praise**   God is <u>sovereign</u>: Holding the position of ruler, royal, reigning; independent of all others; above or superior to all others; controls everything, can do anything.
  - 1 Samuel 2:6-8 "The LORD brings death and makes alive; he brings down to the grave and raises up. The LORD sends poverty and wealth; he humbles and he exalts. He raises the poor from the dust and lifts the needy from the ash heap…for the foundations of the earth are the LORD's; upon them he has set the world."
  - 2 Chronicles 20:5-12 "…O LORD, God of our fathers, are you not the God who is in heaven? You rule over all the kingdoms of the nations. Power and might are in your hand, and no one can withstand you…we have no power to face this vast army that is attacking us. We do not know what to do, but our eyes are upon you.'"
  - Job 42:2 (NIV) "I know that you can do all things; no plan of yours can be thwarted." (TLB) "I know that you can do anything and that no one can stop you."
  - Psalm 33:10-11 (NASB) "The LORD nullifies the counsel of the nations; He frustrates the plans of the peoples. The counsel of the LORD stands forever, The plans of His heart from generation to generation." (AMP) "The Lord brings the counsel of the nations to naught; He makes the thoughts *and* plans of the peoples of no effect. The counsel of the Lord stands forever, the thoughts of His heart through all generations."
  - Isaiah 40:10-12 "See, the Sovereign LORD comes with power, and his arm rules for him…He tends his flock like a shepherd: He gathers the lambs in his arms and carries them close to his heart; he gently leads those that have young. Who has measured the waters in the hollow of his hand, or with the breadth of his hand marked off the heavens? Who has held the dust of the earth in a basket, or weighed the mountains on the scales and the hills in a balance?"
  - Isaiah 46:9-10 "Remember the former things, those of long ago; I am God, and there is no other; I am God, and there is none like me. I make known the end from the beginning, from the ancient times, what is still to come. I say: 'My purpose will stand, and I will do all that I please.'" (NIV) "…Saying, 'My purpose will be established, And I will accomplish all My good pleasure.'" (NASB)

- ♥ **Confession**   Psalm 32:1-5
- ♥ **Thanksgiving**   1) Lord, we thank You that You control everything and can do anything!
  2) We thank You that You use Your mighty power for our good and to bring glory and honor to Your name, that the world may

know that You are the one true God.
3) Thank You, Lord, that You are faithful forever. (Psalm 146:6b)
4) Thank You, Lord, that You are perfect in faithfulness. (Isaiah 25:1)
5)_____

- ♥ **Lord, bless my husband by giving him a <u>wife</u> who**...
  - o casts her burdens upon the Lord...trusts in You...
  - o Psalm 55:22, 23b (NASB) "Cast your burden upon the LORD, and He will sustain you; He will never allow the righteous to be shaken. ["to fall," NIV] I will trust in Thee."

- ♥ **Lord, bless our <u>husbands</u>**   Salvation (if applicable): Ezekiel 36:25-27
  - o May God's Word not come back void but sink in and accomplish God's purposes in his life...
  - o Isaiah 55:10-11 "As the rain and the snow come down from heaven, and do not return to it without watering the earth and making it bud and flourish, so that it yields seed for the sower and bread for the eater, so is my word that goes out from my mouth: It will not return to me empty, but will accomplish what I desire and achieve the purpose for which I sent it."

- ♥ **Lord, bless our <u>marriages</u>**
  - o Ephesians 3:20-21a (personalized and paraphrased) May You do immeasurably more than we could ask or imagine, Lord, in our marriages, according to Your power that is at work within us: You are able. We give You all the glory, Lord.

- ♥ **Lord, bless our <u>homes</u>**
  - o that they will be a place where justice reigns/is lived out, for...
  - o Proverbs 17:15 "Acquitting the guilty and condemning the innocent—the LORD detests them both."

- ♥ **<u>Application</u>**
  - o Luke 6:46-49 May we live Your Word!
  - o Psalm 119:11 May we memorize Your Word!

- ♥ **Lord, bless this <u>prayer ministry</u>**
  - o Zechariah 4:6b "'Not by might nor by power, but by my Spirit,' says the LORD Almighty." By Your Spirit, Lord, may You do all you desire in and through this prayer ministry!

- ♥ **<u>Praise</u>   We praise You, Lord, that You are sovereign!**

Week 35

- ♥ <u>Praise</u>   God is <u>omnipotent</u>:   All powerful; having unlimited power or authority; almighty.
  - o 2 Chronicles 32:7-8 (AMP) "Be strong and courageous. Be not afraid or dismayed before the king of Assyria and all the horde that is with him, for there is Another with us greater than [all those] with him. With him is an arm of flesh, but with us is the Lord our God to help us and to fight our battles. And the people relied on the words of Hezekiah king of Judah." (Thought: I need to rely on the truth of God's Word to me and not on what I see all around me.)
  - o Isaiah 40:28-31 (AMP) "...those who wait for the Lord [who expect, look for, and hope in Him] shall change *and* renew their strength *and* power; they shall lift their wings *and* mount up [close to God] as eagles [mount up to the sun]; they shall run and not be weary, they shall walk and not faint *or* become tired."
  - o Jeremiah 32:17 (NIV) "Ah, Sovereign LORD, you have made the heavens and the earth by your great power and outstretched arm. Nothing is too hard for you." (NASB) "...Nothing is too difficult for Thee." (AMP) "...There is nothing too hard *or* too wonderful for You."
  - o Matthew 19:26 "...With God all things are possible.'"
  - o Ephesians 1:19-20 (TLB) "I pray that you will begin to understand how incredibly great his power is to help those who believe him. It is that same mighty power that raised Christ from the dead and seated him in the place of honor at God's right hand in heaven."

- ♥ <u>Confession</u>   Isaiah 55:6-11
- ♥ <u>Thanksgiving</u>   1) We thank You, Lord, that we can rely on You...
  2) "For He (God) Himself has said, I will not in any way fail you *nor* give you up *nor* leave you without support. [I will] not, [I will] not, [I will] not in any degree leave you helpless *nor* forsake *nor* let [you] down (relax My hold on you)! [Assuredly not!]" Hebrews 13:5b (AMP)
  3) Thank You, Lord, for You, for the power of Your Holy Spirit in our lives, and for the power of prayer...
  4) "We are praying, too, that you will be filled with his mighty, glorious strength so that you can keep going no matter what happens—always full of the joy of the Lord and always thankful to the Father who has made us fit to share all the wonderful things that belong to those who live in the Kingdom of light." Colossians 1:11-12 (TLB)

- ♥ **Lord, bless my husband by giving him a <u>wife</u> who...**

- submits herself to her husband, for that is what the Lord has planned for us...
- Colossians 3:18 (TLB) "You wives, submit yourselves to your husbands, for that is what the Lord has planned for you."
- Colossians 3:18 (AMP) "Wives, be subject to your husbands [subordinate and adapt yourselves to them], as is right *and* fitting *and* your proper duty in the Lord."

♥ **Lord, bless our <u>husbands</u>**   Salvation (if applicable): Isaiah 55:10-11
- Lord, bless him by cleansing him of idols, giving him right desires and an obedient heart...
- Ezekiel 36:25-27 (TLB) "Then it will be as though I had sprinkled clean water on you, for you will be clean—your filthiness will be washed away, your idol worship gone. And I will give you a new heart—I will give you new and right desires—and put a new spirit within you. I will take out your stony hearts of sin and give you new hearts of love. And I will put my Spirit within you so that you will obey my laws and do whatever I command."

♥ **Lord, bless our <u>marriages</u>**
- Hebrews 13:4 (NIV) "Marriage should be honored by all, and the marriage bed kept pure, for God will judge the adulterer and all the sexually immoral." (Thought: In our hearts as well; do not compare in any way, for comparing is a robber of joy.)
- Hebrews 13:4 (TLB) "Honor your marriage and its vows, and be pure; for God will surely punish all those who are immoral or commit adultery."
- Hebrews 13:4 (AMP) "Let marriage be held in honor (esteemed worthy, precious, of great price, and especially dear) in all things. And thus let the marriage bed be undefiled (kept undishonored); for God will judge *and* punish the unchaste [all guilty of sexual vice] and adulterous."

♥ **Lord, bless our <u>homes</u>**
- May we not quarrel and/or build up walls, for...
- Proverbs 17:19 "He who loves a quarrel loves sin; he who builds a high gate invites destruction."

♥ <u>**Application**</u>
- Luke 6:46-49 May we live Your Word!
- Psalm 119:11 May we memorize Your Word!

♥ **Lord, bless this <u>prayer ministry</u>**
- 1 Chronicles 4:10 Bless, enlarge, empower, keep from harm...this ministry.

♥ <u>**Praise**</u> We praise You, Lord, that You are omnipotent!

Week 36

- **Praise**   God is <u>omniscient</u>:   Having infinite knowledge; knowing all things.
    - Psalm 139:1-5 (TLB)   "O Lord, you have examined my heart and know everything about me. You know when I sit or stand. When far away you know my every thought. You chart the path ahead of me, and tell me where to stop and rest. Every moment, you know where I am. You know what I am going to say before I even say it. You both precede and follow me, and place your hand of blessing on my head."
    - Isaiah 65:24 (NIV) "Before they call I will answer; while they are still speaking I will hear." (TLB) "I will answer them before they even call to me. While they are still talking to me about their needs, I will go ahead and answer their prayers!"
    - Matthew 6:8b (TLB) "Remember, your Father knows exactly what you need even before you ask him!"
    - Matthew 10: 29-31 (AMP)   "Are not two little sparrows sold for a penny? And yet not one of them will fall to the ground without your Father's leave (consent) *and* notice. But even the very hairs of your head are all numbered. Fear not, then; you are of more value than many sparrows."
    - Romans 11:33-36 (NIV) "Oh, the depth of the riches of the wisdom and knowledge of God! How unsearchable his judgments, and his paths beyond tracing out! 'Who has known the mind of the Lord? Or who has been his counselor?' 'Who has ever given to God, that God should repay him?' For from him and through him and to him are all things. To him be the glory forever! Amen." (TLB) "...For everything comes from God alone. Everything lives by his power, and everything is for his glory. To him be glory evermore."
    - Hebrews 4:12-13 (TLB) "For whatever God says to us is full of living power; it is sharper than the sharpest dagger, cutting swift and deep into our innermost thoughts and desires with all their parts, exposing us for what we really are. He knows about everyone, everywhere. Everything about us is bare and wide open to the all-seeing eyes of our living God; nothing can be hidden from him to whom we must explain all that we have done." (NIV) "...to whom we must give account."

- **Confession**   1 John 1:8-9
- **Thanksgiving**   1) We thank You, Lord, that You love us so and are so concerned about every detail of our lives.
    2) Thank You, Lord, for Your mercy, grace, and steadfastness.
    3) Thank You, Lord, for the truth of this statement that I learned in Bible study this past week: "Life is hard, but God is good"!

4) Thank You, Lord, that You know our deepest heart cries and You cry with us! You know the prayers we will utter before we even speak them, and You answer our prayers in Your perfect timing and in Your perfect way. You know and want what is best for us all. You know the end from the beginning, and You ever have an eternal perspective. You are always good!

- **Lord, bless my husband by giving him a <u>wife</u> who...**
  - will want only God's will for her life...
  - Psalm 119:33-38 (TLB) "Just tell me what to do and I will do it, Lord As long as I live I'll wholeheartedly obey. Make me walk along the right paths for I know how delightful they really are. Help me to prefer obedience to making money! Turn me away from wanting any other plan than yours. Revive my heart toward you. Reassure me that your promises are for me, for I trust and revere you."

- **Lord, bless our <u>husbands</u>**   Salvation (if applicable): Ephesians 1:17-18
  - For any who are dads and/or may become dads, we pray...
  - Colossians 3:21 (TLB) "Fathers, don't scold your children so much that they become discouraged and quit trying."

- **Lord, bless our <u>marriages</u>**
  - Proverbs 16:3 (personalized for our marriages) Lord, we commit unto You our marriages; may You bring your plans of success to them.

- **Lord, bless our <u>homes</u>**
  - Lord, clean up our hearts and thus our homes; remove from us idols and covetousness...
  - Deuteronomy 7:25-26 May no detestable thing be brought into our homes.

- **<u>Application</u>**
  - Luke. 18:1 May we always pray and not give up!

- **Lord, bless this <u>prayer ministry</u>**
  - Psalm 91:4b May Your faithfulness shield, protect, and defend this ministry, Lord, we pray.

- **<u>Praise</u>** We praise You, Lord, that You are omniscient!

Week 37

- ♥ **Praise** God is <u>omnipresent</u>: Present at all places at all times.
    - o Psalm 46:1-7 "God is our refuge and strength, an ever-present help in trouble. Therefore we will not fear...The LORD Almighty is with us; the God of Jacob is our fortress."
    - o Psalm 139:5-10 (NIV) "You hem me in behind and before: you have laid your hand upon me. Such knowledge is too wonderful for me, too lofty for me to attain. Where can I go from your Spirit? Where can I flee from your presence? If I go up to the heavens, you are there; if I make my bed in the depths, you are there. If I rise on the wings of the dawn, if I settle on the far side of the sea, even there your hand will guide me, your right hand will hold me fast." (TLB) "...even there your hand will guide me, your strength will support me."
    - o Romans 8:38-39 (TLB) "For I am convinced that nothing can ever separate us from his love. Death can't, and life can't. The angels won't, and all the powers of hell itself cannot keep God's love away. Our fears today, our worries about tomorrow, or where we are—high above the sky, or in the deepest ocean—nothing will ever be able to separate us from the love of God demonstrated by our Lord Jesus Christ when he died for us."
    - o Colossians 1:17 (TLB) "He was before all else began and it is his power that holds everything together."
    - o 2 Timothy 4:16-18 "At my first defense, no one came to my support, but everyone deserted me. May it not be held against them. But the Lord stood at my side and gave me strength, so that through me the message might be fully proclaimed and all the Gentiles might hear it. And I was delivered from the lion's mouth. The Lord will rescue me from every evil attack and will bring me safely to his heavenly kingdom. To him be glory forever and ever. Amen."
    - o Hebrews 13:5 (AMP) "Let your character *or* moral disposition be free from love of money [including greed, avarice, lust, and craving for earthly possessions] and be satisfied with your present [circumstances and with what you have]; for He [God] Himself has said, I will not in any way fail you *nor* give you up *nor* leave you without support. [I will] not, [I will] not, [I will] not in any degree leave you helpless *nor* forsake *nor* let [you] down (relax My hold on you)! [Assuredly not!]"

- ♥ <u>**Confession**</u>   1 John 2:1-2
- ♥ <u>**Thanksgiving**</u>   1) We thank You, Lord, for You and the truth of Your Word.
    2) Thank You, Lord, for Your constant encouragement to us all.
    3) Thank You, Lord, that You are always with us; thus we do not need to fear.

4) Thank You, Lord, for the power of prayer.

- ♥ **Lord, bless my husband by giving him a <u>wife</u> who**…
  - o has wholesome talk that builds her husband up…
  - o Ephesians 4:29 "Do not let any unwholesome talk come out of your mouths, but only what is helpful for building others up according to their needs, that it may benefit those who listen."

- ♥ **Lord, bless our <u>husbands</u>**   Salvation (if applicable): Jeremiah 32:40
  - o that they will want only God's will for their life…
  - o Psalm 119:33-38 (TLB) "Just tell me what to do and I will do it, Lord. As long as I live I'll wholeheartedly obey. Make me walk along the right paths for I know how delightful they really are. Help me to prefer obedience to making money! ["Turn my heart toward your statutes and not toward selfish gain," NIV] Turn me away from wanting any other plan than yours. Revive my heart toward you. Reassure me that your promises are for me, for I trust and revere you."

- ♥ **Lord, bless our <u>marriages</u>**
  - o 2 Chronicles 32:7-8 (NASB) (paraphrased/personalized for our marriages) May we be strong and courageous, and not fear the enemy that is all around us trying to destroy our marriages. For God is greater; God is our help and fights our battles. May we rely on Him and the truth of His Word to us.

- ♥ **Lord, bless our <u>homes</u>**
  - o May our homes be filled with pleasant/kind words, for…
  - o Proverbs 16:24 (NIV) "Pleasant words are a honeycomb, sweet to the soul and healing to the bones."
  - o Proverbs 16:24 (TLB) "Kind words are like honey—enjoyable and healthful."
  - o Proverbs 16:24 (AMP) "Pleasant words are as a honeycomb, sweet to the mind and healing to the body."

- ♥ **<u>Application</u>**
  - o Colossians 4:2 (NIV) "Devote yourselves to prayer, being watchful and thankful."
  - o Colossians 4:2 (TLB) "Don't be weary in prayer; keep at it; watch for God's answers and remember to be thankful when they come."

- ♥ **Lord, bless this <u>prayer ministry</u>**
  - o Matthew 9:38 We ask You, the Lord of the harvest, to send out workers.

- ♥ **<u>Praise</u>** We praise You, Lord, that You are omnipresent!

Week 38

- ❤ **Praise**   God is <u>immutable</u>:   Never changing or varying; unchangeable.
    - o 1 Samuel 15:29 "He who is the Glory of Israel does not lie or change his mind; for he is not a man, that he should change his mind."
    - o Psalm 33:11 "But the plans of the LORD stand firm forever, the purposes of his heart through all generations."
    - o Psalm 100:5 "For the LORD is good and his love endures forever; his faithfulness continues through all generations."
    - o Psalm 119:89, 152 "Your word, O LORD, is eternal; it stands firm in the heavens…Long ago I learned from your statutes that you established them to last forever."
    - o Malachi 3:6a "I the LORD do not change."
    - o Hebrews 6:17-19a (AMP) "Accordingly God also, in His desire to show more convincingly *and* beyond doubt to those who were to inherit the promise the unchangeableness of His purpose *and* plan, intervened (mediated) with an oath. This was so that, by two unchangeable things [His promise and His oath] in which it is impossible for God ever to prove false or deceive us, we who have fled [to Him] for refuge might have mighty indwelling strength and strong encouragement to grasp *and* hold fast the hope appointed for us *and* set before [us]. [Now] we have this [hope] as a sure and steadfast anchor of the soul [it cannot slip and it cannot break down under whoever steps out upon it]."

- ❤ **Confession**   Psalm 86:5
- ❤ **Thanksgiving**   1) Thank You and praise You, Lord, for the power of Your Word.
    2) Thank You, Lord, for how praying Your Word works in our hearts, making Your changes in us, week after week.
    3) Thank You, Lord, that You are always the answer, running to You, holding on to You—our "sure and steadfast anchor."
    4) Thank You, Lord, that You are all that we need. You are our all sufficiency. You are our provider, sustainer, helper, our hope, our strength, our joy, our life, our all.
    5)_____

- ❤ Lord, bless my husband by giving him a <u>wife</u> who…
    - o will be quick to listen, slow to speak and slow to become angry…
    - o James 1:19-20 "My dear brothers, take note of this: Everyone should be quick to listen, slow to speak and slow to become angry, ["slow to take offense *and* to get angry," (AMP)] for man's anger does not bring about the righteous life that God desires."

- ❤ Lord, bless our <u>husbands</u>   Salvation (if applicable): Luke 24:45

- o that they will put their confidence in God and trust His Word...
- o Psalm 56:3-4 "When I am afraid. I will trust in you. In God, whose word I praise, in God I trust; I will not be afraid. What can mortal man do to me?"

♥ **Lord, bless our <u>marriages</u>**
- o Scatter the enemies of our marriages (anything that sets itself up against You and Your ways, Lord) with Your mighty arm, we pray...
- o Psalm 89:10b (NASB) "Thou didst scatter Thine enemies with Thy mighty arm."

♥ **Lord, bless our <u>homes</u>**
- o Lord, we thank You that You know the plans that You have for our family. May we rest in Your Truth...
- o Jeremiah 29:11-13 For I know the plans I have for (<u>your family's name</u>), declares the Lord, plans to prosper you and not to harm you, plans to give you hope and a future. May You draw each one of us in our family to call upon You and come and pray to You, and thank You that You will listen. May each one in our family seek You, for Your Word says, "You will seek me and find me when you seek me with all your heart."

♥ **<u>Application</u>**
- o Genesis 2:18, 22 (personal application) Lord, mold us into what our husbands need; make us a gift to them. May we know deep in our hearts that they are a hand-picked blessing from You to us...may we treat them that way...may our body language, attitude, tone of voice, the way we spend our time and energy, etc., display that they are a precious gift/blessing.

♥ **Lord, bless <u>this prayer ministry</u>**
- o Titus 3:1-2 Keep this ministry pure from gossip, complaining, and grumbling. May this ministry always honor You, Lord, and ever honor our husbands/our families. Your Word says, "Remind the people to be subject to rulers and authorities, to be obedient, to be ready to do whatever is good, to slander no one, to be peaceable and considerate, and to show true humility toward all men."

♥ **<u>Praise</u>** We praise You, Lord, that You are immutable!

Week 39

- ♥ <u>Praise</u>   God is <u>faithful</u>:   Constant, loyal, reliable, steadfast, unwavering, devoted, true, dependable.
  - o Deuteronomy 7:9 "Know therefore that the LORD your God is God; he is the faithful God, keeping his covenant of love to a thousand generations of those who love him and keep his commands."
  - o Psalm 33:4 "For the word of the LORD is right and true; he is faithful in all he does."
  - o Psalm 146:5-6 "Blessed is he whose help is the God of Jacob, whose hope is in the LORD his God, the Maker of heaven and earth, the sea, and everything in them—the LORD, who remains faithful forever."
  - o Lamentations 3:21-24 (AMP)   "…great *and* abundant is Your stability *and* faithfulness. The Lord is my portion *or* share, says my living being (my inner self); therefore will I hope in Him *and* wait expectantly for Him."
  - o 2 Timothy 2:13 (AMP) "If we are faithless [do not believe and are untrue to Him], He remains true (faithful to His Word and His righteous character), for He cannot deny Himself."
  - o 1 John 1:9 (AMP) "If we [freely] admit that we have sinned *and* confess our sins, He is faithful and just (true to His own nature and promises) and will forgive our sins [dismiss our lawlessness] and [continuously] cleanse us from all unrighteousness [everything not in conformity to His will in purpose, thought, and action]."

- ♥ <u>Confession</u>   Romans 5:20b
- ♥ <u>Thanksgiving</u>   1) Thank You, Lord, that You are ever faithful to Your Word and to Your character.
  2) Thank You, Lord, for how praying Your Word works in our hearts, making Your changes in us, week after week.
  3) Thank You, Lord, that You are always with us.
  4) Thank You, Lord, that You continuously love us, not because of anything we do or do not do, but just because we are Your children.

- ♥ **Lord, bless my husband by giving him a <u>wife</u> who…**
  - o knows You better and better; knows the hope to which You have called us, Lord…
  - o Ephesians 1:17-18 "I keep asking that the God of our Lord Jesus Christ, the glorious Father, may give you the Spirit of wisdom and revelation, so that you may know him better. I pray also that the eyes of your heart may be enlightened in order that you may know the hope to which he has called you, the riches of his glorious inheritance in the saints."

- ♥ Lord, bless our husbands   Salvation (if applicable): Psalm 18:16-17
    - o that they may know Christ better, know the hope to which God has called them...
    - o Ephesians 1:17-18 "I keep asking that the God of our Lord Jesus Christ, the glorious Father, may give you the Spirit of wisdom and revelation, so that you may know him better. I pray also that the eyes of your heart may be enlightened in order that you may know the hope to which he has called you., the riches of his glorious inheritance in the saints."

- ♥ Lord, bless our marriages
    - o May we wait on the Lord and gain new strength to persevere in our marriages...
    - o Isaiah 40:31a (NASB) "Yet those who wait for the LORD Will gain new strength."
    - o Isaiah 40:31 (AMP) "But those who wait for the Lord [who expect, look for, and hope in Him] shall change *and* renew their strength *and* power; they shall lift their wings *and* mount up [close to God] as eagles [mount up to the sun]; they shall run and not be weary, they shall walk and not faint *or* become tired."

- ♥ Lord, bless our homes
    - o May Your Word be a lamp unto our feet and a light unto our path in our homes, we pray...
    - o Psalm 119:105 (NIV) "Your word is a lamp to my feet and a light for my path."
    - o Psalm 119:105 (TLB) "Your words are a flashlight to light the path ahead of me, and keep me from stumbling."

- ♥ **Application**
    - o Lesson I learned from the book *A Woman After God's Own Heart* by Elizabeth George...
    The better follower I am, the better leader my husband will be.[36] Lord, help us to not just think about and/or not just pray about being a better follower of our husbands, but help us, this week and always, to live it out...teach us, enable us, give us the heart's desire to do so, Lord.

- ♥ Lord, bless this prayer ministry
    - o Ephesians 3:20-21 Do immeasurably more than all we could ask or imagine, Lord...You are able!

- ♥ **Praise** We praise You, Lord, that You are faithful!

---

[36] Elizabeth George, *A Woman After God's Own Heart,* (Eugene, Oregon, Harvest House Publishers, 1997), 60-62.

Week 40

- ♥ **Praise**   God is <u>holy</u>:   Spiritually perfect or pure: sinless; deserving awe, reverence, adoration.
    - o Exodus 15:11 "…Who is like you—majestic in holiness, awesome in glory, working wonders?"
    - o 1 Samuel 2:2 "There is no one holy like the Lord; there is no one besides you; there is no Rock like our God."
    - o Psalm 99:5 "Exalt the Lord our God and worship at his footstool; he is holy."
    - o Isaiah 57:15-16 (TLB) "…I [the Holy One] refresh the humble and give new courage to those with repentant hearts…"
    - o 1 Peter 1:15-16 (AMP) "But as the One Who called you is holy, you yourselves also be holy in all your conduct and manner of living. For it is written, You shall be holy, for I am holy."
    - o Revelation 15:4 (NASB) "Who will not fear, O Lord, and glorify Thy name? For Thou alone art holy; For ALL THE NATIONS WILL COME AND WORSHIP BEFORE THEE, For Thy righteous acts have been revealed."

- ♥ **Confession**   Psalm 139:23-24 along with 1 John 1:8-9
- ♥ **Thanksgiving**
    1) Thank You, Lord, that You are a holy God: You are the one true God: we can trust You and Your ways.
    2) Thank You, Lord, for the privilege to pray to You, the King of the universe!
    3) Thank You, Lord, that You are concerned about every detail of our lives.
    4) Thank You, Lord, that You use the hard times in our lives for our good. It has been in the hard times that I have come to know You better. Thank You that You are always right here by our side.

- ♥ **Lord, bless my husband by giving him a <u>wife</u> who…**
    - o is free from the love of money, is content, for the Lord is her helper…
    - o Hebrews 13:5-6 (NIV) "Keep your lives free from the love of money and be content with what you have, because God has said, 'Never will I leave you; never will I forsake you.' So we say with confidence, 'The Lord is my helper: I will not be afraid. What can man do to me?'"
    - o Hebrews 13:5-6 (TLB) "Stay away from the love of money; be satisfied with what you have. For God has said, 'I will never, *never* fail you nor forsake you.' That is why we can say without any doubt or fear, 'The Lord is my Helper and I am not afraid of anything that mere man can do to me.'"

- ❤ Lord, bless our <u>husbands</u>   Salvation (if applicable): John 6:64-65
    - o that they will not fix their hope on the uncertainty of worldly riches, but on God...
    - o 1 Timothy 6:17-19 (NASB) "Instruct those who are rich in this present world not to be conceited or to fix their hope on the uncertainty of riches, but on God, who richly supplies us with all things to enjoy. Instruct them to do good, to be rich in good works, to be generous and ready to share, storing up for themselves the treasure of a good foundation for the future, so that they may take hold of that which is life indeed."

- ❤ Lord, bless our <u>marriages</u>
    - o May we remember nothing is too difficult for God; that includes whatever struggle we are going through in our marriages right now. God is bigger than any of our problems!
    - o Jeremiah 32:17 (NASB) "Ah LORD God! Behold, Thou hast made the heavens and the earth by Thy great power and by Thine outstretched arm! Nothing is too difficult for Thee."

- ❤ Lord, bless our <u>homes</u>
    - o May the Sabbath be honored in our homes. May it be a day of rest and refreshment. May we honor God by honoring/obeying His Word.
    - o Exodus 20:8 "Remember the Sabbath day by keeping it holy."
    - o Exodus 23:12 "Six days do your work, but on the seventh day do not work, so that your ox and your donkey may rest and the slave born in your household, and the alien as well, may be refreshed."

- ❤ <u>Application</u>
    - o Further applications from lessons I learned from the book *A Woman After God's Own Heart* by Elizabeth George...
        - o Each day this week, and evermore, may we as wives ask ourselves;
        - o Was I a blessing or a burden to my husband today?!
        - o Was I a help or a hindrance to my husband today?!
        - o Did I fit into my husband's plans today or did I fight for my own way?![37]
    - Do a work in our hearts/lives as wives, Lord. Make us a channel of blessing!

- ❤ Lord, bless <u>this prayer ministry</u>
    - o Romans 12:2b May Your good, pleasing, and perfect will be done, Lord.

- ❤ <u>Praise</u>   We praise You, Lord, that You are holy!

---

[37] Ibid.

Always Pray & Don't Give Up (Luke 18:1)

Week 41

- ❤ **Praise**　　God is <u>just</u>: Right or fair; impartial, upright, lawful, correct, true; righteous.
    - Duet. 32:3-4 "I will proclaim the name of the LORD. Oh, praise the greatness of our God! He is the Rock, his works are perfect, and all his ways are just. A faithful God who does no wrong, upright and just is he."
    - Psalm 9:7-10 "The LORD reigns forever; he has established his throne for judgment. He will judge the world in righteousness; he will govern the peoples with justice. The LORD is a refuge for the oppressed, a stronghold in times of trouble. Those who know your name will trust in you, for you, LORD, have never forsaken those who seek you."
    - Psalm 89:14-16 "Righteousness and justice are the foundation of your throne; love and faithfulness go before you. Blessed are those who have learned to acclaim you, who walk in the light of your presence, O LORD. They rejoice in your name all day long; they exult in your righteousness."
    - Isaiah 30:18 "Yet the LORD longs to be gracious to you; he rises to show you compassion. For the LORD is a God of justice. Blessed are all who wait for him!"
    - Zephaniah 3:5 "The LORD within her is righteous; he does no wrong. Morning by morning he dispenses his justice, and every new day he does not fail, yet the unrighteous know no shame."
    - Revelation 15:3-4 (NASB) "And they sang the song of Moses the bond-servant of God and the song of the Lamb, saying, 'Great and marvelous are Thy works, O Lord God, the Almighty; Righteous and true are Thy ways, Thou King of the nations. Who will not fear, O Lord, and glorify Thy name? For Thou alone art holy; For ALL THE NATIONS WILL COME AND WORSHIP BEFORE THEE, For Thy righteous acts have been revealed.'"

- ❤ **Confession**　　Psalm 51:1-2

- ❤ **Thanksgiving**　　1) Thank You, Lord, for Your goodness, faithfulness, and patience, toward us, Your children.
    2) Thank You, Lord, that You speak truth to our hearts if we will simply be still and listen.
    3) Thank You, Lord, that You are always there for us.
    4) Thank You, Lord, that You put Your arm around us and strengthen us to make it through the storms of life. Thank You also that, at times, You will push us out of the nest that we may learn to fly. Oh, how You care for us, Lord. Deuteronomy 32:10-11 says, "In a desert land he found him, in a barren and howling waste. He shielded him and cared for him; he guarded him as the apple of his eye; like an eagle that stirs up its nest and hovers

over its young, that spreads its wings to catch them and carries them on its pinions."

- ❤ **Lord, bless my husband by giving him a <u>wife</u> who…**
    - o fixes her hope on God and not on the uncertainty of worldly riches…
    - o 1 Timothy 6:17 (NASB) "Instruct those who are rich in this present world not to be conceited or to fix their hope on the uncertainty of riches, but on God, who richly supplies us with all things to enjoy."

- ❤ **Lord, bless our <u>husbands</u>**   Salvation (if applicable): Romans 1:20
    - o May they be free from the love of money, being content, the Lord being their helper…
    - o Hebrews 13:5-6 (NASB) "Let your character be free from the love of money, being content with what you have; for He Himself has said, 'I WILL NEVER DESERT YOU, NOR WILL I EVER FORSAKE YOU,' so that we confidently say, 'THE LORD IS MY HELPER, I WILL NOT BE AFRAID. WHAT SHALL MAN DO TO ME?'"

- ❤ **Lord, bless our <u>marriages</u>**
    - o Through the power of Your Holy Spirit, Lord, resurrect our marriages; bring them back from the dead and bring new life to them, Lord, we pray…
    - o Ephesians 1:19-20 (NASB) "…and what is the surpassing greatness of His power toward us who believe. *These are* in accordance with the working of the strength of His might which He brought about in Christ, when He raised Him from the dead, and seated Him at His right hand in the heavenly *places*."

- ❤ **Lord, bless our <u>homes</u>**
    - o Peace…
    - o John 16:33 "I have told you these things, so that in me you may have peace. In this world you will have trouble. But take heart! I have overcome the world."

- ❤ **<u>Application</u>**
    - o 1 John 3:18 "Dear children, let us not love with words or tongue but with actions and in truth." May we not take our husbands for granted, but rather may we appreciate and respect them and the role God has given them as leader of our home. May our actions display this kind of heart attitude.

- ❤ **Lord, bless <u>this prayer ministry</u>**
    - o Zechariah 4:6b "'Not by might nor by power, but by my Spirit,' says the LORD Almighty."

- ❤ **<u>Praise</u>**   We praise You, Lord, that You are just!

Week 42

- ♥ **Praise** God is <u>wise</u>: From root *to know* or *to see*, but wisdom goes past knowledge to understanding and action; having keen perception, discernment; power of judging rightly; always making right choices.
  - o 1 Chronicles 28:9-10 "…The LORD searches every heart and understands every motive behind the thoughts…"
  - o Proverbs 2:6 "For the LORD gives wisdom…"
  - o Isaiah 28:29 "All this also comes from the LORD Almighty, wonderful in counsel and magnificent in wisdom."
  - o Daniel 2:19-22 "…Praise be to the name of God for ever and ever; wisdom and power are his…He reveals deep and hidden things…"
  - o Romans 16:25-27 "…to the only wise God be glory forever through Jesus Christ! Amen."
  - o James 3:17-18 "But the wisdom that comes from heaven is first of all pure; then peace-loving, considerate, submissive, full of mercy and good fruit, impartial and sincere. Peacemakers who sow in peace raise a harvest of righteousness."

- ♥ **Confession**   Psalm 32:3-5 and 1 John 2:1-2

- ♥ **Thanksgiving**   1) Thank You, Lord, that You are "wonderful in counsel."
  2) Thank You, Lord, that we have You to run to.
  3) Thank You, Lord, that You are our Rock. Your works are perfect, Your ways are just. You are faithful, You do no wrong. (See Deuteronomy 32:4.)
  4) Thank You, Lord, that You ride on the heavens to help us… You are our shield, our helper, and our glorious sword. (See Deuteronomy 33:26-29.) We so thank You, Lord, for Your Word, for it is not just idle words for us, but it is indeed our LIFE! (See Deuteronomy 32:47.)

- ♥ **Lord, bless my husband by giving him a <u>wife</u> who…**
  - o throws off everything that hinders and the sin that so easily entangles, runs with perseverance the race marked out for her, fixing her eyes on Jesus and the joy set before her, therefore enduring her cross… not growing weary or losing heart…
  - o Hebrews 12:1-3 "Therefore, since we are surrounded by such a great cloud of witnesses, let us throw off everything that hinders and the sin that so easily entangles, and let us run with perseverance the race marked out for us. Let us fix our eyes on Jesus, the author and perfecter of our faith, who for the joy set before him endured the cross, scorning its shame, and sat down at the

right hand of the throne of God. Consider him who endured such opposition from sinful men, so that you will not grow weary and lose heart."

- ♥ Lord, bless our <u>husbands</u>   Salvation (if applicable): Psalm 46:10
  - o that they may walk in a manner worthy of the Lord...
  - o Colossians 1:10 "And we pray this in order that you may live a life worthy of the Lord and may please him in every way: bearing fruit in every good work, growing in the knowledge of God."

- ♥ Lord, bless our <u>marriages</u>
  - o Do exceedingly, abundantly more than all we could ask or imagine...You are able!
  - o Ephesians 3:20 "Now to him who is able to do immeasurably more than all we ask or imagine, according to his power that is at work within us..."

- ♥ Lord, bless our <u>homes</u>
  - o May they be Christ-centered...that He Himself might come to have first place...
  - o Colossians 1:18b (NASB) "...that He Himself might come to have first place in everything."

- ♥ <u>Application</u>
  - o 1 John 3:18 "Dear children, let us not love with words or tongue but with actions and in truth."
  - o May we love with action and in truth this week, and always, by looking for our husbands' strengths and by choosing to focus on their strengths...may we make the deliberate choice to not focus on their weaknesses and/or on those things that irritate us...for may we remember Your Word, Lord, of Matthew 7:3...may we focus on paying attention to the plank in our own eye, and then the speck will fade away!

- ♥ Lord, bless <u>this prayer ministry</u>
  - o 1 Chronicles 4:10 fourfold prayer of blessing:
    - o Bless this ministry indeed
    - o Enlarge its territory
    - o Empower this ministry; may Your hand be with it
    - o Keep this ministry free from sin...from bringing pain or harm upon itself or others

- ♥ **<u>Praise</u>**   We praise You, Lord, that You are wise!

Week 43

♥ **Praise** God is <u>eternal</u>: Without beginning or end; existing through all time; everlasting.
- Exodus 15:18 "The LORD will reign for ever and ever."
- Deuteronomy 33:26-29 "…The eternal God is your refuge, and underneath are the everlasting arms…"
- Psalm 90:1-2 "Lord, you have been our dwelling place throughout all generations. Before the mountains were born or you brought forth the earth and the world, from everlasting to everlasting you are God."
- Isaiah 26:4 (AMP) "So trust in the Lord (commit yourself to Him, lean on Him, hope confidently in Him) forever; for the Lord God is an everlasting Rock [the Rock of Ages]." (TLB) "Trust in the Lord God always, for in the Lord Jehovah is your everlasting strength."
- Jeremiah 31:3 "…I have loved you with an everlasting love…"
- 1 Timothy 1:17 "Now to the King eternal, immortal, invisible, the only God, be honor and glory for ever and ever. Amen."

♥ **Confession** Psalm 103:8-19

♥ **Thanksgiving**
1) Thank You, Lord, that You are so wonderful, so faithful, so very real.
2) Thank You, Lord, that You love us so much that You sent Your Son to die for us, so that we could live.
3) Thank You, Lord, that You encourage our hearts to keep praying and not give up. Thank You that You are our hope.
4) Thank You, Lord, that as we pray specifically, You answer specifically. You care about every tiny little detail of our lives. 1 Peter 5:7 (TLB) says, "Let him have all your worries and cares, for he is always thinking about you and watching everything that concerns you." Thank You, Lord.
5)_____

♥ **Lord, bless my husband by giving him a <u>wife</u> who…**
- leans on the incomparably great power of the Holy Spirit for us who believe…(Help us lean on the power of the Holy Spirit; that same power that raised Jesus from the dead is in us who believe. Raise us up over our struggles, discouragements, fears, heartaches, etc.)
- Ephesians 1:19-20 (NIV) "…and his incomparably great power for us who believe. That power is like the working of his mighty strength, which he exerted in Christ when he raised him from the dead and seated him at his right hand in the heavenly realms."

- o Ephesians 1:19-20 (TLB) "I pray that you will begin to understand how incredibly great his power is to help those who believe him. It is that same mighty power that raised Christ from the dead and seated him in the place of honor at God's right hand in heaven."

♥ **Lord, bless our <u>husbands</u>**   Salvation (if applicable): Matthew 18:12-14
- o that they will seek the Lord and His strength, seek Him continually...
- o 1 Chronicles 16:11 (NASB) "Seek the LORD and His strength; Seek His face continually."

♥ **Lord, bless our <u>marriages</u>**
- o Isaiah 58:9-12 (NASB) (paraphrased/personalized for our marriages)...
- o v. 9   May we not burden our spouses by "the pointing of the finger and speaking wickedness."
- o v. 11   Lord, continually guide our marriages; help us know that only you satisfy...(May we not look to each other for our needs to be satisfied, but may we look to you, Lord)...give strength to our marriages; make them like a well-watered garden.
- o v. 12 Rebuild, repair, and restore our marriages.

♥ **Lord, bless our <u>homes</u>**
- o May they not be a place of disorder but a place of peace (applying the truth found in this verse to our homes)...
- o 1 Corinthians 14:33a "For God is not a God of disorder but of peace."

♥ **<u>Application</u>**
- o 1 John 3:18 "Dear children, let us not love with words or tongue but with actions and in truth."
  - o Lord, may we not just say the words "I love you" to our husbands, but may our actions and attitudes display that we truly love them. ("Actions speak louder than words!")
  - o May we choose to take the time and energy to do something special for our husband, this week, something just for him!

♥ **Lord, bless this <u>prayer ministry</u>**
- o Psalm 91:4b May Your faithfulness shield, protect, and defend this ministry, Lord.

♥ **<u>Praise</u>**   We praise You, Lord, that You are eternal!

Week 44

- ❤ <u>Praise</u>   God is the <u>Creator</u>:   The one who brought the universe and all matter of life in it into existence.
  - o Genesis 1:1 "In the beginning God created the heavens and the earth."
  - o Psalm 95:1-8 "…In his hand are the depths of the earth, and the mountain peaks belong to him. The sea is his, for he made it, and his hands formed the dry land. Come, let us bow down in worship, let us kneel before the LORD our Maker; for he is our God and we are the people of his pasture, the flock under his care…"
  - o Psalm 100 "…Know that the LORD is God. It is he who made us…"
  - o Psalm 148:1-6 "…Let them praise the name of the LORD, for he commanded and they were created…"
  - o Acts 17:24-28 "…He himself gives all men life and breath and everything else…'in him we live and move and have our being…'"
  - o Colossians 1:15-17 "…All things were created by him and for him…"

- ❤ <u>Confession</u>   Psalm 51:4-12

- ❤ <u>Thanksgiving</u>   1) Thank You, Lord, that You are always with us.
  2) Thank You, Lord, that You are always loving us, watching over us, taking such sovereign, wonderful care of us.
  3) Thank You, Lord, that You provide perfectly for us; You know just what we need (to become more like Jesus).
  4) Thank You, Lord, that You are there, working in our midst, even when we cannot see clearly and cannot understand and/or see all the good You are doing in our lives and the lives of others. Thank You for teaching me that there is a purpose in the pain and a purpose in the waiting! Life is hard, but You are good, Lord!
  5)_____

- ❤ Lord, bless my husband by giving him a <u>wife</u> who…
  - o is strengthened with all power…attaining steadfastness and patience…
  - o Colossians 1:11 (NASB) "…strengthened with all power, according to His glorious might, for the attaining of all steadfastness and patience…"
  - o Colossians 1:11 (NIV) "…being strengthened with all power according to his glorious might so that you may have great endurance and patience…"
  - o Colossians 1:11 (AMP) "[We pray] that you may be invigorated *and* strengthened with all power according to the might of His glory, [to exercise] every kind of endurance and patience (perseverance and forbearance) with joy."

- o Colossians 1:11 (TLB) "We are praying, too, that you will be filled with his mighty, glorious strength so that you can keep going no matter what happens—always full of the joy of the Lord."

♥ Lord, bless our <u>husbands</u>   Salvation (if applicable): 2 Timothy 2:25-26
- o that they will put their hope in God and thus not be downcast or discouraged…may they expect God to act…for God is their help…
- o Psalm 42:5, 11 (TLB) "Why then be downcast? Why be discouraged and sad? Hope in God! I shall yet praise him again. Yes, I shall again praise him for his help…But O my soul, don't be discouraged. Don't be upset. Expect God to act! For I know that I shall again have plenty of reason to praise him for all that he will do. He is my help! He is my God!"

♥ Lord, bless our <u>marriages</u>
- o Give life to dead/dying marriages, Lord, we pray…
- o Romans 4:17b (NASB) (personalized for our marriages) "…God, who gives life to the dead and calls into being that which does not exist" (See vv. 18-22 also.)

♥ Lord, bless our <u>homes</u>
- o Lord, shower Your goodness upon our families as we fear You…may our homes be a refuge for our families from the hardships of the world; may our homes be a place filled with Your presence and Your love…
- o Psalm 31:19-20 (NASB) "How great is Thy goodness, Which Thou hast stored up for those who fear Thee, Which Thou hast wrought for those who take refuge in Thee, Before the sons of men! Thou dost hide them in the secret place of Thy presence from the conspiracies of man; Thou dost keep them secretly in a shelter from the strife of tongues."

♥ <u>Application</u>
- o May we choose to remember/think upon the details of our marriage vows and choose to live them out this week and always!

♥ Lord, bless this <u>prayer ministry</u>
- o Matthew 9:35-38 (paraphrased/personalized for this marriage prayer ministry)…O Lord, may the Truth of Your Word bring healing to every disease that is attacking marriages; have compassion on the hurting, struggling, lost marriages. The harvest is plentiful but the workers are few. Therefore, we ask You, Lord of the harvest, to send out workers into the harvest field of hurting, struggling, lost and dying marriages! (Save them, Lord, we pray!! May Your hand of power and blessing be upon this marriage prayer ministry, Lord, we pray.)

♥ <u>**Praise**</u>   We praise You, Lord, that You are the Creator!

Week 45

- ♥ **Praise** God is good: Virtuous, excellent; upright; God is essentially, absolutely, and consummately good.
    - o Psalm 25:8 (AMP) "Good and upright is the Lord; therefore will He instruct sinners in [His] way."
    - o Psalm 86:5 (AMP) "For You, O Lord, are good, and ready to forgive [our trespasses, sending them away, letting them go completely and forever]; and You are abundant in mercy *and* loving-kindness to all those who call upon You."
    - o Psalm 136:1 "Give thanks to the LORD, for he is good, *His love endures forever*."
    - o Psalm 145:9 "The LORD is good to all; he has compassion on all he has made."
    - o Nahum 1:7 "The LORD is good, a refuge in times of trouble. He cares for those who trust in him."
    - o John 10:11 "I am the good shepherd. The good shepherd lays down his life for the sheep."

- ♥ **Confession**   Psalm 32:1-5

- ♥ **Thanksgiving**   1) Thank You, Lord, that You are always good.
    2) Thank You, Lord, that You are always lovingly and all-powerfully in complete control.
    3) Thank You, Lord, that You are all wise; You have a good plan for each of our lives. You see all the good that will come.
    4) Thank You, Lord, for the truth that Your compassion is intertwined with everything You do (Psalm 145:9b, TLB).
    5)_____

- ♥ Lord, bless my husband by giving him a **wife** who...
    - o is very patient and kind, never jealous or envious, never boastful or proud...
    - o 1 Corinthians 13:4 (TLB) "Love is very patient and kind, never jealous or envious, never boastful or proud."

- ♥ Lord, bless our **husbands**   Salvation (if applicable): Acts 26:18
    - o that they will strengthen themselves in the Lord when things are hard all around them and they are distressed...
    - o 1 Samuel 30:6 (NASB) "Moreover David was greatly distressed because the people spoke of stoning him, for all the people were embittered, each one because of his sons and his daughters. But David strengthened himself in the LORD his God."

- ♥ Lord, bless our **marriages**

- o Psalm 31:19-24 (TLB) (personalized/paraphrased for our marriages) Know/trust God's Truth...
- o v. 19 God has great blessings stored up for those who trust and reverence Him.
- o v. 20 Hide and shelter our marriages from the conspiracies of the enemy.
- o v. 21 May God's never-failing love protect our marriages like the walls of a fort!
- o v. 22 God will never desert us or our marriages.
- o v. 23 God protects those loyal to Him.
- o v. 24 Depend on the Lord.

♥ **Lord, bless our <u>homes</u>**
- o May the joy of the Lord be our strength in all things...
- o Nehemiah 8:10b "Do not grieve, for the joy of the LORD is your strength."
- o 1 Timothy 6:17 (NASB) "Instruct those who are rich in this present world not to be conceited or to fix their hope on the uncertainty of riches, but on God, who richly supplies us with all things to enjoy."

♥ **<u>Application</u>**
- o May we choose to appreciate, admire, accept, and adapt to our husbands.[38]

♥ **Lord, bless this <u>prayer ministry</u>**
- o Titus 3:1-2 Lord, keep this ministry pure from the sin of gossip, complaining, and grumbling. May this ministry always and completely honor You, Lord, and ever honor our husbands/our families. Your Word says, "Remind the people to be subject to rulers and authorities, to be obedient, to be ready to do whatever is good, to slander no one, to be peaceable and considerate, and to show true humility toward all men."

♥ **<u>Praise</u>** We praise You, Lord, that You are good!

---

[38] I first learned this principle of the 4 A's [appreciate, admire, accept, adapt to your husband] while attending a women's weekly small-group Bible study, in 2001. The Bible study leader's words struck a cord with me, so much so, that I decided to implement them into the "application" section of the prayer sheets.

Week 46

- ♥ **Praise**   God is <u>Love</u>:
  - Psalm 136:1-4 "Give thanks to the L<small>ORD</small>, for he is good, *His love endures forever*…to him who alone does great wonders, *His love endures forever.*"
  - Romans 5:5-8 "And hope does not disappoint us, because God has poured out his love into our hearts by the Holy Spirit, whom he has given us. You see, at just the right time, when we were still powerless, Christ died for the ungodly…God demonstrates his own love for us in this: While we were still sinners, Christ died for us."
  - Romans 8:35-39 (TLB) "Who then can ever keep Christ's love from us? When we have trouble or calamity, when we are hunted down or destroyed, is it because he doesn't love us anymore? And if we are hungry, or penniless, or in danger, or threatened with death, has God deserted us? No, for the Scriptures tell us that for his sake we must be ready to face death at every moment of the day—we are like sheep awaiting slaughter; but despite all this, overwhelming victory is ours through Christ who loved us enough to die for us. For I am convinced that nothing can ever separate us from his love. Death can't, and life can't. The angels won't, and all the powers of hell itself cannot keep God's love away. Our fears for today, our worries about tomorrow, or where we are—high above the sky, or in the deepest ocean—nothing will ever be able to separate us from the love of God demonstrated by our Lord Jesus Christ when he died for us."
  - Ephesians 3:14-19 "…to grasp how wide and long and high and deep is the love of Christ…"
  - 1 John 3:1 and 4:10-12 "How great is the love the Father has lavished on us, that we should be called children of God! …This is love: not that we loved God, but that he loved us and sent his Son as an atoning sacrifice for our sins. Dear friends, since God so loved us, we also ought to love one another…"

- ♥ **Confession**   Isaiah 55:6-10
- ♥ **Thanksgiving**   1) Thank You, Lord, that You love us so.
  2) Thank You, Lord, that our lives are in Your hands.
  3) Thank You, Lord, that we can trust You.
  4) Thank You, Lord, that You bless obedience; You are our perseverance.
  5)_____

- ♥ **Lord, bless my husband by giving him a <u>wife</u> who…**
  - by yielding to the power of Your Holy Spirit, lives out the Truth of Your Word of…

- o 1 Corinthians 13:5 (TLB) "[Love is]...never haughty or selfish or rude. Love does not demand its own way. It is not irritable or touchy. It does not hold grudges and will hardly even notice when others do it wrong."

♥ **Lord, bless our <u>husbands</u>**   Salvation (if applicable): 2 Corinthians 4:3-6
- o Lord, may You inspire them to fear You, so that they will never turn away from You...
- o Jeremiah 32:40 "I will make an everlasting covenant with them: I will never stop doing good to them, and I will inspire them to fear me, so that they will never turn away from me."

♥ **Lord, bless our <u>marriages</u>**
- o Colossians 3:23 (personalized/paraphrased for our marriages) Lord, help us to work at our marriages with all our hearts, as working for You, Lord, not for men.

♥ **Lord, bless our <u>homes</u>**
- o To be filled with love...
- o Romans 5:5 (NASB) "...and hope does not disappoint, because the love of God has been poured out within our hearts through the Holy Spirit who was given to us."
- o 1 Corinthians 13:2b (NIV) "If I have a faith that can move mountains, but have not love, I am nothing."
- o 1 Corinthians 16:14 (NIV) "Do everything in love."

♥ **<u>Application</u>**
- o May we:
  - o Think only Truth: Philippians 4:8 and Joshua 1:8
  - o Live only Truth: Luke 6:46-49 and Joshua 1:8
  - o Think only about today (thus not worrying about tomorrow): Matthew 6:33-34
  - o Delight in correction: Proverbs 3:11-12
- o In my heart this is a lifelong assignment God has given me as His child.

♥ **Lord, bless this <u>prayer ministry</u>**
- o Ephesians 3:20-21 May You do immeasurably more than we could ask or imagine, Lord, through the power of Your Holy Spirit, throughout the generations...You are able!

♥ **<u>Praise</u>** We praise You, Lord, that You are Love!

Week 47

- ♥ **Praise**   God is <u>Light</u>:
  - o Psalm 104:1-2 "Praise the LORD, O my soul. O LORD my God, you are very great; you are clothed with splendor and majesty. He wraps himself in light as with a garment; he stretches out the heavens like a tent."
  - o Psalm 119:105 (TLB) "Your words are a flashlight to light the path ahead of me, and keep me from stumbling." (Thought/Application: As we choose to walk in obedience to God's Word, fear is removed, truth is revealed, we are guided in the path God has for us; He is able to protect us from stumbling and getting hurt. Obedience equals protection! Oh, may we not beat ourselves up over times we have stumbled, but may we "look back only to learn"!)
  - o John 8:12 (AMP) "Once more Jesus addressed the crowd. He said, I am the Light of the world. He who follows Me will not be walking in the dark, but will have the Light which is Life."
  - o 2 Corinthians 4:5-6 (KJV) "For we preach not ourselves, but Christ Jesus the Lord; and ourselves your servants for Jesus' sake. For God, who commanded the light to shine out of darkness, hath shined in our hearts, to *give* the light of the knowledge of the glory of God in the face of Jesus Christ."
  - o 1 John 1:5-7 "This is the message we have heard from him and declare to you: God is light; in him there is no darkness at all. If we claim to have fellowship with him yet walk in the darkness, we lie and do not live by the truth. But if we walk in the light, as he is in the light, we have fellowship with one another, and the blood of Jesus, his Son, purifies us from all sin."
  - o Revelation 21:22-27 "...The glory of God gives it light, and the Lamb is its lamp. The nations will walk by its light..."

- ♥ **Confession**   1 John 1:8-9
- ♥ **Thanksgiving**   1) Thank You, Lord, that You give us the Truth of Your Word to bless and help us.
  2) Thank You, Lord, for the gift of this day.
  3) Thank You, Lord, for the gift of being Your children.
  4) Thank You, Lord, for the gift of our husbands. Thank You for the gift of this powerful prayer ministry and how You have done miracles in our hearts, lives, marriages, and families through it, Lord. It's all about You, Lord. It's all about You!

- ♥ Lord, bless my husband by giving him a <u>wife</u> who...
  - o rejoices in Truth...
  - o 1 Corinthians 13:6 (TLB) "It [love] is never glad about injustice, but rejoices whenever truth wins out."

- 💗 **Lord, bless our <u>husbands</u>**   Salvation (if applicable): 2 Corinthians 10:3-5 (see TLB)
  - o May they fear You, Lord, and thus be blessed…
  - o Psalm 34:9 (NASB) "O fear the LORD, you His saints; For to those who fear Him, there is no want."
  - o Psalm 34:9 (NIV) "Fear the LORD, you his saints, for those who fear him lack nothing."
  - o Psalm 34:9 (TLB) "If you belong to the Lord, reverence him; for everyone who does this has everything he needs."
  - o Psalm 34:9 (AMP) "O fear the Lord, you His saints [revere and worship Him]! For there is no want to those who truly revere *and* worship Him *with* godly fear."

- 💗 **Lord, bless our <u>marriages</u>**
  - o Hebrews 13:5-6 (applying this Scripture to our marriages, we pray) Keep our lives free from the love of money, and may we be content with what we have. (Thought: May we be content with the spouse You have given us, Lord. May we accept and love one another right where we are.) May we do this because God has said, "Never will I leave you; never will I forsake you." So we say with confidence, "The Lord is our helper." (Thought: When we are struggling in our marriages, may we remember that You—Lord of heaven and earth, Creator of all things—You are our helper! There is no problem in our lives that is too big for You!) We will not be afraid. What can man do to us?

- 💗 **Lord, bless our <u>homes</u>**
  - o To be filled with right heart attitudes…
  - o Psalm 139: 23-24 (do this work in us, Lord, we pray) "Search me, O God, and know my heart; test me and know my anxious thoughts. See if there is any offensive way in me, and lead me in the way everlasting."

- 💗 **<u>Application</u>**
  - o Genesis 2:18 "The LORD God said, 'It is not good for the man to be alone. I will make a helper suitable for him.'" (Thought: O Lord, mold me little by little into the helper my husband needs me to be. Make me a gift and blessing to him. I pray you will show me how I can help him in a specific way each day.)

- 💗 **Lord, bless this <u>prayer ministry</u>**
  - o Romans 12:2b God's good, pleasing, and perfect will be done.

- 💗 ## <u>Praise</u> We praise You, Lord, that You are Light!

Week 48

- ❤ **Praise**   God is our <u>Father</u>:
    - o Deuteronomy 1:29-31 "Then I said to you, 'Do not be terrified; do not be afraid of them. The LORD your God, who is going before you, will fight for you, as he did for you in Egypt, before your very eyes, and in the desert. There you saw how the LORD your God carried you, as a father carries his son...'" (Application: Thank You, Lord, that I do not need to be afraid of any circumstance or situation in my life, for the Truth of Your Word tells me that You go before me...You will fight for me...You will carry me!)
    - o Psalm 68:4-6 "...a father to the fatherless..."
    - o Luke 11:11-13 "...If you then, though you are evil, know how to give good gifts to your children, how much more will your Father in heaven give the Holy Spirit to those who ask him!"
    - o John 1:12-13 "Yet to all who received him, to those who believed in his name, he gave the right to become children of God—children born not of natural descent, nor of human decision or a husband's will, but born of God."
    - o 2 Corinthians 6:18 "'I will be a Father to you, and you will be my sons and daughters,' says the Lord Almighty."
    - o Galatians 4:4-7 "But when the time had fully come, God sent his Son, born of a woman, born under law, to redeem those under law, that we might receive the full rights of sons. Because you are sons, God sent the Spirit of his Son into our hearts, the Spirit who calls out, '*Abba*, Father.' So you are no longer a slave, but a son; and since you are a son, God has made you also an heir."

- ❤ **Confession**   1 John 2:1-2

- ❤ **Thanksgiving**   1) Thank You, Lord, for the amazing, glorious gift of being Your children.
    2) Thank You, Lord, that You have plans for our lives, sovereign plans for us before we were even born.
    3) Thank You, Lord, that no matter what this day holds and/or what our life holds, You are with us.
    4) Thank You, Lord, that You are good and Your plans are good. We can trust You. You ride on the heavens to help us. You are our shield, our helper, our glorious sword. (See Deuteronomy 33:26-29.)
    5)_____

- ❤ **Lord, bless my husband by giving him a <u>wife</u> who...**
    - o loves him...

- o 1 Corinthians 13:7 (TLB) "If you love someone you will be loyal to him no matter what the cost. You will always believe in him, always expect the best of him, and always stand your ground in defending him."

♥ **Lord, bless our <u>husbands</u>**   Salvation (if applicable): 2 Peter 3:8-9 (see TLB)
  - o May You instruct them in Your ways; for You are good and upright, Lord…
  - o Psalm 25:8 "Good and upright is the LORD; therefore he instructs sinners in his ways."

♥ **Lord, bless our <u>marriages</u>**
  - o Give us singleness of heart in our marriages, Lord, we pray…
  - o Jeremiah 32:39 "I [God] will give them singleness of heart and action, so that they will always fear me for their own good and the good of their children after them."

♥ **Lord, bless our <u>homes</u>**
  - o Lord, make our homes peaceful dwelling places, secure, undisturbed places of rest for our families…
  - o Isaiah 32:17-18 "The fruit of righteousness will be peace; the effect of righteousness will be quietness and confidence forever. My people will live in peaceful dwelling places, in secure homes, in undisturbed places of rest."

♥ **<u>Application</u>**
  - o Philippians 2:3-4 May we study our husband, seeking to know what his interests are, and then may we choose to line ourselves up with him and his interests: "Do nothing out of selfish ambition or vain conceit, but in humility consider others better than yourselves. Each of you should look not only to your own interests, but also to the interests of others."

♥ **Lord, bless this <u>prayer ministry</u>**
  - o Zechariah 4:6b "'Not by might nor by power, but by my Spirit,' says the LORD Almighty."

♥ **<u>Praise</u> We praise You, Lord, that You are our Father!**

Week 49

- ♥ **Praise**   God is our <u>Joy</u>:
    - o 1 Chronicles 16:27 (AMP) "Honor and majesty are [found] in His presence; strength and joy are [found] in His sanctuary." (NIV) "Splendor and majesty are before him; strength and joy in his dwelling place." (TLB) "Majesty and honor march before him, Strength and gladness walk beside him."
    - o Nehemiah 8:9-12 "…Do not grieve, for the joy of the LORD is your strength…"
    - o Psalm 4:6-8 "Many are asking, 'Who can show us any good?' Let the light of your face shine upon us, O LORD. You have filled my heart with greater joy than when their grain and new wine abound. I will lie down and sleep in peace, for you alone, O LORD, make me dwell in safety."
    - o Psalm 30:1-5, 11-12 (NASB) "…Weeping may last for the night, But a shout of joy *comes* in the morning…"
    - o Psalm 43:3-5 "…to God, my joy and my delight…Why are you downcast, O my soul? Why so disturbed within me? Put your hope in God…"
    - o Zephaniah 3:17 (NASB) "The LORD your God is in your midst, A victorious warrior. He will exult over you with joy, He will be quiet in His love, He will rejoice over you with shouts of joy." (NIV) "The LORD your God is with you, he is mighty to save. He will take great delight in you, he will quiet you with his love, he will rejoice over you with singing."

- ♥ <u>**Confession**</u>   Psalm 86:5

- ♥ <u>**Thanksgiving**</u>   1) Thank You, Lord, for who You are and how You love us so; that You would take great delight in us is an amazing and humbling thought.
    2) Thank You, Lord, that You are real. You are good.
    3) Thank You, Lord, that You go before us and You are ever with us.
    4) Thank You, Lord, that our life struggles do not last forever; You have the power to turn our weeping into rejoicing. You have the power to take our pain and cause it to bring glory and honor to Your name. May not a single tear be wasted. May we ever thank and praise You, and may we ever keep our eyes fixed on You, Lord.
    5)_____

- ♥ Lord, bless my husband by giving him a <u>wife</u> who…
    - o seeks the Lord…
    - o 1 Chronicles 16:11 (NASB) "Seek the LORD and His strength; Seek His face continually."

- o 1 Chronicles 16:11 (NIV) "Look to the Lord and his strength; seek his face always."
- o 1 Chronicles 16:11 (TLB) "Seek the Lord; yes, seek his strength And seek his face untiringly."

♥ **Lord, bless our <u>husbands</u>**   Salvation (if applicable): Ezekiel 36:25-27 (see TLB)
- o May they be humble that they may receive Your guidance, Lord, and be taught Your ways...
- o Psalm 25:9 "[The Lord] guides the humble in what is right and teaches them his way."

♥ **Lord, bless our <u>marriages</u>**
- o Build up our marriages; rebuild the areas of our marriages where we have done things our way instead of Your way, Lord. Draw us to You and Your ways with Your lovingkindness...
- o Jeremiah 31:3b-4a (NASB) "I have loved you with an everlasting love; Therefore I have drawn you with lovingkindness. Again I will build you, and you shall be rebuilt."

♥ **Lord, bless our <u>homes</u>**
- o May they be places of encouragement and building up...
- o Ephesians 4:29 (NIV) "Do not let any unwholesome talk come out of your mouths, but only what is helpful for building others up according to their needs, that it may benefit those who listen."
- o Ephesians 4:29 (NASB) "Let no unwholesome word proceed from your mouth, but only such *a word* as is good for edification according to the need *of the moment*, that it may give grace to those who hear."
- o Ephesians 4:29 (TLB) "Don't use bad language. Say only what is good and helpful to those you are talking to, and what will give them a blessing."

♥ **<u>Application</u>**
- o 1 Corinthians 7:4a Lord, ever give me an attitude of the heart, and may I ever live out, that my body is not my own but rather a gift from myself and You, Lord, to my husband: "The wife's body does not belong to her alone but also to her husband."

♥ **Lord, bless this <u>prayer ministry</u>**
- o 1 Chronicles 4:10 Bless, enlarge, empower, keep from harm...this ministry.

♥ **<u>Praise</u>** We praise You, Lord, that You are our Joy!

Week 50

- ♥ **Praise** God is our <u>Miracle Worker</u>:
    - o 1 Chronicles 16:8-12 "...Remember the wonders he has done, his miracles..."
    - o Psalm 77:11-14 "I will remember the deeds of the LORD; yes, I will remember your miracles of long ago...You are the God who performs miracles; you display your power among the peoples."
    - o Psalm 111:2-5 "...He has caused his wonders to be remembered..."
    - o Luke 7:20-23 "...Go back and report to John what you have seen and heard: The blind receive sight, the lame walk, those who have leprosy are cured, the deaf hear, the dead are raised, and the good news is preached to the poor..."
    - o John 20:30-31 "Jesus did many other miraculous signs in the presence of his disciples, which are not recorded in this book. But these are written that you may believe that Jesus is the Christ, the Son of God, and that by believing you may have life in his name."
    - o John 21:25 "Jesus did many other things as well. If every one of them were written down, I suppose that even the whole world would not have room for the books that would be written."

- ♥ **<u>Confession</u>**   Romans 5:20b

- ♥ **<u>Thanksgiving</u>**   1) Thank You, Lord, that You work miracles still today.
    2) Thank You, Lord, that we can trust You always.
    3) Thank You, Lord, that You are working out Your sovereign plans in each of our lives.
    4) Thank You, Lord, that as Your children, we will see You work all things out for good in our lives. (Romans 8:28)
    5)_____

- ♥ Lord, bless my husband by giving him a <u>wife</u> who...
    - o against all hope, puts her hope in God and believes in God's power to work miracles...
    - o Romans 4:18 (NIV) "Against all hope, Abraham in hope believed and so became the father of many nations, just as it had been said to him, 'So shall your offspring be.'"
    - o Romans 4:18 (MSG) "When everything was hopeless, Abraham believed anyway, deciding to live not on the basis of what he saw he *couldn't* do but on what God said he *would* do. And so he was made father of a multitude of peoples. God himself said to him, 'You're going to have a big family, Abraham!'"

- ♥ Lord, bless our <u>husbands</u>   Salvation (if applicable): Isaiah 55:10-11

- o   Lord, may You put mature Christian men in their lives to set them an example, and may they be encouraged to live as You desire them to live…
- o   Titus 2:1-2, 6-7 "You must teach what is in accord with sound doctrine. Teach the older men to be temperate, worthy of respect, self-controlled, and sound in faith, in love and in endurance…Similarly, encourage the young men to be self-controlled. In everything set them an example by doing what is good. In your teaching show integrity, seriousness."

♥ **Lord, bless our <u>marriages</u>**
- o   Applying this Scripture to our marriages, we pray…Lord, hold our marriages in Your everlasting arms; drive out our enemies (the enemies against our marriages, trying to destroy our marriages, e.g., wrong priorities, pride, selfishness, self-centeredness, pushing for our own way, lies from the enemy, lies of the world, unforgiveness, doubt, fear, discouragement, despair…You are our hope, Lord. You are our Miracle Worker!) May our marriages be secure in You, Lord; You are our shield, helper, and glorious sword.
- o   Deuteronomy 33:26-29 "There is no one like the God of Jeshurun, who rides on the heavens to help you (personalizing: to help us in our marriage) and on the clouds in his majesty. The eternal God is your refuge, and underneath are the everlasting arms. He will drive out your enemy before you, saying, 'Destroy him!' So Israel will live in safety alone; Jacob's spring is secure in a land of grain and new wine, where the heavens drop dew. Blessed are you, O Israel! Who is like you, a people saved by the LORD? He is your shield and helper and your glorious sword. Your enemies will cower before you, and you will trample down their high places."

♥ **Lord, bless our <u>homes</u>**
- o   Protection from the evil one and his snares, traps, schemes, and deceit…
- o   Psalm 141:9-10 "Keep me from the snares they have laid for me, from the traps set by evildoers. Let the wicked fall into their own nets, while I pass by in safety."

♥ **<u>Application</u>**
- o   Luke 6:46-49 May we come to You and put Your Word into practice!
- o   Psalm 119:11 May we hide Your Word in our hearts that we might not sin against You!

♥ **Lord, bless this <u>prayer ministry</u>**
- o   Psalm 91:4b May Your faithfulness shield, protect, and defend this ministry, Lord.

♥ **<u>Praise</u>**   We praise You, Lord, that You are our Miracle Worker!

Week 51

- **Praise**   God is <u>compassionate</u>:
    - Nehemiah 9:16-21 (NIV) "...Because of your great compassion you did not abandon them in the desert. By day the pillar of cloud did not cease to guide them on their path, nor the pillar of fire by night to shine on the way they were to take..." (TLB) "...but in your great mercy you didn't abandon them to die in the wilderness! The pillar of cloud led them forward day by day, and the pillar of fire showed them the way through the night..."
    - Psalm 103:8-22 (NIV) "The LORD is compassionate and gracious, slow to anger, abounding in love...For as high as the heavens are above the earth, so great is his love for those who fear him..." (TLB) "He is merciful and tender toward those who don't deserve it; he is slow to get angry and full of kindness and love...for his mercy toward those who fear and honor him is as great as the height of the heavens above the earth..."
    - Psalm 145:8-9 "The LORD is gracious and compassionate, slow to anger and rich in love. The LORD is good to all; he has compassion on all he has made."
    - Isaiah 30:18 "Yet the LORD longs to be gracious to you; he rises to show you compassion. For the LORD is a God of justice. Blessed are all who wait for him!"
    - Isaiah 49:13-16 "Shout for joy, O heavens; rejoice, O earth; burst into song, O mountains! For the LORD comforts his people and will have compassion on his afflicted ones. But Zion said, 'The LORD has forsaken me, the Lord has forgotten me.' 'Can a mother forget the baby at her breast and have no compassion on the child she has borne? Though she may forget, I will not forget you! See, I have engraved you on the palms of my hands; your walls are ever before me.'"
    - Matthew 9:36 "When he saw the crowds, he had compassion on them, because they were harassed and helpless, like sheep without a shepherd."

- **<u>Confession</u>**   Psalm 139:23-24 and 1 John 1:8-9
- **<u>Thanksgiving</u>**   1) Thank You, Lord, that You are so very compassionate toward us.
    2) Thank You, Lord, that You love us and care about every detail of our lives.
    3) Thank You, Lord, that You are always with us.
    4) Thank You, Lord, that You are perfect in faithfulness. (Isaiah 25:1)
    5)_____

- Lord, bless my husband by giving him a <u>wife</u> who...

- o does not weaken in faith but is strengthened in faith giving glory to God, being fully persuaded that God has the power to do what He has promised…
- o Romans 4:19-21 "Without weakening in his faith, he faced the fact that his body was as good as dead—since he was about a hundred years old—and that Sarah's womb was also dead. Yet he did not waver through unbelief regarding the promise of God, but was strengthened in his faith and gave glory to God, being fully persuaded that God had power to do what he had promised."

♥ **Lord, bless our <u>husbands</u>**   Salvation (if applicable): Ephesians 1:17-18
- o May they not repay anyone evil for evil, but may they be careful to do what is right in the eyes of everyone…
- o Romans 12:17-18 "Do not repay anyone evil for evil. Be careful to do what is right in the eyes of everybody. If it is possible, as far as it depends on you, live at peace with everyone."

♥ **Lord, bless our <u>marriages</u>**
- o Lord, restore and build up our marriages, we pray; restoring honor and comforting us once again through it all…
- o Psalm 71:20-21 "Though you have made me see troubles, many and bitter, you will restore my life again; from the depths of the earth you will again bring me up. You will increase my honor and comfort me once again."

♥ **Lord, bless our <u>homes</u>**
- o May they be a place of truthfulness…
  - o John 8:32 know the truth
  - o John 14:6 Jesus is the truth
  - o Zechariah 8:16 speak the truth to each other
  - o Ephesians 4:15 speak the truth in love

♥ <u>**Application**</u>
- o Luke 6:46-49 May we come to You, Lord, and put Your Word into practice (live it!)…dig down deep that we will stand through the storms of life!
- o Psalm 119:11 "I have hidden your word in my heart that I might not sin against you." May we desire and choose to memorize Your Word, Lord that we might not sin against You!

♥ **Lord, bless this <u>prayer ministry</u>**
- o Matthew 9:38 "Ask the Lord of the harvest, therefore, to send out workers into his harvest field."

♥ <u>**Praise**</u> We praise You, Lord, that You are compassionate!

Week 52

- ♥ **Praise** God is our <u>Rock</u>:
  - o 1 Samuel 2:1-2 "…There is no Rock like our God."
  - o 2 Samuel 22:47 "The LORD lives! Praise be to my Rock!…"
  - o Psalm 18:31-36, 46-50 "For who is God besides the LORD? And who is the Rock except our God? It is God who arms me with strength…he enables me to stand on the heights. He trains my hands for battle…You give me your shield of victory, and your right hand sustains me…You broaden the path beneath me, so that my ankles do not turn…"
  - o Psalm 62:1-8 "…Find rest, O my soul, in God alone; my hope comes from him. He alone is my rock and my salvation; he is my fortress, I will not be shaken. My salvation and my honor depend on God; he is my mighty rock, my refuge. Trust in him at all times, O people; pour out your hearts to him, for God is our refuge."
  - o Matthew 7:24-25 "Therefore everyone who hears these words of mine and puts them into practice is like a wise man who built his house on the rock. The rain came down, the streams rose, and the winds blew and beat against that house; yet it did not fall, because it had its foundation on the rock."
  - o 1 Corinthians 10:4b "…for they drank from the spiritual rock that accompanied them, and that rock was Christ."
- ♥ **Confession**   Psalm 51:1-2
- ♥ **Thanksgiving**   1) Thank You, Lord, that You are our stability, support, our foundation, our source of strength, our Rock.
  2) Thank You, Lord, that we can find rest in You, trust You, pour our hearts out to You. You are so wonderful, so very real, so very good—always!
- ♥ **Lord, bless my husband by giving him a <u>wife</u> who…**
  - o has a tight rein on her tongue (My thoughts: allowing the Holy Spirit to be a bridle in her mouth, directing her words)…
  - o James 1:26 (NIV) "If anyone considers himself religious and yet does not keep a tight rein on his tongue, he deceives himself and his religion is worthless."
  - o James 1:26 (NASB) "If anyone thinks himself to be religious, and yet does not bridle his tongue but deceives his *own* heart, this man's religion is worthless."
  - o James 1:26 (KJV) "If any man among you seem to be religious, and bridleth not his tongue, but deceiveth his own heart, this man's religion *is* vain."
- ♥ **Lord, bless our <u>husbands</u>**   Salvation (if applicable): Jeremiah 32:40

- o May they allow God's hand to strengthen them...
- o 1 Chronicles 29:11-13 (NASB) "Thine, O LORD, is the greatness and the power and the glory and the victory and the majesty, indeed everything that is in the heavens and the earth; Thine is the dominion, O LORD, and Thou dost exalt Thyself as head over all. Both riches and honor *come* from Thee, and Thou dost rule over all, and in Thy hand is power and might; and it lies in Thy hand to make great, and to strengthen everyone. Now therefore, our God, we thank Thee, and praise Thy glorious name."

♥ **Lord, bless our <u>marriages</u>**
- o Lord, may You help us that our marriages will not die...when we are slipping, thank You that Your love supports us...when we are anxious, console us and bring joy to our souls, we pray and thank You, Lord...
- o Psalm 94:17-19 "Unless the LORD had given me help, I would soon have dwelt in the silence of death. When I said, 'My foot is slipping,' your love, O LORD, supported me. When anxiety was great within me, your consolation brought joy to my soul."

♥ **Lord, bless our <u>homes</u>**
- o May they be a place of comfort; a place of protection/a fortress from the harshness of the world...a place where all can be themselves and not a place of perfectionism or materialism where children or husbands feel that things, or getting things done, is more important than their hearts...
- o Psalm 59:9, 17 "O my Strength, I watch for you; you, O God, are my fortress, my loving God...O my Strength, I sing praise to you; you, O God, are my fortress, my loving God."
- o Psalm 139:1-3 "O LORD, you have searched me and you know me. You know when I sit and when I rise; you perceive my thoughts from afar. You discern my going out and my lying down; you are familiar with all my ways."

♥ <u>**Application**</u>
- o Luke 18:1b Always pray and don't give up!

♥ **Lord, bless this <u>prayer ministry</u>**
- o Titus 3:1-2 Keep this ministry pure, Lord, may we "be ready to do whatever is good, to slander no one, to be peaceable and considerate, and to show true humility toward all men."

♥ <u>**Praise**</u> We praise You, Lord, that You are our Rock!

Week 53

- ♥ **Praise**   God is our <u>Shield</u>:   "A person or thing that protects or defends; defense; shelter."[39]
    - o 2 Samuel 22:1-4, 36 "…The LORD is my rock, my fortress and my deliverer; my God is my rock, in whom I take refuge, my shield…You give me your shield of victory…"
    - o Psalm 3 "…You are a shield around me, O LORD…I lie down and sleep; I wake again, because the LORD sustains me. I will not fear the tens of thousands drawn up against me on every side…From the LORD comes deliverance…"
    - o Psalm 5:11-12 "But let all who take refuge in you be glad; let them ever sing for joy. Spread your protection over them, that those who love your name may rejoice in you. For surely, O LORD, you bless the righteous; you surround them with your favor as with a shield."
    - o Psalm 84:10-12 "…The LORD God is a sun and shield…no good thing does he withhold from those whose walk is blameless. O LORD Almighty, blessed is the man who trusts in you."
    - o Psalm 115:9-15 "…You who fear him, trust in the LORD—he is their help and shield…he will bless those who fear the LORD—small and great alike…May you be blessed by the LORD, the Maker of heaven and earth."
    - o Proverbs 2:7-8 "He holds victory in store for the upright, he is a shield to those whose walk is blameless, for he guards the course of the just and protects the way of his faithful ones."

- ♥ **Confession**   Proverbs 28:13-14

- ♥ **Thanksgiving**   1) Thank You, Lord, that You are our shield, our protector and defender.
    2) Thank You, Lord, for the Truth of Your Word.
    3) Thank You, Lord, that we can always come to You, turn to You.
    4) We thank You, Lord, that You are always there.

- ♥ Lord, bless my husband by giving him a <u>wife</u> who…
    - o stays away from complaining and arguing…
    - o Philippians 2:14-16a (TLB) "In everything you do, stay away from complaining and arguing, so that no one can speak a word of blame against you. You are to live clean, innocent lives as children of God in a dark world full of people who are crooked and stubborn. Shine out among them like beacon lights, holding out to them the Word of Life."

---

[39] "Shield." Def. 2. A Merriam-Webster, *Webster's Collegiate Dictionary*, Fifth Edition (Springfield: G. & C. Merriam Co., Publishers, 1943), 917.

- ♥ **Lord, bless our <u>husbands</u>**   Salvation (if applicable): Luke 24:45
    - o Lord, give them wholehearted devotion to obey Your commands; give them the desire to follow Your will for their lives, doing everything You ask them to do...
    - o 1 Chronicles 29:19 (David prayed this for his son Solomon; God had a specific task for Solomon to do. Personalizing this verse...Lord, we pray this Scripture for our husbands acknowledging that You have specific tasks for them to do.) "And give my son Solomon the wholehearted devotion to keep your commands, requirements and decrees and to do everything to build the palatial structure for which I have provided."

- ♥ **Lord, bless our <u>marriages</u>**
    - o Lord, thwart the way of the wicked...protect/defend/shelter/support our marriages with Your faithfulness, we pray...
    - o Psalm 146:9b (NASB) "[The LORD] thwarts the way of the wicked."
    - o Psalm 91:4b (NASB) "And under His wings you may seek refuge; His faithfulness is a shield and bulwark."
    - o Bulwark: "Any strong support, defense, or safeguard."[40]

- ♥ **Lord, bless our <u>homes</u>**
    - o Lord, cleanse our homes/our hearts from idol worship, giving us right desires...
    - o Ezekiel 36:25-27 (TLB) "Then it will be as though I had sprinkled clean water on you, for you will be clean—your filthiness will be washed away, your idol worship gone. And I will give you a new heart—I will give you new and right desires—and put a new spirit within you. I will take out your stony hearts of sin and give you new hearts of love. [*hearts of love*, literally, "hearts of flesh," in contrast to "hearts of stone"] And I will put my Spirit within you so that you will obey my laws and do whatever I command."

- ♥ **<u>Application</u>**
    - o Colossians 4:2 (NIV) "Devote yourselves to prayer, being watchful and thankful."
    - o Colossians 4:2 (TLB) "Don't be weary in prayer; keep at it; watch for God's answers and remember to be thankful when they come."

- ♥ **Lord, bless this <u>prayer ministry</u>**
    - o Ephesians 3:20-21 Do immeasurably more than all we could ask or imagine.

- ♥ **<u>Praise</u>** We praise You, Lord, that You are our Shield!

---

[40] "Bulwark." Def. 2. Ibid., 134.

Week 54

- ♥ **Praise**   God is our <u>Fortress</u>
  - Psalm 18:1-3 (AMP)   "I LOVE You fervently *and* devotedly, O Lord, my Strength. The Lord is my Rock, my Fortress, and my Deliverer; my God, my keen *and* firm Strength in Whom I will trust *and* take refuge, my Shield, and the Horn of my salvation, my High Tower. I will call upon the Lord, Who is to be praised; so shall I be saved from my enemies."
  - Psalm 59:17 (AMP)   "Unto You, O my Strength, I will sing praises; for God is my Defense, my Fortress, *and* High Tower, the God Who shows me mercy *and* steadfast love."
  - Psalm 91:1-2 (AMP)   "HE WHO dwells in the secret place of the Most High shall remain stable *and* fixed under the shadow of the Almighty [Whose power no foe can withstand]. I will say of the Lord, He is my Refuge and my Fortress, my God; on Him I lean *and* rely, *and* in Him I [confidently] trust!"
  - Psalm 144:1-2 (NASB)   "BLESSED be the LORD, my rock, Who trains my hands for war, And my fingers for battle; My lovingkindness and my fortress, My stronghold and my deliverer; My shield and He in whom I take refuge…"
  - Proverbs 14:26 (AMP)   "In the reverent *and* worshipful fear of the Lord there is strong confidence, and His children shall always have a place of refuge."
  - Jeremiah 16:19a (NASB)   "O LORD, my strength and my stronghold, And my refuge in the day of distress…"

- ♥ **Confession**   Psalm 32:3-5 and 1 John 2:1-2

- ♥ **Thanksgiving**   1) Thank You, Lord, that You are our source of protection and support.
  2) Thank You, Lord, that You are always there for us to run to.
  3) Thank You, Lord, that You will never fail us nor leave us without support. (Hebrews 13:5, AMP)
  4) We thank You, Lord, that You love us so; You are so amazing and wonderful, forgiving and merciful, strong and gentle, all at the same time.
  5)_____

- ♥ Lord, bless my husband by giving him a <u>wife</u> who…
  - thinks before she speaks…weighs her answers…ponders her answers…
  - Proverbs 15:28 (TLB)   "A good man thinks before he speaks; the evil man pours out his evil words without a thought."
  - Proverbs 15:28 (NIV)   "The heart of the righteous weighs its answers, but the mouth of the wicked gushes evil."

- o Proverbs 15:28 (NASB) "The heart of the righteous ponders how to answer, But the mouth of the wicked pours out evil things."

♥ **Lord, bless our <u>husbands</u>**   Salvation (if applicable): Psalm 18:16-17
- o May they hold to Your teaching/to Your Word... and thus know the Truth, that the Truth may set them free (from worry, discouragement, deceit of the enemy, etc.)...
- o John 8:31-32 "To the Jews who had believed him, Jesus said, 'If you hold to my teaching, you are really my disciples. Then you will know the truth, and the truth will set you free.'"

♥ **Lord, bless our <u>marriages</u>**
- o We pray Your blessings upon our marriages...
- o John 1:16 "From the fullness of his grace we have all received one blessing after another."

♥ **Lord, bless our <u>homes</u>**
- o May Your Word—keeping it, obeying it, being led by it—be the foundation of our homes/families, we pray...
- o Deuteronomy 6:17-18a "Be sure to keep the commands of the LORD your God...Do what is right and good in the LORD's sight, so that it may go well with you."
- o John 14:21 "Whoever has my commands and obeys them, he is the one who loves me. He who loves me will be loved by my Father, and I too will love him and show myself to him."
- o Psalm 119:105 (NIV) "Your word is a lamp to my feet and a light for my path." (TLB) "Your words are a flashlight to light the path ahead of me, and keep me from stumbling."

♥ **<u>Application</u>**
- o May we apply what we pray—that our husbands are a hand-picked gift to us from God. May we treat them that way. May our body language, attitude, and tone of voice display that they are indeed a hand-picked gift from God to us.

♥ **Lord, bless this <u>prayer ministry</u>**
- o Romans 12:2b God's good, pleasing, and perfect will be done.

♥ **<u>Praise</u>**   We praise You, Lord, that You are our Fortress!

Week 55

- ❤ **Praise** God is our <u>Friend</u>: "1) A person whom one knows, likes, and trusts. 2) One with whom one is allied in a struggle or cause; a comrade. 3) One who supports, sympathizes with..."[41]
  - Exodus 33:7-11a "...The Lord would speak to Moses face to face, as a man speaks with his friend."
  - Proverbs 18:24b (KJV) "There is a friend *that* sticketh closer than a brother."
  - Isaiah 41:8-10 (NASB) "But you, Israel, My servant, Jacob whom I have chosen, Descendant of Abraham My friend,... 'You are My servant, I have chosen you and not rejected you. Do not fear, for I am with you; Do not anxiously look about you, for I am your God. I will strengthen you, surely I will help you, Surely I will uphold you with My righteous right hand.'"
  - John 15:9-17 "...Greater love has no one than this, that he lay down his life for his friends. You are my friends if you do what I command."
  - James 2:23 "And the scripture was fulfilled that says, 'Abraham believed God, and it was credited to him as righteousness,' and he was called God's friend."

- ❤ **Confession** Psalm 103:8-19

- ❤ **Thanksgiving** 1) Thank You, Lord, that You strengthen us, uphold us, and encourage us.
  2) Thank You, Lord, for the things You are doing that we cannot see, the battles You are fighting in the heavenly realms.
  3) Thank You, Lord, that You are our hope, joy, strength, perseverance. Your love for us is so great.

- ❤ **Lord, bless my husband by giving him a <u>wife</u> who...**
  - strengthens herself in the Lord when things are hard all around her...
  - 1 Samuel 30:6 (NASB) "Moreover David was greatly distressed because the people spoke of stoning him, for all the people were embittered, each one because of his sons and his daughters. But David strengthened himself in the Lord his God."
  - 1 Samuel 30:6 (AMP) "David was greatly distressed, for the men spoke of stoning him because the souls of them all were bitterly grieved, each man for

---

[41] "Friend." Def. 1, 4, 5. William Morris, *The American Heritage Dictionary of the English Language*, New College Edition. (Boston: Houghton Mifflin Company, 1976), 527.

his sons and daughters. But David encouraged *and* strengthened himself in the Lord his God."

- ❤ **Lord, bless our <u>husbands</u>**   Salvation (if applicable): John 6:64-65
    - May they submit themselves to God and resist the devil. May they come near to You and not be double-minded...
    - James 4:7-8 (NIV) "Submit yourselves, then, to God. Resist the devil, and he will flee from you. Come near to God and he will come near to you. Wash your hands, you sinners, and purify your hearts, you double-minded."
    - James 4:7-8 (AMP) "So be subject to God. Resist the devil [stand firm against him], and he will flee from you. Come close to God and He will come close to you. [Recognize that you are] sinners, get your soiled hands clean; [realize that you have been disloyal] wavering individuals with divided interests, and purify your hearts [of your spiritual adultery]."
    - James 4:7-8 (TLB) "So give yourselves humbly to God. Resist the devil and he will flee from you. And when you draw close to God, God will draw close to you. Wash your hands, you sinners, and let your hearts be filled with God alone to make them pure and true to him."

- ❤ **Lord, bless our <u>marriages</u>**
    - Lord, we run to You with our marriages; in the name of Jesus we pray that You will make our marriages strong in You and keep them safe from the enemy, who would love to destroy them. Keep our marriages safe from the enemies of pride, stubbornness, business, discouragement, and wrong priorities, we pray...
    - Proverbs 18:10 "The name of the LORD is a strong tower; the righteous run to it and are safe."

- ❤ **Lord, bless our <u>homes</u>**
    - May our homes be a place where the Lord is feared and His name is honored. May a precious scroll of remembrance be written in Your presence, Lord...
    - Malachi 3:16 "Then those who feared the LORD talked with each other, and the LORD listened and heard. A scroll of remembrance was written in his presence concerning those who feared the LORD and honored his name."

- ❤ <u>**Application**</u>
    - Genesis 2:22 Mold us into what our husbands need; may we be a gift to them!

- ❤ **Lord, bless this <u>prayer ministry</u>**
    - Zechariah 4:6b "'Not by might nor by power, but by my Spirit,' says the LORD Almighty."

- ❤ <u>Praise</u> We praise You, Lord, that You are our Friend!

Week 56

- ♥ **Praise** God is our <u>Counselor</u>: "An adviser."[42]
    - o Psalm 119:24 "Your statutes are my delight; they are my counselors."
    - o Isaiah 9:6 (TLB) "For unto us a Child is born; unto us a Son is given; and the government shall be upon his shoulder. These will be his royal titles: 'Wonderful,' 'Counselor,' 'The Mighty God,' 'The Everlasting Father,' 'The Prince of Peace.'"
    - o Isaiah 28:29 "All this also comes from the LORD Almighty, wonderful in counsel and magnificent in wisdom."
    - o John 14:15-17, 25-27 (NASB) "If you love Me, you will keep My commandments. And I will ask the Father, and He will give you another Helper, that He may be with you forever; *that* is the Spirit of truth…These things I have spoken to you, while abiding with you. But the Helper, the Holy Spirit, whom the Father will send in My name, He will teach you all things, and bring to your remembrance all that I said to you…"
    - o John 15:26 "When the Counselor comes, whom I will send to you from the Father, the Spirit of truth who goes out from the Father, he will testify about me."
    - o John 16:13a (NASB) "But when He, the Spirit of truth, comes, He will guide you into all the truth." (See vv. 7-15.)
- ♥ **Confession**   Psalm 51:4-12 (TLB)
- ♥ **Thanksgiving**   1) Thank You, Lord, that You are with us. You are wonderful.
    2) Thank You, Lord, that You are there to talk to, to go to for counsel, for guidance, for help.
    3) Thank You, Lord, that Your power and love are more than we can measure.
- ♥ Lord, bless my husband by giving him a <u>wife</u> who…
    - o will not hold onto her anger ("don't sin by nursing your grudge," TLB) and thus not give the devil a foothold …
    - o Ephesians 4:26-27 (NIV) "'In your anger do not sin.' Do not let the sun go down while you are still angry, and do not give the devil a foothold."
    - o Ephesians 4:26-27 (TLB) "If you are angry, don't sin by nursing your grudge. Don't let the sun go down with you still angry—get over it quickly; for when you are angry you give a mighty foothold to the devil."

---

[42] "Counselor." Def. 1. A Merriam-Webster, *Webster's Collegiate Dictionary*, Fifth Edition. (Springfield, Mass.: G. & C. Merriam Co., Publishers, 1943), 231.

- o Ephesians 4:26–27 (NASB) "BE ANGRY, AND *yet* DO NOT SIN; do not let the sun go down on your anger, and do not give the devil an opportunity [James 4:7 *a place*]."

♥ **Lord, bless our <u>husbands</u>**   Salvation (if applicable): Romans 1:20
- o Show them Your ways, Lord, teach them Your paths; guide them in Your Truth… may their hope be in You…
- o Psalm 25:4-5 Show (<u>husband's name</u>) Your ways, O Lord, teach him Your paths; guide him in Your truth and teach him, for You are God my Savior, may (<u>husband's name</u>) put <u>his</u> hope in You all day long, we pray.

♥ **Lord, bless our <u>marriages</u>**
- o May we be good listeners to one another as husband and wife, for…
- o Proverbs 18:13 "He who answers before listening—that is his folly and his shame."

♥ **Lord, bless our <u>homes</u>**
- o May they be a place where the Truths of God's Word are passed down/taught to our children, from generation to generation…
- o Deuteronomy 6:4-9 "Hear, O Israel: The LORD our God, the LORD is one. Love the LORD your God with all your heart and with all your soul and with all your strength. These commandments that I give you today are to be upon your hearts. Impress them on your children. Talk about them when you sit at home and when you walk along the road, when you lie down and when you get up. Tie them as symbols on your hands and bind them on your foreheads. Write them on the doorframes of your houses and on your gates."

♥ **<u>Application</u>**
- o Lesson I learned from the book *A Woman After God's Own Heart* by Elizabeth George… The better follower I am, the better leader my husband will be.[43] Lord, help us to not just think about and/or not just pray about being a better follower of our husbands, but help us, this week and always, to live it out …teach us, enable us, give us the heart's desire to do so.

♥ **Lord, bless this <u>prayer ministry</u>**
- o 1 Chronicles 4:10 Bless, enlarge, empower, keep from harm…this ministry.

♥ **<u>Praise</u>   We praise You, Lord, that You are our Counselor!**

---

[43] Elizabeth George, *A Woman After God's Own Heart*, (Eugene, Oregon, Harvest House Publishers, 1997), 60-62.

Week 57

- ♥ **Praise** God is our <u>Comforter</u>: "One who or that which gives comfort, as aid, cheer, etc."[44] Comfort: "1) To assist; to aid... 2) To impart strength and hope to...Comfort suggests relief afforded by imparting positive cheer, hope, or strength, as well as by diminution of pain."[45]
    - o Psalm 23:4 (AMP) "...Your rod [to protect] and Your staff [to guide], they comfort me."
    - o Psalm 71:17-22 (NIV) "...Who, O God, is like you? Though you have made me see troubles, many and bitter, you will restore my life again; from the depths of the earth you will again bring me up. You will increase my honor and comfort me once again..." (KJV) "...comfort me on every side..."
    - o Psalm 94:17-19 (KJV) "Unless the LORD *had been* my help, my soul had almost dwelt in silence. When I said, My foot slippeth; thy mercy, O LORD, held me up. In the multitude of my thoughts within me thy comforts delight my soul."
    - o Isaiah 66:13 (AMP) "As one whom his mother comforts, so will I comfort you; you shall be comforted in Jerusalem."
    - o Matthew 5:4 (AMP) "Blessed *and* enviably happy [with a happiness produced by the experience of God's favor and especially conditioned by the revelation of His matchless grace] are those who mourn, for they shall be comforted!"
    - o 2 Corinthians 1:3-5 (TLB) "What a wonderful God we have...who so wonderfully comforts and strengthens us in our hardships and trials...You can be sure that the more we undergo sufferings for Christ, the more he will shower us with his comfort and encouragement."

- ♥ **Confession** Psalm 32:1-5
- ♥ **Thanksgiving** 1) Thank You, Lord, that there is power in Your Name.
    2) Thank You, Lord, that we can always talk with You.
    3) Thank You, Lord, that You are our strength, joy, and help.
    4) Thank You, Lord, that You have a wonderful, sovereign plan.

- ♥ **Lord, bless my husband by giving him a <u>wife</u> who**...
    - o will be inspired to fear You, so that we will never turn away from You, Lord...
    - o Jeremiah 32:40b "I will inspire them to fear me, so that they will never turn away from me."

---

[44] "Comforter." Def. 1. A Merriam-Webster, *Webster's Collegiate Dictionary*, Fifth Edition. (Springfield, Mass.: G. & C. Merriam Co., Publishers, 1943), 200.
[45] "Comfort." Def. 1, 2. Ibid.

- ♥ Lord, bless our <u>husbands</u>   Salvation (if applicable): Psalm 46:10a
  - May Your Holy Spirit lovingly speak Your Truth to our husbands' hearts that…
  - Proverbs 15:16-17 "Better a little with the fear of the LORD than great wealth with turmoil. Better a meal of vegetables where there is love than a fattened calf with hatred."

- ♥ Lord, bless our <u>marriages</u>
  - May we know and remember that…
  - Proverbs 18:24b "There is a friend who sticks closer than a brother." (Jesus!) Friend: "1) A person whom one knows, likes, and trusts. 2) A favored companion… 3) One with whom one is allied in a struggle or cause; a comrade. 4) One who supports, sympathizes with…"[46] May we remember that You, Lord Jesus, are our comrade and supporter. (My thoughts: With You this marriage can stand and be wonderful.) Lord, help us to be a friend to each other as husband and wife, we pray.

- ♥ Lord, bless our <u>homes</u>
  - May our homes be a place where forgiveness abounds, showing kindness and compassion to one another…
  - Ephesians 4:32 "Be kind and compassionate to one another, forgiving each other, just as in Christ God forgave you."
  - Colossians 3:12-14 "Therefore, as God's chosen people, holy and dearly loved, clothe yourselves with compassion, kindness, humility, gentleness and patience. Bear with each other and forgive whatever grievances you may have against one another. Forgive as the Lord forgave you. And over all these virtues put on love, which binds them all together in perfect unity."

- ♥ <u>Application</u>
  - Further applications from lessons I learned from the book *A Woman After God's Own Heart* by Elizabeth George… to ask myself daily: was I a blessing or a burden to my husband today? Was I a help or a hindrance to my husband today? Did I fit into my husband's plans today or did I fight for my own way?[47]

- ♥ Lord, bless this <u>prayer ministry</u>
  - Psalm 91:4b May Your faithfulness shield, protect, and defend this ministry.

- ♥ **<u>Praise</u>** We praise You, Lord, that You are our Comforter!

---

[46] "Friend." Def. 1, 3, 4, 5. William Morris, *The American Heritage Dictionary of the English Language*, New College Edition. (Boston: Houghton Mifflin Company, 1976), 527.

[47] Elizabeth George, *A Woman After God's Own Heart*, (Eugene, Oregon, Harvest House Publishers, 1997), 60-62.

Week 58

- ♥ **Praise**   God is our <u>Communicator</u>:
  - o 1 Samuel 3:8b-10 "Then Eli realized that the LORD was calling the boy. So Eli told Samuel, 'Go and lie down, and if he calls you, say, "Speak, LORD, for your servant is listening…"'"
  - o Job 33:13-18 "Why do you complain to him that he answers none of man's words? For God does speak—now one way, now another—though man may not perceive it. In a dream, in a vision of the night, when deep sleep falls on men as they slumber in their beds, he may speak in their ears and terrify them with warnings, to turn man from wrongdoing and keep him from pride, to preserve his soul from the pit, his life from perishing by the sword."
  - o Isaiah 30:19-21 "…Whether you turn to the right or to the left, your ears will hear a voice behind you, saying, 'This is the way; walk in it.'"
  - o Matthew 10:18-20 (AMP) "And you will be brought before governors and kings for My sake, as a witness to bear testimony before them and to the Gentiles (the nations). But when they deliver you up, do not be anxious about how *or* what you are to speak; for what you are to say will be given you in that very hour *and* moment. For it is not you who are speaking, but the Spirit of your Father speaking through you."
  - o John 10:27-28 (AMP) "The sheep that are My own hear *and* are listening to My voice; and I know them, and they follow Me. And I give them eternal life, and they shall never lose it *or* perish throughout the ages. [To all eternity they shall never by any means be destroyed.] And no one is able to snatch them out of My hand."
  - o 1 Corinthians 2:9-13 (AMP) "But, on the contrary, as the Scripture says, What eye has not seen and ear has not heard and has not entered into the heart of man, [all that] God has prepared (made and keeps ready) for those who love Him [who hold Him in affectionate reverence, promptly obeying Him and gratefully recognizing the benefits He has bestowed]. Yet to us God has unveiled *and* revealed them by *and* through His Spirit…Now we have not received the spirit [that belongs to] the world, but the [Holy] Spirit Who is from God, [given to us] that we might realize *and* comprehend *and* appreciate the gifts [of divine favor and blessing so freely and lavishly] bestowed on us by God…"

- ♥ **Confession**   Isaiah 55:6-10

- ♥ **Thanksgiving**
  1) Thank You, Lord, that You love us so very much.
  2) Thank You, Lord, for the gift of being Yours.
  3) Thank You, Lord, that You are always there.
  4) Thank You, Lord, that You are greater and mightier than all.

- ♥ Lord, bless my husband by giving him a <u>wife</u> who…
    - o rids herself of all such things as anger, rage, malice, slander, and filthy language…
    - o Colossians 3:7-8 "You used to walk in these ways, in the life you once lived. But now you must rid yourselves of all such things as these: anger, rage, malice, slander, and filthy language from your lips."
- ♥ Lord, bless our <u>husbands</u>   Salvation (if applicable): Matthew 18:12-14
    - o May they be patient men who calm quarrels, for Your Word says…
    - o Proverbs 15:18 "A hot-tempered man stirs up dissension, but a patient man calms a quarrel." Patient: "1) Capable of bearing affliction with calmness. 2) Tolerant; understanding. 3) Persevering; constant. 4) Capable of bearing delay and waiting for the right moment."[48]
- ♥ Lord, bless our <u>marriages</u>
    - o May our marriages be like a tree planted by streams of water, which yields its fruit in season and whose leaf does not wither…
    - o Psalm 1:1-3 "Blessed is the man who does not walk in the counsel of the wicked…But his delight is in the law of the LORD, and on his law he meditates day and night. He is like a tree planted by streams of water, which yields its fruit in season and whose leaf does not wither. Whatever he does prospers."
- ♥ Lord, bless our <u>homes</u>
    - o May they be a place where we are filled with God's grace toward each other…
    - o Romans 5:20b "But where sin increased, grace increased all the more."
- ♥ <u>Application</u>
    - o 1 John 3:18 says, "Dear children, let us not love with words or tongue but with actions and in truth." May we love with action this week by taking the action of writing our husbands a note telling them how much we appreciate them. (O Lord, help us to appreciate our husbands and not take them for granted!)
- ♥ Lord, bless this <u>prayer ministry</u>
    - o Matthew 9:38 "Ask the Lord of the harvest, therefore, to send out workers into his harvest field."
- ♥ **<u>Praise</u>** We praise You, Lord, that You are our Communicator!

---

[48] "Patient." Def. 1, 2, 3, 4. William Morris, *The American Heritage Dictionary of the English Language*, New College Edition. (Boston: Houghton Mifflin Company, 1976), 961.

Week 59

- ♥ **Praise**   God is our <u>Savior</u>:
  - o Psalm 68:19-20 (AMP) "Blessed be the Lord, Who bears our burdens *and* carries us day by day, even the God Who is our salvation! Selah [pause, and calmly think of that]! God is to us a God of deliverances *and* salvation; and to God the Lord belongs escape from death [setting us free]."
  - o Isaiah 43:11-13 (NASB) "I, even I, am the LORD; And there is no savior besides Me…Even from eternity I am He; And there is none who can deliver out of My hand; I act and who can reverse it?"
  - o Matthew 1:20-21 (NASB) "But when he had considered this, behold, an angel of the Lord appeared to him in a dream, saying, 'Joseph, son of David, do not be afraid to take Mary as your wife; for that which has been conceived in her is of the Holy Spirit. And she will bear a Son; and you shall call His name Jesus, for it is He who will save His people from their sins.'"
  - o Acts 5:30-31 (AMP) "The God of our forefathers raised up Jesus, Whom you killed by hanging Him on a tree (cross). God exalted Him to His right hand to be Prince *and* Leader and Savior *and* Deliverer *and* Preserver, in order to grant repentance to Israel and to bestow forgiveness *and* release from sins."
  - o Titus 3:3-6 (NASB) "For we also once were foolish ourselves, disobedient, deceived, enslaved to various lusts and pleasures, spending our life in malice and envy, hateful, hating one another. But when the kindness of God our Savior and *His* love for mankind appeared, He saved us, not on the basis of deeds which we have done in righteousness, but according to His mercy…"
  - o 1 John 4:14-15 (NIV) "And we have seen and testify that the Father has sent his Son to be the Savior of the world. If anyone acknowledges that Jesus is the Son of God, God lives in him and he in God."

- ♥ **Confession**   1 John 1:8-9

- ♥ **Thanksgiving**   1) Thank You, Lord, that You are so forgiving when we come to You with repentant hearts.
  2) Thank You, Lord, that You turn lives of pain into lives that bring great praise to Your name.
  3) Thank You, Lord, that You are still a God of miracles today.
  4) Thank You, Lord, for the power of prayer.

- ♥ **Lord, bless my husband by giving him a <u>wife</u> who…**
  - o does not lie…
  - o Colossians 3:9-10 "Do not lie to each other, since you have taken off your old self with its practices and have put on the new self, which is being renewed in knowledge in the image of its Creator."

- ♥ Lord, bless our <u>husbands</u>   Salvation (if applicable): 2 Timothy 2:25-26
  - that they will have a timely, apt reply…
  - Proverbs 15:23 "A man finds joy in giving an apt reply—and how good is a timely word!"
- ♥ Lord, bless our <u>marriages</u>
  - Psalm 40:11-14 (paraphrasing/personalizing for our marriages) Do not withhold Your mercy from us, O Lord; may Your love and Your truth always protect us/this marriage. For troubles without number surround us (business, discouragement, wrong priorities); our sins have overtaken us and we cannot see. They are more than the hairs of my head, and our hearts fail within us. Be pleased, O Lord, to save this marriage; O Lord, come quickly to help us. May all who seek to take the life of this marriage be put to shame and confusion. May all who desire the ruin of this marriage be turned back in disgrace.
- ♥ Lord, bless our <u>homes</u>
  - Bring perfect peace, helping us trust in You forever, our everlasting Rock…
  - Isaiah 26:3-4 (TLB) "He will keep in perfect peace all those who trust in him, whose thoughts turn often to the Lord! Trust in the Lord God always, for in the Lord Jehovah is your everlasting strength."
  - Isaiah 26:3-4 (AMP) "You will guard him *and* keep him in perfect *and* constant peace whose mind [both its inclination and its character] is stayed on You, because he commits himself to You, leans on You, *and* hopes confidently in You. So trust in the Lord (commit yourself to Him, lean on Him, hope confidently in Him) forever; for the Lord God is an everlasting Rock [Rock of Ages]."
- ♥ <u>Application</u>
  - 1 John 3:18 "Dear children, let us not love with words or tongue but with actions and in truth." May we love with action by choosing to look for/focus on our husbands' strengths!
- ♥ Lord, bless this <u>prayer ministry</u>
  - Keep this ministry pure from gossip, complaining, and grumbling. May this ministry honor You, Lord, and honor our husbands and families…
  - Titus 3:1-2 "Remind the people to be subject to rulers and authorities, to be obedient, to be ready to do whatever is good, to slander no one, to be peaceable and considerate, and to show true humility toward all men."
- ♥ **<u>Praise</u>** We praise You, Lord, that You are our Savior!

Week 60

- ♥ **Praise**   God is our <u>Deliverer</u>:   Deliver: "To release or rescue from bondage, danger, or evil of any kind; set free."[49]
  - 2 Samuel 22:17-22 (NASB) "He sent from on high, He took me; He drew me out of many waters. He delivered me from my strong enemy, From those who hated me, for they were too strong for me. They confronted me in the day of my calamity, But the LORD was my support. He also brought me forth into a broad place; He rescued me, because He delighted in me…"
  - Psalm 22:4-5 (AMP) "Our fathers trusted in You; they trusted (leaned on, relied on You, and were confident) and You delivered them. They cried to You and were delivered; they trusted in, leaned on, *and* confidently relied on You, and were not ashamed *or* confounded *or* disappointed."
  - Psalm 34:1-7, 15-19 (AMP) "…I sought (inquired of) the Lord *and* required Him [of necessity and on the authority of His Word], and He heard me, and delivered me from all my fears…Many evils confront the [consistently] righteous, but the Lord delivers him out of them all."
  - Psalm 91:9-16 (AMP) "Because you have made the Lord your refuge, and the Most High your dwelling place, There shall no evil befall you, nor any plague *or* calamity come near your tent. For He will give His angels [especial] charge over you to accompany *and* defend *and* preserve you in all your ways [of obedience and service]…Because he has set his love upon Me, therefore will I deliver him; I will set him on high, because he knows *and* understands My name [has a personal knowledge of My mercy, love, and kindness—trusts and relies on Me, knowing I will never forsake him, no, never]. He shall call upon Me, and I will answer him; I will be with him in trouble, I will deliver him and honor him. With long life will I satisfy him and show him My salvation."
  - Isaiah 46:3-4 "Listen to me, O house of Jacob, all you who remain of the house of Israel, you whom I have upheld since you were conceived, and have carried since your birth. Even to your old age and gray hairs I am he, I am he who will sustain you. I have made you and I will carry you; I will sustain you and I will rescue you."
  - 2 Corinthians 1:8-10 "…We were under great pressure, far beyond our ability to endure, so that we despaired even of life. Indeed, in our hearts we felt the sentence of death. But this happened that we might not rely on ourselves but on God, who raises the dead. He has delivered us from such a deadly peril, and he will deliver us. On him we have set our hope that he will continue to deliver us."

- ♥ **Confession**   1 John 2:1-2

---

[49] "Deliver." Def. 1. Ibid., 349.

- ❤ <u>Thanksgiving</u>   1) Thank You, Lord, that You are so very faithful.
  2) Thank You, Lord, that You are in complete control.
  3) Thank You, Lord, that we can trust You.
  4) Thank You, Lord, for the encouragement of Your Word.

- ❤ Lord, bless my husband by giving him a <u>wife</u> who…
  - o puts her trust in God when she is afraid…
  - o Psalm 56:3-4 (TLB) "But when I am afraid, I will put my confidence in you. Yes, I will trust the promises of God. And since I am trusting him, what can mere man do to me?"

- ❤ Lord, bless our <u>husbands</u>   Salvation (if applicable): Acts 26:18 (TLB)
  - o May they fear the Lord and avoid evil, for…
  - o Proverbs 16:6 "Through love and faithfulness sin is atoned for; through the fear of the LORD a man avoids evil."

- ❤ Lord, bless our <u>marriages</u>
  - o Psalm 18:16-19 (paraphrasing/personalizing for our marriages) Reach down from on high and take hold of our marriages, Lord. Draw them up out of deep waters. Rescue our marriages from our powerful enemy, from our foes (My thoughts: enemies of pride, stubbornness, wrong priorities, unforgiveness, hard hearts, Satan, fatigue, despair, discouragement, business) who are too strong for us. They confront us in the day of our disaster, but You, Lord, are our support. Bring us out into a spacious place; rescue our marriages because You delight in us/them.

- ❤ Lord, bless our <u>homes</u>
  - o Build our families up and rebuild us (where necessary) on Your solid foundation…
  - o Jeremiah 31:3b-4a (NASB) "I have loved you with an everlasting love; Therefore I have drawn you with lovingkindness. Again I will build you, and you shall be rebuilt."

- ❤ <u>Application</u>
  - o Do something special for your husband this week, just for him!

- ❤ Lord, bless this <u>prayer ministry</u>
  - o Ephesians 3:20-21 Do immeasurably more than all we could ask or imagine, Lord…You are able!

- ❤ **<u>Praise</u>** We praise You, Lord, that You are our Deliverer!

Week 61

- ♥ **Praise**   God is <u>merciful</u>:   Mercy: "1) Forbearance from inflicting harm, esp. as punishment,....compassionate treatment of an offender or adversary. 2) Disposition to exercise compassion or forgiveness; willingness to spare."[50]
    - o Micah 7:18-20   "Who is a God like you, who pardons sin and forgives the transgression of the remnant of his inheritance? You do not stay angry forever but delight to show mercy...You will be true to Jacob, and show mercy to Abraham, as you pledged on oath to our fathers in days long ago."
    - o Luke 1:46-55   "...The Mighty One has done great things for me—holy is his name. His mercy extends to those who fear him, from generation to generation..."
    - o Luke 6:35-36   "But love your enemies, do good to them, and lend to them without expecting to get anything back. Then your reward will be great, and you will be sons of the Most High, because he is kind to the ungrateful and wicked. Be merciful, just as your Father is merciful."
    - o Romans 9:14-16 (AMP)   "...He says to Moses, I will have mercy on whom I will have mercy and I will have compassion (pity) on whom I will have compassion. [Exod. 33:19.] So then [God's gift] is not a question of human will and human effort, but of God's mercy. [It depends not on one's own willingness nor on his strenuous exertion as in running a race, but on God's having mercy on him.]"
    - o Ephesians 2:3-9 (TLB)   "...God is so rich in mercy...Because of his kindness you have been saved through trusting Christ..."
    - o Titus 3:5-7 (TLB) "Then he saved us—not because we were good enough to be saved, but because of his kindness and pity—by washing away our sins and giving us the new joy of the indwelling Holy Spirit whom he poured out upon us with wonderful fullness—and all because of what Jesus Christ our Savior did...all because of his great kindness..."
- ♥ **Confession**   Psalm 86:5 (TLB)
- ♥ **Thanksgiving**   1) Thank You, Lord, for Your mercy, kindness, and compassion.
    2) Thank You, Lord, that we can look to You for hope.
    3) Thank You, Lord, that You are our strength.
    4) Thank You, Lord, that You are so very, very faithful, worthy of all praise.
    5)_____

---

[50] "Mercy." Def. 1, 2. A Merriam-Webster, *Webster's Collegiate Dictionary*, Fifth Edition. (Springfield, Mass.: G. & C. Merriam Co., Publishers, 1943), 625-626.

- ♥ **Lord, bless my husband by giving him a <u>wife</u> who…**
    - o guards her lips…
    - o Proverbs 13:3 (NIV) "He who guards his lips guards his life, but he who speaks rashly will come to ruin."
    - o Proverbs 13:3 (TLB) "Self-control means controlling the tongue! A quick retort can ruin everything."
- ♥ **Lord, bless our <u>husbands</u>**   Salvation (if applicable): 2 Corinthians 4:3-6
    - o May their ways be pleasing to You, Lord, that even their enemies will live at peace with them…
    - o Proverbs 16:7 "When a man's ways are pleasing to the LORD, he makes even his enemies live at peace with him."
- ♥ **Lord, bless our <u>marriages</u>**
    - o Jeremiah 20:11a (paraphrasing/personalizing for our marriages) May we remember that the Lord is with us like a mighty warrior…fighting for our marriages, fighting so that our enemy will not prevail.
- ♥ **Lord, bless our <u>homes</u>**
    - o God's blessings upon our homes/families, for…
    - o John 1:16 "From the fullness of his grace we have all received one blessing after another."
- ♥ **<u>Application</u>**
    - o May we remember/think upon the details of our marriage vows and live them out this week and always!
- ♥ **Lord, bless this <u>prayer ministry</u>**
    - o Romans 12:2b God's good, pleasing, and perfect will be done in and through this prayer ministry, we pray!
- ♥ **<u>Praise</u>**   We praise You, Lord, that You are merciful!

Week 62

- ♥ **Praise**   God is our <u>Intercessor</u>:   Intercede: "To plead on another's behalf."[51]
    - o Job 16:19   "Even now my witness is in heaven; my advocate is on high." Advocate: "1) A person who argues for a cause; supporter or defender. 2) A person who pleads in another's behalf; an intercessor."[52]
    - o Romans 8:26-27 (AMP) "So too the [Holy] Spirit comes to our aid *and* bears us up in our weakness; for we do not know what prayer to offer *nor* how to offer it worthily as we ought, but the Spirit Himself goes to meet our supplication *and* pleads in our behalf with unspeakable yearnings *and* groanings too deep for utterance...the Spirit intercedes *and* pleads [before God] in behalf of the saints according to *and* in harmony with God's will."
    - o 1 Timothy 2:5-6 "For there is one God and one mediator between God and men, the man Christ Jesus, who gave himself as a ransom for all men..."
    - o Hebrews 7:25 (AMP) "Therefore He is able also to save to the uttermost (completely, perfectly, finally, and for all time and eternity) those who come to God through Him, since He is always living to make petition to God *and* intercede with Him *and* intervene for them."
    - o Hebrews 9:24 (AMP)   "For Christ (The Messiah) has not entered into a sanctuary made with [human] hands...but [He has entered] into heaven itself, now to appear in the [very] presence of God on our behalf."
    - o 1 John 2:1-3 "...We have one who speaks to the Father in our defense—Jesus Christ, the Righteous One. He is the atoning sacrifice for our sins, and not only for ours but also for the sins of the whole world. We know that we have come to know him if we obey his commands."

- ♥ **Confession**   Romans 5:20b

- ♥ **Thanksgiving**   1) Thank You, Lord, for providing forgiveness of sin through the gift of Your Son, Christ Jesus.
    2) Thank You, Lord, for the gift of being Your children.
    3) Thank You, Lord, for Your faithful, loving, sovereign care of our lives.

- ♥ Lord, bless my husband by giving him a <u>wife</u> who…
    - o perseveres and does not shrink back, but lives by faith…
    - o Hebrews 10:35-38 "So do not throw away your confidence; it will be richly rewarded. You need to persevere so that when you have done the will of God,

---

[51] "Intercede." Def. 1. William Morris, *The American Heritage Dictionary of the English Language*, New College Edition. (Boston: Houghton Mifflin Company, 1976), 683.
[52] "Advocate." Def. 1, 2. Ibid., 19.

you will receive what he has promised. For in just a very little while, 'He who is coming will come and will not delay. But my righteous one will live by faith. And if he shrinks back, I will not be pleased with him.'"

- ♥ **Lord, bless our <u>husbands</u>**   Salvation (if applicable): 2 Corinthians 10:4-5 (TLB)
    - o Teach them Your ways, O Lord; give them an undivided heart for You…
    - o Psalm 86:11 Teach (<u>husband's name</u>) Your ways, O Lord, and may he walk in Your truth; give (<u>husband's name</u>) an undivided heart, that he may fear Your name.

- ♥ **Lord, bless our <u>marriages</u>**
    - o Psalm 3:3a (paraphrasing/personalizing for our marriages) O Lord, be a shield around us/our marriages, we pray. (Application: Shield our marriages from the world's ways, false hopes and/or expectations, Satan, the tinsel of this world, discouragement, despair, wrong priorities, deception from the evil one, business, laziness, unforgiveness, pride, pushing for our own way, stubbornness, etc.)

- ♥ **Lord, bless our <u>homes</u>**
    - o May they be a place where Your Word is honored and respected in the heart, obeyed…
    - o James 1:22 (NIV) "Do not merely listen to the word, and so deceive yourselves. Do what it says."
    - o James 1:22 (MSG) "Don't fool yourself into thinking that you are a listener when you are anything but, letting the Word go in one ear and out the other. *Act* on what you hear!"

- ♥ **<u>Application</u>**
    - o May we choose to appreciate, admire, accept, and adapt to our husbands.[53]

- ♥ **Lord, bless this <u>prayer ministry</u>**
    - o Zechariah 4:6b "Not by might nor by power, but by my Spirit,' says the LORD Almighty."

- ♥ **<u>Praise</u>** We praise You, Lord, that You are our Intercessor!

---

[53] I first learned this principle of the 4 A's [appreciate, admire, accept, adapt to your husband] while attending a women's weekly small-group Bible study, in 2001. The Bible study leader's words struck a cord with me, so much so, that I decided to implement them into the "application" section of the prayer sheets.

Week 63

- ❤ **Praise**   God is <u>perfect</u>:   "1) Lacking nothing essential to the whole... 2) In a state of undiminished or highest excellence; without defect; flawless. 3) Completely skilled or talented in a certain field or area. 4) ...accurate; exact. 5) Complete; thorough..."[54]
  - Deuteronomy 32:1-4 "Listen, O heavens, and I will speak; hear, O earth, the words of my mouth. Let my teaching fall like rain and my words descend like dew, like showers on new grass, like abundant rain on tender plants. I will proclaim the name of the Lord. Oh, praise the greatness of our God! He is the Rock, his works are perfect, and all his ways are just. A faithful God who does no wrong, upright and just is he."
  - 2 Samuel 22:31 "As for God, his way is perfect; the word of the Lord is flawless. He is a shield for all who take refuge in him."
  - Psalm 12:6 (AMP) "The words *and* promises of the Lord are pure words, like silver refined in an earthen furnace, purified seven times over."
  - Psalm 19:7-8 (NIV) "The law of the Lord is perfect, reviving the soul. The statutes of the Lord are trustworthy, making wise the simple. The precepts of the Lord are right, giving joy to the heart. The commands of the Lord are radiant, giving light to the eyes." (TLB) "God's laws are perfect. They protect us, make us wise, and give us joy and light."
  - Isaiah 25:1 "O Lord, you are my God; I will exalt you and praise your name, for in perfect faithfulness you have done marvelous things, things planned long ago."

- ❤ **Confession**   Psalm 139:23-24 and 1 John 1:8-9

- ❤ **Thanksgiving**   1) Thank You, Lord, for the Truth of Your Word that guides us, corrects us, encourages us, and blesses us so.
  2) Thank You, Lord, that we can trust You and Your ways; Your purposes are perfect.
  3) Thank You, Lord, that through the hard times You are growing us up in You.
  4) Thank You, Lord, for loving us so.

- ❤ **Lord, bless my husband by giving him a <u>wife</u> who...**
  - gives God all her worries and cares, for...

---

[54] "Perfect." Def. 1, 2, 3, 4, 5. William Morris, *The American Heritage Dictionary of the English Language*, New College Edition. (Boston: Houghton Mifflin Company, 1976), 973.

- o 1 Peter 5:7 (TLB) "Let him have all your worries and cares, for he is always thinking about you and watching everything that concerns you."

♥ **Lord, bless our <u>husbands</u>**   Salvation (if applicable): 2 Peter 3:8-9
- o May they be honest and speak the truth…
- o Proverbs 16:13 "Kings take pleasure in honest lips; they value a man who speaks the truth."

♥ **Lord, bless our <u>marriages</u>**
- o We commit them unto Your faithful care…
- o 1 Peter 4:19 (NIV) (paraphrasing/personalizing for our marriages) Whenever we/our marriages suffer according to God's will, we should commit ourselves/our marriage to You, our faithful Creator, and continue to do good.
- o 1 Peter 4:19 (TLB) (paraphrasing/personalizing for our marriages) So if we/our marriage is suffering according to God's will, may we keep on doing what is right and trust ourselves/our marriage to the God who made us, for He will never fail us.

♥ **Lord, bless our <u>homes</u>**
- o May they be a place where prayer abounds, for…
- o Proverbs 15:8b (NIV) "The prayer of the upright pleases him."
- o Proverbs 15:8 (TLB) "The Lord…delights in the prayers of his people."

♥ **<u>Application</u>**
- o May we:
  - o Think only Truth: Philippians 4:8 and Joshua 1:8
  - o Live only Truth: Luke 6:46-49 and Joshua 1:8
  - o Think only about today (not worrying about tomorrow): Matthew 6:33-34
  - o Delight in correction: Proverbs 3:11-12
- o In my heart this is a lifelong assignment God has given me as his child.

♥ **Lord, bless this <u>prayer ministry</u>**
- o 1 Chronicles 4:10 fourfold prayer of blessing:
  - o Bless this ministry indeed
  - o Enlarge its territory
  - o Empower this ministry; may Your hand be with it
  - o Keep this ministry free from sin…from bringing pain or harm upon itself or others

♥ **<u>Praise</u>**   We praise You, Lord, that You are perfect!

Week 64

- ♥ **Praise**   God is the <u>Way</u>:
    - o 2 Samuel 22:31-34 "As for God, his way is perfect; the word of the LORD is flawless. He is a shield for all who take refuge in him. For who is God besides the LORD? And who is the Rock except our God? It is God who arms me with strength and makes my way perfect. He makes my feet like the feet of a deer; he enables me to stand on the heights."
    - o Psalm 16:11 (KJV) "Thou wilt shew me the path of life; in thy presence *is* fullness of joy; at thy right hand *there are* pleasures for evermore."
    - o Isaiah 48:16-18 "Come near me and listen to this: 'From the first announcement I have not spoken in secret; at the time it happens, I am there.' And now the Sovereign LORD has sent me, with his Spirit. This is what the LORD says—your Redeemer, the Holy One of Israel: 'I am the LORD your God, who teaches you what is best for you, who directs you in the way you should go. If only you had paid attention to my commands, your peace would have been like a river, your righteousness like the waves of the sea.'"
    - o Isaiah 55:6-9 (NASB) "Seek the LORD while He may be found; Call upon Him while He is near. Let the wicked forsake his way, And the unrighteous man his thoughts; And let him return to the LORD, And He will have compassion on him, And to our God, For He will abundantly pardon. 'For My thoughts are not your thoughts, Neither are your ways My ways,' declares the LORD. 'For as the heavens are higher than the earth, So are My ways higher than your ways, And My thoughts than your thoughts.'"
    - o John 14:4-7 (AMP) "And [to the place] where I am going, you know the way. Thomas said to Him, Lord, we do not know where You are going, so how can we know the way? Jesus said to him, I am the Way and the Truth and the Life; no one comes to the Father except by (through) Me. If you had known Me [had learned to recognize Me], you would also have known My Father. From now on, you know Him and have seen Him."
    - o 1 Corinthians 10:13 (NASB) "No temptation has overtaken you but such as is common to man; and God is faithful, who will not allow you to be tempted beyond what you are able, but with the temptation will provide the way of escape also, that you may be able to endure it."

- ♥ **Confession**   Psalm 51:1-2
- ♥ **Thanksgiving**   1) Thank You, Lord, for Your goodness, grace, and faithfulness.
    2) Thank You, Lord, that You are always right there to help us.
    3) Thank You, Lord, for the gift of life.
    4) Thank You, Lord, for the gift of You in our lives.
    5)_____

- ♥ Lord, bless my husband by giving him a <u>wife</u> who…
    - o believes that You are good and chooses to take refuge in You/trusts in You…
    - o Nahum 1:7 (NASB) "The LORD is good, A stronghold in the day of trouble, And He knows those who take refuge in Him."
    - o Nahum 1:7 (TLB) "The Lord is good. When trouble comes, he is the place to go! And he knows everyone who trusts in him!"

- ♥ Lord, bless our <u>husbands</u>   Salvation (if applicable): Ezekiel 36:25-27 (TLB)
    - o May they be patient and control their temper, for Your Word says…
    - o Proverbs 16:32 "Better a patient man than a warrior, a man who controls his temper than one who takes a city."

- ♥ Lord, bless our <u>marriages</u>
    - o O Lord, teach us and give us the desire and enable us, as a married couple, to walk together…
    - o Amos 3:3 "Do two walk together unless they have agreed to do so?"

- ♥ Lord, bless our <u>homes</u>
    - o May our families pursue righteousness…
    - o Proverbs 15:9b "He loves those who pursue righteousness."

- ♥ <u>Application</u>
    - o Genesis 2:18 "The LORD God said, 'It is not good for the man to be alone. I will make a helper suitable for him.'" (Application: O Lord, mold me little by little into the helper my husband needs me to be. Make me a gift and blessing to him! I pray that You will show me how I can help him in a specific way each day.)

- ♥ Lord, bless this <u>prayer ministry</u>
    - o Psalm 91:4b May Your faithfulness shield, protect, and defend this ministry.

- ♥ **<u>Praise</u>**   We praise You, Lord, that You are the Way!

Week 65

- ❤ <u>**Praise**</u>   God is <u>Truth</u>:
    - o Psalm 119:160 "All your words are true; all your righteous laws are eternal."
    - o John 1:17b "Grace and truth came through Jesus Christ."
    - o John 8:31-32 "To the Jews who had believed him, Jesus said, 'If you hold to my teaching, you are really my disciples. Then you will know the truth, and the truth will set you free.'"
    - o John 16:13 "But when he, the Spirit of truth, comes, he will guide you into all truth."
    - o John 17:3, 17 "Now this is eternal life: that they may know you, the only true God, and Jesus Christ, whom you have sent...Sanctify them by the truth; your word is truth."
    - o 1 John 5:20 "We know also that the Son of God has come and has given us understanding, so that we may know him who is true. And we are in him who is true—even in his Son Jesus Christ. He is the true God and eternal life."

- ❤ <u>**Confession**</u>   Proverbs 28:13-14
- ❤ <u>**Thanksgiving**</u>   1) Thank You, Lord, for providing forgiveness for our sins.
    2) Thank You, Lord, that You are in complete control of all things.
    3) Thank You, Lord, for the gift of each day.
    4) Thank You, Lord, for loving us so and for being so very real.
    5)_____

- ❤ **Lord, bless my husband by giving him a <u>wife</u> who**...
    - o follows Your Truths (Lord, may You put mature Christian women in our lives to train us in Your Truths and to set us good examples)...
    - o Titus 2:3-5 "Likewise, teach the older women to be reverent in the way they live, not to be slanderers or addicted to much wine, but to teach what is good. Then they can train the younger women to love their husbands and children, to be self-controlled and pure, to be busy at home, to be kind, and to be subject to their husbands, so that no one will malign the word of God." "...that the word of God may not be dishonored." (NASB)

- ❤ **Lord, bless our <u>husbands</u>**   Salvation (if applicable): Isaiah 55:10-11
    - o May they be humble, for Your Word says...
    - o Proverbs 18:12 "Before his downfall a man's heart is proud, but humility comes before honor."

- ❤ **Lord, bless our <u>marriages</u>**
    - o May Your favor rest upon our marriages...

- o Psalm 90:17 "May the favor of the Lord our God rest upon us; establish the work of our hands for us—yes, establish the work of our hands."
- o Establish: "1) To make firm or secure; fix in a stable condition. 2) To originate on a firm, lasting basis; to found. 3) To introduce as a permanent entity..."[55]
- o Application: O Lord, may our marriages be firm and secure, grounded in You and the Truth of Your Word.

♥ **Lord, bless our <u>homes</u>**
- o May they be filled with peace and quiet and not strife...
- o Proverbs 17:1 "Better a dry crust with peace and quiet than a house full of feasting, with strife."

♥ **<u>Application</u>**
- o Philippians 2:3-4 "Do nothing out of selfish ambition or vain conceit, but in humility consider others better than yourselves. Each of you should look not only to your own interests, but also to the interest of others."
- o Application: May we study our husband...what are his interests, his dreams, etc. Then may we choose to line ourselves up with him and what is important to him.

♥ **Lord, bless this <u>prayer ministry</u>**
- o Matthew 9:38 "Ask the Lord of the harvest, therefore, to send out workers into his harvest field." (Application: of lost and dying marriages!)

♥ **<u>Praise</u>** We praise You, Lord, that You are Truth!

---

[55] "Establish." Def. 1, 4, 6. Ibid., 448.

Always Pray & Don't Give Up (Luke 18:1)

Week 66

- ♥ **Praise** God is <u>Life</u>:
    - o Deuteronomy 30:19-20 "This day I call heaven and earth as witnesses against you that I have set before you life and death, blessings and curses. Now choose life, so that you and your children may live and that you may love the LORD your God, listen to his voice, and hold fast to him. For the LORD is your life and he will give you many years in the land he swore to give to your fathers, Abraham, Isaac and Jacob."
    - o Deuteronomy 32:47a "They are not just idle words for you—they are your life."
    - o Nehemiah 9:6 "You alone are the LORD. You made the heavens, even the highest heavens, and all their starry host, the earth and all that is on it, the seas and all that is in them. You give life to everything, and the multitudes of heaven worship you."
    - o John 6:35 "Then Jesus declared, 'I am the bread of life. He who comes to me will never go hungry, and he who believes in me will never be thirsty.'"
    - o John 11:25-26 "Jesus said to her, 'I am the resurrection and the life. He who believes in me will live, even though he dies; and whoever lives and believes in me will never die. Do you believe this?'"
    - o Acts 17:25 "And he is not served by human hands, as if he needed anything, because he himself gives all men life and breath and everything else."

- ♥ **Confession** Psalm 25:11-12

- ♥ **Thanksgiving** 1) Thank You, Lord, for loving us all so very much! Thank You for loving us just because You made us.
    2) Thank You, Lord, that we can really deep down trust You.
    3) Thank You, Lord, that You are always with us.
    4) Thank You, Lord, that You are always good and always do what is right.

- ♥ **Lord, bless my husband by giving him a <u>wife</u> who...**
    - o lives at peace with everyone...
    - o Romans 12:18-19a, 21 (NIV) "If it is possible, as far as it depends on you, live at peace with everyone. Do not take revenge, my friends, but leave room for God's wrath...Do not be overcome by evil, but overcome evil with good."
    - o Romans 12:18-19a, 21 (TLB) "Don't quarrel with anyone. Be at peace with everyone, just as much as possible. Dear friends, never avenge yourselves. Leave that to God...Don't let evil get the upper hand but conquer evil by doing good."

- ♥ **Lord, bless our <u>husbands</u>**   Salvation (if applicable): Ephesians 1:17-18
  - o May this be their heart, we pray…
  - o Psalm 18:1-3 "I love you, O L<small>ORD</small>, my strength. The L<small>ORD</small> is my rock, my fortress and my deliverer; my God is my rock, in whom I take refuge. He is my shield and the horn of my salvation, my stronghold. I call to the L<small>ORD</small>, who is worthy of praise, and I am saved from my enemies."
- ♥ **Lord, bless our <u>marriages</u>**
  - o Thank You, Lord, for this Truth…
  - o Jeremiah 29:11 For I know the plans I have for <u>(husband's and my name)</u>, declares the Lord, plans to prosper them and not to harm them, plans to give them hope and a future.
  - o Thought: All the while remembering the Truth from v. 10 as well…i.e., though your marriage may be struggling, going through hard and painful times right now, God knows how long these hard times will last; only He knows the future. God knows all the good that will come as a result of going through these hard times; He knows the blessings He has planned for you. O dear child of God, persevere holding on tightly to God and His ways. Jesus is your hope, an anchor for your soul, firm and secure (Hebrews 6:18-19).
- ♥ **Lord, bless our <u>homes</u>**
  - o May our families promote love…
  - o Proverbs 17:9 (NIV) "He who covers over an offense promotes love, but whoever repeats the matter separates close friends."
  - o Proverbs 17:9 (TLB) "Love forgets mistakes; nagging about them parts the best of friends."
- ♥ <u>**Application**</u>
  - o 1 Corinthians 7:4a Lord, ever give me an attitude of the heart, and may I ever live out, that my body is not my own but rather a gift from myself and You, Lord, to my husband: "The wife's body does not belong to her alone but also to her husband."
- ♥ **Lord, bless this <u>prayer ministry</u>**
  - o Keep this ministry pure from gossip, complaining, and grumbling. May this ministry honor You, Lord, and honor our husbands and families…
  - o Titus 3:1-2 "Remind the people to be subject to rulers and authorities, to be obedient, to be ready to do whatever is good, to slander no one, to be peaceable and considerate, and to show true humility toward all men."
- ♥ <u>Praise</u> We praise You, Lord, that You are Life!

Week 67

- ♥ **Praise**   God is our <u>Victor</u>:   "1) One who defeats or vanquishes an adversary; the winner in a fight, battle, or war. 2) A winner of a contest or struggle."[56]
    - o Deuteronomy 20:1-4 (NASB) "WHEN you go out to battle against your enemies and see horses and chariots *and* people more numerous than you, do not be afraid of them; for the LORD your God, who brought you up from the land of Egypt, is with you...Do not be fainthearted. Do not be afraid, or panic, or tremble before them, for the LORD your God is the one who goes with you, to fight for you against your enemies, to save you."
    - o Joshua 21:43-45 (NASB) "So the LORD gave Israel all the land which He had sworn to give to their fathers, and they possessed it and lived in it. And the LORD gave them rest on every side, according to all that He had sworn to their fathers, and no one of all their enemies stood before them; the LORD gave all their enemies into their hand. Not one of the good promises which the LORD had made to the house of Israel failed; all came to pass."
    - o Psalm 44:1-8 (NASB)   "...Thou with Thine own hand didst drive out the nations...For by their own sword they did not possess the land; And their own arm did not save them; But Thy right hand, and Thine arm, and the light of Thy presence, For Thou didst favor them...Through Thee we will push back our adversaries; Through Thy name we will trample down those who rise up against us. For I will not trust in my bow, Nor will my sword save me. But Thou hast saved us from our adversaries...In God we have boasted all day long, And we will give thanks to Thy name forever."
    - o Psalm 118:13-17 (AMP) "You [my adversary] thrust sorely at me that I might fall, but the Lord helped me. The Lord is my Strength and Song; and He has become my Salvation. The voice of rejoicing and salvation is in the tents *and* private dwellings of the [uncompromisingly] righteous: the right hand of the Lord does valiantly *and* achieves strength!...I shall not die but live, and shall declare the works *and* recount the illustrious acts of the Lord."
    - o Proverbs 21:30-31 (AMP) "There is no [human] wisdom or understanding or counsel [that can prevail] against the Lord. The horse is prepared for the day of battle, but deliverance *and* victory are of the Lord."
    - o 1 Corinthians 15:51-58 There is victory over death through Jesus; therefore, may we stand firm. "...Always give yourselves fully to the work of the Lord, because you know that your labor in the Lord is not in vain."

- ♥ **Confession**   Psalm 130:4-5

---

[56] "Victor." Def. 1, 2. Ibid., 1428.

- ♥ <u>Thanksgiving</u>
  1) Thank You, Lord, that You are so patient and persevering in our lives.
  2) Thank You, Lord, that You teach us how truly dependent we are upon You.
  3) Thank You, Lord, that You do give us rest.
  4) Thank You, Lord, that You are our hope, our help, our victor!

- ♥ Lord, bless my husband by giving him a <u>wife</u>…
  - o whose love is sincere…
  - o Romans 12:9, 11-12 (NIV) "Love must be sincere. Hate what is evil; cling to what is good…Never be lacking in zeal, but keep your spiritual fervor, serving the Lord. Be joyful in hope, patient in affliction, faithful in prayer."
  - o Romans 12:9, 11-12 (TLB) "Don't just pretend that you love others; really love them. Hate what is wrong. Stand on the side of the good…Never be lazy in your work but serve the Lord enthusiastically. Be glad for all God is planning for you. Be patient in trouble, and prayerful always."

- ♥ Lord, bless our <u>husbands</u>   Salvation (if applicable): Jeremiah 32:40
  - o May You guide them and hold them fast…
  - o Psalm 139:10 (see vv. 5-10) (NIV) "…even there your hand will guide me, your right hand will hold me fast."
  - o Psalm 139:10 (see vv. 5-10) (NASB) "Even there Thy hand will lead me, And Thy right hand will lay hold of me."

- ♥ Lord, bless our <u>marriages</u>
  - o May You strengthen our marriages in You, Lord…
  - o Zechariah 10:12 (see vv. 8-12) (NASB) "'And I shall strengthen them in the LORD, And in His name they will walk,' declares the LORD."

- ♥ Lord, bless our <u>homes</u>
  - o May they be a place where justice reigns/is lived out, for…
  - o Proverbs 17:15 "Acquitting the guilty and condemning the innocent—the LORD detests them both."

- ♥ <u>Application</u>
  - o Luke 18:1 May we always pray and not give up!

- ♥ Lord, bless this <u>prayer ministry</u>
  - o Ephesians 3:20-21 Do immeasurably more than all we could ask or imagine, Lord…You are able!

- ♥ <u>Praise</u>   We praise You, Lord, that You are our Victor!

Week 68

- ❤ **Praise**   God is our <u>Hope</u>:   "To be confident; trust. To look forward to with confidence of fulfillment; expect with desire… —Hope against hope. To persist in hoping for something against the odds."[57]
  - Isaiah 40:28-31 (NASB) "Do you not know? Have you not heard? The Everlasting God, the LORD, the Creator of the ends of the earth Does not become weary or tired. His understanding is inscrutable. He gives strength to the weary, And to *him who* lacks might He increases power. Though youths grow weary and tired, And vigorous young men stumble badly, Yet those who wait for (hope in) the LORD Will gain new strength; They will mount up *with* wings like eagles, They will run and not get tired, They will walk and not become weary."
  - Jeremiah 29:11-13 (TLB) "For I know the plans I have for you, says the Lord. They are plans for good and not for evil, to give you a future and a hope. In those days when you pray, I will listen. You will find me when you seek me, if you look for me in earnest."
  - Lamentations 3:21-25 (NASB) "This I recall to mind, Therefore I have hope. The LORD's lovingkindness indeed never cease, For His compassions never fail. *They* are new every morning; Great is Thy faithfulness. 'The LORD is my portion,' says my soul, 'Therefore I have hope in Him.' The LORD is good to those who wait for Him, To the person who seeks Him."
  - Romans 15:4, 13 (NASB) "For whatever was written in earlier times was written for our instruction, that through perseverance and the encouragement of the Scriptures we might have hope…Now may the God of hope fill you with all joy and peace in believing, that you may abound in hope by the power of the Holy Spirit."
  - Hebrews 6:17-20a "Because God wanted to make the unchanging nature of his purpose very clear to the heirs of what was promised, he confirmed it with and oath. God did this so that, by two unchangeable things in which it is impossible for God to lie, we who have fled to take hold of the hope offered to us may be greatly encouraged. We have this hope as an anchor for the soul, firm and secure. It enters the inner sanctuary behind the curtain, where Jesus, who went before us, has entered on our behalf."
  - 1 Peter 1:3 (TLB) "All honor to God, the God and Father of our Lord Jesus Christ; for it is his boundless mercy that has given us the privilege of being born again, so that we are now members of God's own family. Now we live in the hope of eternal life because Christ rose again from the dead."

---

[57] "Hope." Def. 2. Ibid., 634.

- ♥ <u>Confession</u>   Psalm 32:3-5 and 1 John 2:1-2
- ♥ <u>Thanksgiving</u>   1) Thank You, Lord, that You are our hope!
  2) Thank You, Lord, that You never grow tired or weary.
  3) Thank You, Lord, that You do not give up on us.
  4) Thank You, Lord, that You are always with us.
  5)_____

♥ Lord, bless my husband by giving him a <u>wife</u> who…
  - lives out the Truth of Your Word of…
  - Matthew 5:44 (NASB) "But I say to you, love your enemies, and pray for those who persecute you."
  - Luke 6:28 (NASB) "Bless those who curse you, pray for those who mistreat you."

♥ Lord, bless our <u>husbands</u>   Salvation (if applicable): Luke. 24:45
  - May You answer them when they are in distress, may You protect them and help them, Lord…
  - Psalm 20:1-2 "May the LORD answer you when you are in distress; may the name of the God of Jacob protect you. May he send you help from the sanctuary and grant you support from Zion."

♥ Lord, bless our <u>marriages</u>
  - May no weapon formed against our marriages prosper, we pray…
  - Isaiah 54:17a (NASB) "No weapon that is formed against you shall prosper."

♥ Lord, bless our <u>homes</u>
  - May we not quarrel and/or build up high walls…
  - Proverbs 17:19 "He who loves a quarrel loves sin; he who builds a high gate invites destruction."

♥ <u>Application</u>
  - Luke 18:1 May we always pray and not give up!
  - May we apply what we pray—that our husbands are a hand-picked gift to us from God. May we treat them that way. May our body language, attitude, and tone of voice display it.

♥ Lord, bless this <u>prayer ministry</u>
  - Romans 12:2b God's good, pleasing and perfect will be done in and through this prayer ministry, we pray!

♥ **<u>Praise</u>**   We praise You, Lord, that You are our Hope!

Week 69

- ♥ **Praise**   God is <u>Jehovah</u>:   The Self-Existent One, I Am
  - o Exodus 3:13-15 "…God said to Moses, 'I AM WHO I AM. This is what you are to say to the Israelites: "I AM has sent me to you."' God also said to Moses, 'Say to the Israelites, "The LORD, the God of your fathers—the God of Abraham, the God of Isaac and the God of Jacob—has sent me to you."' This is my name forever, the name by which I am to be remembered from generation to generation."
  - o 1 Chronicles 16:23-30 (NASB) "…Ascribe to the LORD the glory due His name…"
  - o Psalm 102:27 (NASB) "But Thou art the same, And Thy years will not come to an end."
  - o Psalm 105:1-7 (NASB) "…Call upon His name…Glory in His holy name…"
  - o Jeremiah 16:19-21 (KJV) "…I will cause them to know mine hand and my might; and they shall know that my name *is* The LORD."
  - o John 8:58 (AMP) "Jesus replied, I assure you, most solemnly I tell you, before Abraham was born, I AM."

- ♥ **<u>Confession</u>**   Psalm 103:8-19

- ♥ **<u>Thanksgiving</u>**   1) Thank You, Lord, that You understand us better than we understand ourselves.
  2) Thank You, Lord, that You are in complete control.
  3) Thank You, Lord, that You go before us.
  4) Thank You, Lord, that You are always with us.
  5)_____

- ♥ Lord, bless my husband by giving him a <u>wife</u> who…
  - o does not conform any longer to the pattern of this world…
  - o Romans 12:2 (NIV) "Do not conform any longer to the pattern of this world, but be transformed by the renewing of your mind. Then you will be able to test and approve what God's will is—his good, pleasing and perfect will."
  - o Romans 12:2 (TLB) "Don't copy the behavior and customs of this world, but be a new and different person with a fresh newness in all you do and think. Then you will learn from your own experience how his ways will really satisfy you."

- ♥ Lord, bless our <u>husbands</u>   Salvation (if applicable): Psalm 18:16-17
  - o Lord, may You instruct and teach them in the way they should go; counsel them and watch over them…

- Psalm 32:8-10 "I will instruct you and teach you in the way you should go; I will counsel you and watch over you. Do not be like the horse or the mule, which have no understanding but must be controlled by bit and bridle or they will not come to you. Many are the woes of the wicked, but the LORD's unfailing love surrounds the man who trusts in him."

❤ Lord, bless our <u>marriages</u>
- May we be inclined to fear You and obey You, Lord...
- Deuteronomy 5:29 "Oh, that their hearts would be inclined to fear me and keep all my commands always, so that it might go well with them and their children forever!" (Personalizing this Scripture, I would pray: O Lord, may my husband and I be inclined to fear You and keep all Your commands always, so that it might go well with us and our children forever!)

❤ Lord, bless our <u>homes</u>
- May no detestable thing be brought into our houses. Lord, clean up our hearts and thus our homes. Remove from us idols and covetousness...
- Deuteronomy 7:25-26 "The images of their gods you are to burn in the fire. Do not covet the silver and gold on them, and do not take it for yourselves, or you will be ensnared by it, for it is detestable to the LORD your God. Do not bring a detestable thing into your house or you, like it, will be set apart for destruction. Utterly abhor and detest it, for it is set apart for destruction."

❤ <u>Application</u>
- Genesis 2:22 "Then the LORD God made a woman from the rib he had taken out of the man, and he brought her to the man."
  - Lord, mold us into what our husbands need; make us a gift to them!

❤ Lord, bless this <u>prayer ministry</u>
- Zechariah 4:6b "Not by might nor by power, but by my Spirit,' says the LORD Almighty."

❤ **<u>Praise</u>** We praise You, Lord, that You are Jehovah!

Week 70

- ♥ **Praise**   God is <u>Jehovah Tsidkenu</u>:   The Lord Our Righteousness
    - o Jeremiah 23:5-6 (KJV) "Behold, the days come, saith the Lord, that I will raise unto David a righteous Branch, and a King shall reign and prosper, and shall execute judgment and justice in the earth. In his days Judah shall be saved, and Israel shall dwell safely: and this *is* his name whereby he shall be called, THE LORD OUR RIGHTEOUSNESS."
    - o Ezekiel 36:25-26 (TLB) "Then it will be as though I had sprinkled clean water on you, for you will be clean—your filthiness will be washed away, your idol worship gone. And I will give you a new heart—I will give you new and right desires—and put a new spirit within you. I will take out your stony hearts of sin and give you new hearts of love."
    - o Romans 3:21-22 (AMP) "But now the righteousness of God has been revealed independently *and* altogether apart from the Law, although actually it is attested by the Law and the Prophets, Namely, the righteousness of God which comes by believing *with* personal trust *and* confident reliance on Jesus Christ (the Messiah). [And it is meant] for all who believe…"
    - o Romans 5:17-19 "For if, by the trespass of the one man, death reigned through that one man, how much more will those who receive God's abundant provision of grace and of the gift of righteousness reign in life through the one man, Jesus Christ…"
    - o 2 Corinthians 5:21 (NASB) "He made Him who knew no sin to be sin on our behalf, that we might become the righteousness of God in Him." (MSG) "…In Christ. God put the wrong on him who never did anything wrong, so we could be put right with God."
    - o 1 John 1:7-9 (TLB) "But if we are living in the light of God's presence, just as Christ does, then we have wonderful fellowship and joy with each other, and the blood of Jesus his Son cleanses us from every sin. If we say that we have no sin, we are only fooling ourselves, and refusing to accept the truth. But if we confess our sins to him, he can be depended on to forgive us and to cleanse us from every wrong. [And it is perfectly proper for God to do this for us because Christ died to wash away our sins.]"
- ♥ **Confession**   Psalm 51:4-12 (TLB)
- ♥ **Thanksgiving**
    1) Thank You, Lord, for Your mercy, grace, and love.
    2) Thank You, Lord, that You just want us to love and trust You.
    3) Thank You, Lord, that You are so patient with us.
    4) Thank You, Lord, that You are always with us.
    5)_____

- ♥ Lord, bless my husband by giving him a <u>wife</u> who...
    - o does not think of herself more highly than she ought, but has an honest evaluation of herself through God's eyes...
    - o Romans 12:3 "For by the grace given me I say to every one of you: Do not think of yourself more highly than you ought, but rather think of yourself with sober judgment, in accordance with the measure of faith God has given you."
- ♥ Lord, bless our <u>husbands</u>   Salvation (if applicable): John 6:64-65
    - o May they put their trust in You, Lord, and not in their own strength, for Your Word says...
    - o Psalm 20:7-8 "Some trust in chariots and some in horses, but we trust in the name of the LORD our God. They are brought to their knees and fall, but we rise up and stand firm."
- ♥ Lord, bless our <u>marriages</u>
    - o May we not be afraid of any enemies against our marriages. For You, Lord, will fight for us/for our marriages, we pray...
    - o Deuteronomy 3:22 "Do not be afraid of them; the LORD your God himself will fight for you."
- ♥ Lord, bless our <u>homes</u>
    - o May our homes be filled with pleasant words, for...
    - o Proverbs 16:24 "Pleasant words are a honeycomb, sweet to the soul and healing to the bones."
- ♥ <u>Application</u>
    - o Lesson I learned from the book *A Woman After God's Own Heart* by Elizabeth George...
        - o The better follower I am, the better leader my husband will be![58]
        - o O Lord, I pray that You will make me a better follower!
- ♥ Lord, bless this <u>prayer ministry</u>
    - o 1 Chronicles 4:10 Bless, enlarge, empower, keep from harm...this ministry.
- ♥ <u>**Praise**</u> We praise You, Lord, that You are our Righteousness!

---

[58] Elizabeth George, *A Woman After God's Own Heart*, (Eugene, Oregon, Harvest House Publishers, 1997), 60-62.

Week 71

- ♥ **Praise** God is <u>Jehovah M'Kaddesh</u>: The Lord Who Sanctifies
    - o Exodus 31:12-13 (NASB) "'…I am the LORD who sanctifies you.'"
    - o Ephesians 4:11-16 (TLB) "…Lovingly follow the truth at all times—speaking truly, dealing truly, living truly—and so become more and more in every way like Christ…"
    - o Philippians 1:6 (TLB) "And I am sure that God who began the good work within you will keep right on helping you grow in his grace until his task within you is finally finished on that day when Jesus Christ returns."
    - o 1 Thessalonians 5:23-24 (AMP) "…Faithful is He Who is calling you [to Himself] *and* utterly trustworthy, and He will also do it [fulfill His call by hallowing and keeping you]."
    - o 1 Peter 2:9 (TLB) "…you are God's very own—all this so that you may show to others how God called you out of the darkness into his wonderful light."

- ♥ **Confession** Psalm 32:1-5

- ♥ **Thanksgiving** 1) Thank You, Lord, for loving us and making us each one.
    2) Thank You, Lord, that we are always in Your sight and always in Your care.
    3) Thank You, Father, that You are faithful to complete Your work in us.

- ♥ **Lord, bless my husband by giving him a <u>wife</u> who…**
    - o rejoices in the Lord, though there are hard times in life…
    - o Habakkuk 3:17-19 "Though the fig tree does not bud and there are no grapes on the vines, though the olive crop fails and the fields produce no food, though there are no sheep in the pen and no cattle in the stalls, yet I will rejoice in the LORD, I will be joyful in God my Savior. The Sovereign LORD is my strength; he makes my feet like the feet of a deer, he enables me to go on the heights."
    - o Habakkuk 3:17-19 (personalizing this Scripture) Though (your personal struggle or hardship), yet I will rejoice in the Lord, I will be joyful in God my Savior. The Sovereign Lord is my strength; He makes my feet like the feet of a deer, He enables me to go on the heights. (My thoughts: God enables me to persevere, carry on, climb the mountains in life!)

- ♥ **Lord, bless our <u>husbands</u>** Salvation (if applicable): Romans 1:20
    - o May they seek first Your kingdom and Your righteousness, Lord, and thus not worry…
    - o Matthew 6:33-34 (NIV) "But seek first his kingdom and his righteousness, and all these things will be given to you as well. Therefore do not worry about

tomorrow, for tomorrow will worry about itself. Each day has enough trouble of its own."
- o Matthew 6:33-34 (TLB) "…and he will give them to you if you give him first place in your life and live as he wants you to. So don't be anxious about tomorrow. God will take care of your tomorrow too. Live one day at a time."
- o Matthew 6:33-34 (MSG) "Give your entire attention to what God is doing right now, and don't get worked up about what may or may not happen tomorrow. God will help you deal with whatever hard things come up when the time comes."

♥ **Lord, bless our marriages**
- o We are one as husband and wife; may no man separate us, we pray…
- o Mark 10:6-9 (NASB) "But from the beginning of creation, God MADE THEM MALE AND FEMALE. FOR THIS CAUSE A MAN SHALL LEAVE HIS FATHER AND MOTHER, AND THE TWO SHALL BECOME ONE FLESH; consequently they are no longer two, but one flesh. What therefore God has joined together, let no man separate."

♥ **Lord, bless our homes**
- o Thank You, Lord, that You know the plans You have for our families…
- o Jeremiah 29:11-13 "For I know the plans I have for you," declares the LORD, "plans to prosper you and not to harm you, plans to give you hope and a future." Lord, may You cause/draw each one of us in our family to call upon You and come and pray to You. Thank You, Lord, that You will listen. May each one in our family seek You with all their heart. For Your Word says, "You will seek me and find me when you seek me with all your heart."

♥ **Application**
- o Further applications from lessons I learned from *A Woman After God's Own Heart* by Elizabeth George…
    - o Be a blessing and not a burden to my husband daily!
    - o Be a help and not a hindrance to my husband daily!
    - o Fit into my husband's plans daily and not fight for my own way![59]

♥ **Lord, bless this prayer ministry**
- o Psalm 91:4b May Your faithfulness shield and defend this prayer ministry, we pray!

♥ **Praise** We praise You, Lord, that You are the Lord Who Sanctifies!

---
[59] Ibid.

Week 72

- ❤ **Praise**   God is <u>Jehovah Shalom</u>:   The Lord Our Peace
    - o Judges 6:22-24a "When Gideon realized that it was an angel of the LORD, he exclaimed, 'Ah, Sovereign LORD! I have seen the angel of the LORD face to face!' But the LORD said to him, 'Peace! Do not be afraid. You are not going to die.' So Gideon built an altar to the LORD there and called it The LORD is Peace."
    - o Isaiah 9:6 (TLB) "For unto us a Child is born; unto us a Son is given; and the government shall be upon his shoulder. These will be his royal titles: 'Wonderful,' 'Counselor,' 'The Mighty God,' 'The Everlasting Father,' 'The Prince of Peace.'"
    - o Isaiah 26:3-4 (TLB) "He will keep in perfect peace all those who trust in him, whose thoughts turn often to the Lord! Trust in the Lord God always, for in the Lord Jehovah is your everlasting strength."
    - o John 14:27 (NASB) "Peace I leave with you; My peace I give to you; not as the world gives, do I give to you. Let not your heart be troubled, nor let it be fearful."
    - o Ephesians 2:11-18 "…But now in Christ Jesus you who once were far away have been brought near through the blood of Christ. For he himself is our peace…"
    - o Colossians 1:15-20 "…For God was pleased to have all his fullness dwell in him, and through him to reconcile to himself all things…by making peace through his blood, shed on the cross."

- ❤ **Confession**   Isaiah 55:6-11
- ❤ **Thanksgiving**   1) Thank You, Lord, for being in complete control.
    2) Thank You, Lord, for making a way for us to be reconciled to You. Thank You that You are always with us.
    3) Thank You, Lord, that You made us each one and You have unique, wonderful plans for us each one as well.

- ❤ **Lord, bless my husband by giving him a <u>wife</u> who…**
    - o rejoices in the Lord always…
    - o Philippians 4:4 (NIV) "Rejoice in the Lord always. I will say it again: Rejoice!"
    - o Philippians 4:4 (TLB) "Always be full of joy in the Lord; I say it again, rejoice!"
    - o Philippians 4:4 (MSG) "Celebrate God all day, every day. I mean, *revel* in him!"

- ❤ **Lord, bless our <u>husbands</u>**   Salvation (if applicable): Psalm 46:10
    - o Show them the way they should go, rescue them from their enemies, teach them to do Your will, lead them on level ground…

- o Psalm 143:8-10 (personalizing this Scripture) Let the morning bring (<u>husband's name</u>) word of Your unfailing love; may he put his trust in You. Show (<u>husband's name</u>) the way he should go; to You may he lift up his soul. Rescue (<u>husband's name</u>) from his enemies, O Lord; may he hide himself in You. Teach (<u>husband's name</u>) to do Your will, for You are his God. May Your good Spirit lead (<u>husband's name</u>) on level ground.

♥ Lord, bless our <u>marriages</u>
- o O Lord, may we truly leave and cleave and be one as Your Word says to us...
- o Genesis 2:20-24 (NASB) "And the man gave names to all the cattle, and to the birds of the sky, and to every beast of the field, but for Adam there was not found a helper suitable for him. So the LORD God caused a deep sleep to fall upon the man, and he slept; then He took one of his ribs, and closed up the flesh at that place. And the LORD God fashioned into a woman the rib which He had taken from the man, and brought her to the man. And the man said, 'This is now bone of my bones, And flesh of my flesh; She shall be called Woman, Because she was taken out of Man.' For this cause a man shall leave his father and his mother, and shall cleave to his wife; and they shall become one flesh."

♥ Lord, bless our <u>homes</u>
- o May Your Word be a lamp unto our feet and a light unto our path in our homes, we pray...
- o Psalm 119:105 (NASB) "Thy word is a lamp to my feet, And a light to my path."
- o Psalm 119:105 (TLB) "Your words are a flashlight to light the path ahead of me, and keep me from stumbling."

♥ <u>Application</u>
- o 1 John 3:18 (TLB) "Little children, let us stop just *saying* we love people; let us *really* love them, and *show it* by our *actions*."
  - o May we take the action to write our husband a note this week, telling him how much we appreciate him!
  - o May we truly appreciate our husbands and not take them for granted, Lord!

♥ Lord, bless this <u>prayer ministry</u>
- o Matthew 9:35-38 (TLB) (applying this Scripture to lost, hurting, struggling marriages) O Lord, there is such a harvest of marriages needing Your healing touch, needing the healing power of the Truth of Your Word. You are our Good Shepherd. Lead us and teach us Your ways, we pray. We ask You, Lord of the harvest, to send out workers into Your harvest field.

♥ **<u>Praise</u>**   We praise You, Lord, that You are our Peace!

Week 73

- ♥ **Praise** God is <u>Jehovah Shammah</u>: The Lord Is There—This name promises His presence…
    - o Exodus 33:14-17 "The LORD replied, 'My Presence will go with you, and I will give you rest…'"
    - o Deuteronomy 31:1-8 "…Be strong and courageous. Do not be afraid or terrified because of them, for the LORD your God goes with you; he will never leave you nor forsake you. The LORD himself goes before you and will be with you; he will never leave you nor forsake you. Do not be afraid; do not be discouraged." (Thought: O Lord, may we not be afraid or discouraged, because the Truth is that You go before us and You, Lord, are with us! Thank You, Lord, for the Truth. Help us to think upon and be controlled by the Truth and not by our emotions! You are real. You are God. You are good. We can trust You!)
    - o Psalm 139:1-10 "…You hem me in behind and before; you have laid your hand upon me…Where can I go from your Spirit?…Your hand will guide me, your right hand will hold me fast."
    - o Isaiah 12:6 (NASB) "…Great in your midst is the Holy One of Israel."
    - o Matthew 28:16-20 (TLB) "…Be sure of this—that I am with you always, even to the end of the world." (MSG) "…I'll be with you as you do this, day after day after day, right up to the end of the age."
    - o 1 Corinthians 3:16 "Don't you know that you yourselves are God's temple and that God's Spirit lives in you?" (Thought: Wow, You are not only with us, Lord, but as Your children, we have Your Holy Spirit in us!)

- ♥ **Confession**   1 John 1:8-9
- ♥ **Thanksgiving**   1) Thank You, Lord, for the blessing of sisters in Christ.
    2) Thank You, Lord, for the Truth of Your Word.
    3) Thank You, Lord, for the encouragement, guidance, help, and hope we receive through Your Word.
    4) Thank You, Lord, that You are always with us.

- ♥ **Lord, bless my husband by giving him a <u>wife</u> who…**
    - o lets her gentleness be evident to all, for the Lord is near…
    - o Philippians 4:5 (NIV) "Let your gentleness be evident to all. The Lord is near. "Gentle: "1) Considerate or kindly in disposition; amiable; patient. 2) Not harsh, severe, or violent; mild; soft. 3) Easily managed or handled; docile; tame."[60]

- ♥ **Lord, bless our <u>husbands</u>**   Salvation (if applicable): Matthew 18:12-14

---

[60] "Gentle." Def. 1, 2, 3. William Morris, *The American Heritage Dictionary of the English Language*, New College Edition. (Boston: Houghton Mifflin Company, 1976), 550.

- o Lord, give them wisdom and patience to overlook an offense…
- o Proverbs 19:11 "A man's wisdom gives him patience; it is to his glory to overlook an offense."
- o Patience: "1) The capacity of calm endurance. 2) Tolerant understanding."[61]

♥ **Lord, bless our <u>marriages</u>**
- o May each husband love his wife, and may we wives see to it that we respect our husbands, as Your Word says…
- o Ephesians 5:33 (NASB) "Nevertheless let each individual among you also love his own wife even as himself; and let the wife *see to it* that she respect her husband."

♥ **Lord, bless our <u>homes</u>**
- o May the Sabbath be honored in our hearts and homes, we pray. May it be a day of rest and refreshment. May we honor God by honoring/obeying His Word…
- o Exodus 23:12 "Six days do your work, but on the seventh day do not work, so that your ox and your donkey may rest and the slave born in your household, and the alien as well, may be refreshed."
- o Exodus 20:8 "Remember the Sabbath day by keeping it holy."

♥ **<u>Application</u>**
- o 1 John 3:18 (TLB) "Little children, let us stop just *saying* we love people; let us *really* love them, and *show it* by our *actions*." May we put love into action by choosing to focus on our husband's strengths and not his weaknesses and/or those things that irritate us, etc. May we ever remember what Matthew 7:3 says: "Why do you look at the speck of sawdust in your brother's eye and pay no attention to the plank in your own eye?"

♥ **Lord, bless this <u>prayer ministry</u>**
- o Keep it pure from grumbling, complaining, and gossip. May this ministry honor You, Lord, and honor our husbands and families…
- o Titus 3:1-2 "Remind the people to be subject to rulers and authorities, to be obedient, to be ready to do whatever is good, to slander no one, to be peaceable and considerate, and to show true humility toward all men."

♥ **<u>Praise</u>** We praise You, Lord, that You are there!

---

[61] "Patience." Def. 1, 2. Ibid., 961.

Week 74

- ♥ **Praise**   God is <u>Jehovah Rapha</u>:   The Lord Heals
    - o Exodus 15:22-26 (NASB) God has the power to turn "bitter to sweet"…bitter hearts, bitter situations, etc. Praise You, Lord! May we cry out to You! Help us to see what we need to see. "…The people grumbled at Moses, saying, 'What shall we drink?' Then he cried out to the LORD, and the LORD showed him a tree; and he threw it into the waters, and the waters became sweet…And He said, 'If you will give earnest heed to the voice of the LORD your God, and do what is right in His sight, and give ear to His commandments, and keep all His statutes, I will put none of the diseases on you which I have put on the Egyptians; for I, the LORD am your healer.'" O the blessings of obedience!
    - o Deuteronomy 32:39 (NASB) "…It is I who heal; And there is no one who can deliver from My hand."
    - o Psalm 103:1-4 (AMP) "BLESS (AFFECTIONATELY, gratefully praise) the Lord, O my soul; and all that is [deepest] within me, bless His holy name!...forget not [one of] all His benefits—Who forgives [every one of] all your iniquities, Who heals [each one of] all your diseases, Who redeems your life from the pit *and* corruption, Who beautifies, dignifies, *and* crowns you with loving-kindness and tender mercy."
    - o Psalm 147:3 (AMP) "He heals the brokenhearted and binds up their wounds [curing their pains and their sorrows]."
    - o Isaiah 53:4-5 (NASB) "Surely our griefs He Himself bore, and our sorrows He carried…He was pierced through for our transgressions, He was crushed for our iniquities; The chastening for our well-being *fell* upon Him; And by His scourging we are healed."
    - o Matthew 8:16-17 (NASB) "And when evening had come, they brought to Him many who were demon-possessed; and He cast out the spirits with a word, and healed all who were ill in order that what was spoken through Isaiah the prophet might be fulfilled, saying, 'HE HIMSELF TOOK OUR INFIRMITIES, AND CARRIED AWAY OUR DISEASES.'" Oh, the power of Your Word, Lord! You have the power to do what we cannot. May we put our hope and trust in You, Lord!
- ♥ **Confession**   1 John 2:1-2
- ♥ **Thanksgiving**   1) Thank You, Lord, for what You see.
    2) Thank You, Lord, for Your perfect loving, sovereign care.
    3) Thank You, Lord, for being our healer/for being our God.
- ♥ **Lord, bless my husband by giving him a <u>wife</u> who…**
    - o allows You, Lord, to quiet/calm her heart with Your love …

- o Zephaniah 3:17 "The LORD your God is with you, he is mighty to save. He will take great delight in you, he will quiet you with his love, he will rejoice over you with singing."

♥ **Lord, bless our <u>husbands</u>**   Salvation (if applicable): 2 Timothy 2:25-26 (TLB)
- o May You, the God of peace, equip them with everything good for doing Your will, and may You work in them what is pleasing to You, Lord…
- o Hebrews 13:20-21 "May the God of peace, who through the blood of the eternal covenant brought back from the dead our Lord Jesus, that great Shepherd of the sheep, equip you with everything good for doing his will, and may he work in us what is pleasing to him, through Jesus Christ, to whom be glory for ever and ever. Amen."

♥ **Lord, bless our <u>marriages</u>**
- o Hold our marriages together, we pray…
- o Colossians 1:17 (NASB) "And He is before all things, and in Him all things hold together."

♥ **Lord, bless our <u>homes</u>**
- o May they be filled with Your peace …
- o John 16:33 (NIV) "I have told you these things, so that in me you may have peace. In this world you will have trouble. But take heart! I have overcome the world."
- o John 16:33 (TLB) "I have told you all this so that you will have peace of heart and mind. Here on earth you will have many trials and sorrows; but cheer up, for I have overcome the world."
- o John 16:33 (AMP) "I have told you these things, so that in Me you may have [perfect] peace *and* confidence. In the world you have tribulation *and* trials distress *and* frustration; but be of good cheer [take courage; be confident, certain, undaunted]! For I have overcome the world. [I have deprived it of power to harm you and have conquered it for you.]"

♥ **<u>Application</u>**
- o 1 John 3:18 (TLB) "Little children, let us stop just *saying* we love people; let us *really* love them, and *show it* by our *actions*."
  - o May we do something special for our husbands this week, just for them!

♥ **Lord, bless this <u>prayer ministry</u>**
- o Ephesians 3:20-21 Do immeasurably more that all we could ask or imagine, Lord…You are able!

♥ **<u>Praise</u>** We praise You, Lord, that You are the Lord who heals!

Week 75

- ♥ **Praise**   God is <u>Jehovah Jireh</u>:   The Lord Will Provide—From the root word 'to see,' God would foresee our need of redemption. This name tells us God is willing and able to meet every need of His people.
  - Genesis 22:8, 13-14 (NASB) "And Abraham said, 'God will provide for Himself the lamb for the burnt offering, my son.' So the two of them walked on together…Then Abraham raised his eyes and looked, and behold, behind *him* a ram caught in the thicket by his horns; and Abraham went and took the ram, and offered him up for a burnt offering in the place of his son. And Abraham called the name of that place The Lord Will Provide…"
  - Acts 14:17 "…He has shown kindness by giving you rain from heaven and crops in their seasons; he provides you with plenty of food and fills your hearts with joy."
  - Romans 8:32 (AMP) "He who did not withhold *or* spare [even] His own Son but gave Him up for us all, will He not also with Him freely *and* graciously give us all [other] things?"
  - 2 Corinthians 9:8 "And God is able to make all grace abound to you, so that in all things at all times, having all that you need, you will abound in every good work."
  - Matthew 6:8b (TLB) "Remember, your Father knows exactly what you need even before you ask him!"
  - 1 Timothy 6:17 "Command those who are rich in this present world not to be arrogant nor to put their hope in wealth, which is so uncertain, but to put their hope in God, who richly provides us with everything for our enjoyment."
- ♥ **Confession**   Psalm 86:5
- ♥ **Thanksgiving**   1) Thank You, Lord, for providing for us so miraculously, abundantly, sacrificially, completely, amazingly, and steadfastly!
  2) Thank You, Lord, for the gift of being Your children.
  3) Thank You, Lord, for the gift of grace, and that You are faithful to complete the work in us that You have begun.
  4) Thank You, Lord, that You are always with us.
  5)_____
- ♥ Lord, bless my husband by giving him a <u>wife</u> who…
  - humbles herself before the Lord …
  - James 4:10 "Humble yourselves before the Lord, and he will lift you up."
- ♥ Lord, bless our <u>husbands</u>   Salvation (if applicable): Acts 26:18 (TLB)

- o   May Your favor rest upon them, Lord; establish the work of their hands…
- o   Psalm 90:17 May the favor of the Lord our God rest upon (husband's name); establish the work of his hands for him—yes, establish the work of his hands.
- o   Establish: "To make firm or secure; fix in a stable condition."[62]

♥ Lord, bless our <u>marriages</u>
- o   Lord, may Your divine order be lived out in us, with thankfulness…
- o   Colossians 3:17-21 "And whatever you do, whether in word or deed, do it all in the name of the Lord Jesus, giving thanks to God the Father through him. Wives, submit to your husbands, as is fitting in the Lord. Husbands, love your wives and do not be harsh with them. Children, obey your parents in everything, for this pleases the Lord. Fathers, do not embitter your children, or they will become discouraged."

♥ Lord, bless our <u>homes</u>
- o   May You, Lord, have first place in our hearts and in our homes …
- o   Colossians 1:18b (NASB) "…that He Himself might come to have first place in everything."

♥ <u>Application</u>
- o   May we choose to remember and think upon the details of our marriage vows and live them out this week and always!

♥ Lord, bless this <u>prayer ministry</u>
- o   Romans 12:2b God's good, pleasing, and perfect will be done in and through this prayer ministry, we pray!

♥ <u>Praise</u>   We praise You, Lord, that You will provide!

---

[62] "Establish." Def. 1. Ibid., 448.

Week 76

- ♥ **Praise**   God is <u>Jehovah Raah</u>:   The Lord Our Shepherd—Raah is also translated "companion" or "friend."
    - o Psalm 23 (TLB) "Because the Lord is my Shepherd, I have everything I need!...He gives me new strength. He helps me do what honors him the most...I will not be afraid, for you are close beside me, guarding, guiding all the way. You provide...blessings overflow!..."
    - o Isaiah 40:11 "He tends his flock like a shepherd: He gathers the lambs in his arms and carries them close to his heart; he gently leads those that have young."
    - o Ezekiel 34:11-16 "For this is what the Sovereign LORD says: I myself will search for my sheep and look after them. As a shepherd looks after his scattered flock when he is with them, so will I look after my sheep. I will rescue them...I will search for the lost and bring back the strays. I will bind up the injured and strengthen the weak...I will shepherd the flock with justice."
    - o Matthew 18:10-14 "...Your Father in heaven is not willing that any of these little ones should be lost."
    - o John 10:11-12, 27-30 "I am the good shepherd. The good shepherd lays down his life for the sheep."...Jesus does not abandon us..."My sheep listen to my voice; I know them, and they follow me. I give them eternal life, and they shall never perish; no one can snatch them out of my hand. My Father, who has given them to me, is greater than all; no one can snatch them out of my Father's hand. I and the Father are one."
    - o Revelation 7:17 "For the Lamb at the center of the throne will be their shepherd; he will lead them to springs of living water. And God will wipe away every tear from their eyes."
- ♥ **Confession**   Romans 5:20b
- ♥ **Thanksgiving**   1) Thank You, Lord, for being our Good Shepherd.
        2) Thank You, Lord, for the gift of this day.
- ♥ **Lord, bless my husband by giving him a <u>wife</u> who**...
    - o cooperates with God's plan for her life/marriage and lets perseverance finish its work so that she may be mature and complete, not lacking anything...
    - o James 1:2-4 (NIV) "Consider it pure joy...whenever you face trials of many kinds, because you know that the testing of your faith develops perseverance. Perseverance must finish its work so that you may be mature and complete, not lacking anything."
    - o James 1:2-4 (TLB) "...Is your life full of difficulties and temptations? Then be happy, for when the way is rough, your patience has a chance to grow. So let it

grow, and don't try to squirm out of your problems. For when your patience is finally in full bloom, then you will be ready for anything, strong in character, full and complete."

- ♥ **Lord, bless our <u>husbands</u>**   Salvation (if applicable): 2 Corinthians 4:3-6
  - o May they keep away from every kind of evil, and may You sanctify them through and through...
  - o 1 Thessalonians 5:22-24 (NIV) "Avoid every kind of evil. May God himself, the God of peace, sanctify you through and through. May your whole spirit, soul and body be kept blameless at the coming of our Lord Jesus Christ. The one who calls you is faithful and he will do it."
  - o 1 Thessalonians 5:22-24 (TLB) (personalized) Keep away from every kind of evil. May the God of peace himself make (<u>husband's name</u>) entirely pure and devoted to God; and may <u>his</u> spirit and soul and body be kept strong and blameless until that day when our Lord Jesus Christ comes back again. God who called you to become His child, will do all this for you, just as He promised.

- ♥ **Lord, bless our <u>marriages</u>**
  - o Lord, may You be the head of our marriages, have all supremacy in our marriages...
  - o Colossians 1:18 "And he is the head of the body, the church; he is the beginning and the firstborn from among the dead, so that in everything he might have the supremacy."
  - o 1 Corinthians 11:3 "Now I want you to realize that the head of every man is Christ, and head of the woman is man, and the head of Christ is God."

- ♥ **Lord, bless our <u>homes</u>**
  - o May they be a place of order, not chaos but peace...
  - o 1 Corinthians 14:33a "For God is not a God of disorder but of peace."

- ♥ **Application**
  - o May we choose to appreciate, admire, accept, and adapt to our husbands.[63]

- ♥ **Lord, bless this <u>prayer ministry</u>**
  - o Zechariah 4:6b "'Not by might nor by power, but by my Spirit,' says the LORD Almighty."

- ♥ <u>**Praise**</u> We praise You, Lord, that You are our Shepherd!

---

[63] I first learned this principle of the 4 A's [appreciate, admire, accept, adapt to your husband] while attending a women's weekly small-group Bible study, in 2001. The Bible study leader's words struck a cord with me, so much so, that I decided to implement them into the "application" section of the prayer sheets.

Week 77

- ♥ **Praise** God is <u>Jehovah Nissi</u>: The Lord Our Banner—Nissi is also translated "ensign" or "standard," and represents His cause, His victory.
  - o Exodus 17:15-16 (AMP) "And Moses built an altar and called the name of it, The Lord is my Banner; And he said, Because [theirs] is a hand against the throne of the Lord, the Lord will have war with Amalek from generation to generation."
  - o Psalm 20:5-8 "We will shout for joy when you are victorious and will lift up our banners in the name of our God…Some trust in chariots and some in horses, but we trust in the name of the LORD our God. They are brought to their knees and fall, but we rise up and stand firm."
  - o Psalm 60:4 (KJV) "Thou hast given a banner to them that fear thee, that it may be displayed because of the truth. Selah."
  - o Song of Solomon 2:4 (AMP) "He brought me to the banqueting house, and his banner over me was love [for love waved as a protecting and comforting banner over my head when I was near him]."
  - o Isaiah 11:10 "In that day the Root of Jesse will stand as a banner for the peoples; the nations will rally to him, and his place of rest will be glorious."
  - o 1 Corinthians 15:56-58 "The sting of death is sin, and the power of sin is the law. But thanks be to God! He gives us the victory through our Lord Jesus Christ. Therefore, my dear brothers, stand firm. Let nothing move you. Always give yourselves fully to the work of the Lord, because you know that your labor in the Lord is not in vain."

- ♥ **Confession** Psalm 139:23-24 and 1 John 1:8-9
- ♥ **Thanksgiving**
  1) Thank You, Lord, for who You are.
  2) Thank You, Lord, for what You are doing in our lives and our marriages.
  3) Thank You, Lord, for the power of prayer!
  4) Thank You, Lord, that You are always with us.
  5)_____

- ♥ Lord, bless my husband by giving him a <u>wife</u> who…
  - o has pleasant/kind words…sweet to the soul and healing to the bones…
  - o Proverbs 16:24 (NIV) "Pleasant words are a honeycomb, sweet to the soul and healing to the bones."
  - o Proverbs 16:24 (TLB) "Kind words are like honey—enjoyable and healthful."

- ♥ Lord, bless our <u>husbands</u>   Salvation (if applicable): 2 Corinthians 10:4-5

- o May we as wives be confident of the Truth of Your Word, Lord, and thus leave Your work in your hands …
- o Philippians 1:6 (personalized) He who began a good work in (husband's name) will carry it on to completion until the day of Christ Jesus.

♥ **Lord, bless our <u>marriages</u>**
- o Protect them from divorce, we pray…
- o Psalm 31:21b (TLB) "His never-failing love protects me like the walls of a fort!" (May Your never-failing love protect our marriages like the walls of a fort, we pray!)
- o Psalm 91:4b (NIV) "His faithfulness will be your shield and rampart." (May Your faithfulness shield, protect, and defend our marriages, we pray!)

♥ **Lord, bless our <u>homes</u>**
- o May You shower your goodness upon our families as we fear You…May our homes be a refuge for our families from the harshness of the world …
- o Psalm 31:19-20 (NASB) "How great is Thy goodness, Which Thou hast stored up for those who fear Thee, Which Thou hast wrought for those who take refuge in Thee, Before the sons of men! Thou dost hide them in the secret place of Thy presence from the conspiracies of man; Thou dost keep them secretly in a shelter from the strife of tongues."

♥ **<u>Application</u>**
- o May we:
  - o Think only Truth: Philippians 4:8 and Joshua 1:8
  - o Live only Truth: Luke 6:46-49 and Joshua 1:8
  - o Think only about today (thus not worrying about tomorrow): Matthew 6:33-34
  - o Delight in correction: Proverbs 3:11-12
- o In my heart, this is a lifelong assignment God has given me as His child.

♥ **Lord, bless this <u>prayer ministry</u>**
- o 1 Chronicles 4:10 fourfold prayer of blessing…
  - o Bless this ministry indeed
  - o Enlarge its territory
  - o Empower this ministry; may Your hand be with it
  - o Keep this ministry free from sin…from bringing pain or harm upon itself or others

♥ **<u>Praise</u>** We praise You, Lord, that You are our Banner!

Week 78

- ♥ **Praise** God is <u>Jehovah Sabaoth</u>: The Lord of Hosts—Commander of all the armies of heaven.
    - o Deuteronomy 20:1-4 (NASB) "WHEN you go out to battle against your enemies and see horses and chariots and people more numerous than you, do not be afraid of them; for the LORD your God, who brought you up from the land of Egypt, is with you...'Hear, O Israel, you are approaching the battle against your enemies today. Do not be fainthearted. Do not be afraid, or panic, or tremble before them, for the LORD your God is the one who goes with you, to fight for you against your enemies, to save you.'"
    - o 1 Samuel 17:41-47 "...David said to the Philistine, 'You come against me with sword and spear and javelin, but I come against you in the name of the LORD Almighty...'"
    - o Nehemiah 9:5-6 (NASB) "...Arise, bless the LORD your God forever and ever! O may Thy glorious name be blessed And exalted above all blessing and praise! Thou alone art the LORD. Thou hast made the heavens, The heaven of heavens with all their host..."
    - o Psalm 103:19-22 "The LORD has established his throne in heaven, and his kingdom rules over all. Praise the LORD, you his angels, you mighty ones who do his bidding, who obey his word. Praise the LORD, all his heavenly hosts, you his servants who do his will. Praise the LORD, all his works everywhere..."
    - o Zechariah 14:9 (KJV) "And the LORD shall be king over all the earth..."
    - o Revelation 11:15 "...He will reign for ever and ever."
- ♥ **Confession**   Psalm 51:1-2
- ♥ **Thanksgiving**   1) Thank You, Lord, for who You are.
    2) Thank You, Lord, that You are so very real.
    3) Thank You, Lord, for Your faithfulness.

- ♥ Lord, bless my husband by giving him a <u>wife</u> who...
    - o is humble...
    - o Proverbs 16:18 (NIV) "Pride goes before destruction, a haughty spirit before a fall."

- ♥ Lord, bless our <u>husbands</u>   Salvation (if applicable): 2 Peter 3:8-9
    - o May they be still and know that You are God, You are with them, You are their fortress/stronghold/refuge...
    - o Psalm 46:10-11 (NIV) "'Be still, and know that I am God; I will be exalted among the nations, I will be exalted in the earth.' The LORD Almighty is with us; the God of Jacob is our fortress."

- o   Psalm 46:10-11 (NASB) "'Cease *striving* and know that I am God; I will be exalted among the nations, I will be exalted in the earth.' The LORD of hosts is with us; The God of Jacob is our stronghold."
- o   Psalm 46:10-11 (TLB) "'Stand silent! Know that I am God! I will be honored by every nation in the world!' The Commander of the heavenly armies is here among *us!* He, the God of Jacob, has come to rescue *us!*"
- o   Psalm 46:10-11 (AMP) "Let be *and* be still, and know (recognize and understand) that I am God. I will be exalted among the nations! I will be exalted in the earth! The Lord of hosts is with us; the God of Jacob is our Refuge (our High Tower and Stronghold). Selah [pause, and calmly think of that]!"

♥ Lord, bless our <u>marriages</u>
- o   May they be filled with Your love, Lord...
- o   Romans 5:5 (NASB) "...and hope does not disappoint, because the love of God has been poured out within our hearts through the Holy Spirit who was given to us."
- o   1 Corinthians 13:2b (NIV) "If I have a faith that can move mountains, but have not love, I am nothing."
- o   1 Corinthians 16:14 (NIV) "Do everything in love."

♥ Lord, bless our <u>homes</u>
- o   May they be filled with laughter...
- o   Nehemiah 8:10b (NIV) "Do not grieve, for the joy of the LORD is your strength."
- o   1 Timothy 6:17 (NASB) "Instruct those who are rich in this present world not to be conceited or to fix their hope on the uncertainty of riches, but on God, who richly supplies us with all things to enjoy."

♥ <u>Application</u>
- o   Genesis 2:18 (NASB) "Then the LORD God said, 'It is not good for the man to be alone; I will make him a helper suitable for him.'" (Application: May we live out being a suitable helper to our husbands each day!)

♥ Lord, bless this <u>prayer ministry</u>
- o   Psalm 91:4b May Your faithfulness shield, protect, and defend this prayer ministry, we pray!

♥ **<u>Praise</u>**   We praise You, Lord, that You are the Lord of Hosts!

Week 79

- ❤ **Praise**　　God is <u>El</u>:　　The God of Power and Might
    - o Exodus 15:13　"In your unfailing love you will lead the people you have redeemed. In your strength you will guide them to your holy dwelling."
    - o Deuteronomy 3:24　"O Sovereign LORD, you have begun to show to your servant your greatness and your strong hand. For what god is there in heaven or on earth who can do the deeds and mighty works you do?"
    - o 2 Chronicles 20:5-12　"… 'O LORD, God of our fathers, are you not the God who is in heaven? You rule over all the kingdoms of the nations. Power and might are in your hand, and no one can withstand you…For we have no power to face this vast army that is attacking us. We do not know what to do, but our eyes are upon you.'"
    - o Psalm 18:1-3　"I love you, O LORD, my strength. The LORD is my rock, my fortress and my deliverer…in whom I take refuge. He is my shield…I call to the LORD, who is worthy of praise, and I am saved from my enemies."
    - o Psalm 89:8　"O LORD God Almighty, who is like you? You are mighty, O LORD, and your faithfulness surrounds you."
    - o Isaiah 43:10-13　"'You are my witnesses,' declares the LORD, 'and my servant whom I have chosen, so that you may know and believe me and understand that I am he. Before me no god was formed, nor will there be one after me. I, even I, am the LORD, and apart from me there is no savior. I have revealed and saved and proclaimed—I, and not some foreign god among you. You are my witnesses,' declares the LORD, 'that I am God. Yes, and from ancient days I am he. No one can deliver out of my hand. When I act, who can reverse it?'"

- ❤ **Confession**　　Proverbs 28:13-14
- ❤ **Thanksgiving**　　1) Thank You, Lord, that You are a God of power and might.
    　　　　　　　　　　2) Thank You, Lord, that You are so very faithful.
    　　　　　　　　　　3) Thank You, Lord, for Your love.
    　　　　　　　　　　4) Thank You, Lord, that You are always with us.

- ❤ **Lord, bless my husband by giving him a <u>wife</u> who…**
    - o gives heed to instruction and trusts in You, Lord…
    - o Proverbs 16:20 (NIV)　"Whoever gives heed to instruction prospers, and blessed is he who trusts in the LORD."
    - o Proverbs 16:20 (NASB)　"He who gives attention to the word shall find good, And blessed is he who trusts in the LORD."
    - o Proverbs 16:20 (TLB)　"God blesses those who obey him; happy the man who puts his trust in the Lord."

- ♥ Lord, bless our <u>husbands</u>   Salvation (if applicable): Ezekiel 36:25-27
  - o O Lord, bless them, we pray...
  - o Numbers 6:24-26 "The LORD bless you and keep you; the LORD make his face shine upon you and be gracious to you; the LORD turn his face toward you and give you peace."

- ♥ Lord, bless our <u>marriages</u>
  - o Applying this Scripture to our marriages, we pray that we will not be quarrelsome but kind, teachable, and patient when wronged, and that we will correct with gentleness those in opposition to God's Word/God's Truth...
  - o 2 Timothy 2:24-25 (NASB) "And the Lord's bond-servant must not be quarrelsome, but be kind to all, able to teach, patient when wronged, with gentleness correcting those who are in opposition, if perhaps God may grant them repentance leading to the knowledge of the truth."
  - o 2 Timothy 2:24-25 (TLB) "God's people must not be quarrelsome; they must be gentle, patient teachers of those who are wrong. Be humble when you are trying to teach those who are mixed up concerning the truth. For if you talk meekly and courteously to them they are more likely, with God's help, to turn away from their wrong ideas and believe what is true."

- ♥ Lord, bless our <u>homes</u>
  - o May they be filled with Your love...
  - o Romans 5:5 (NASB) "...and hope does not disappoint, because the love of God has been poured out within our hearts through the Holy Spirit who was given to us."
  - o 1 Corinthians 13:2b (NIV) "If I have a faith that can move mountains, but have not love, I am nothing."
  - o 1 Corinthians 16:14 (NIV) "Do everything in love."

- ♥ <u>Application</u>
  - o Philippians 2:3-4 "Do nothing out of selfish ambition or vain conceit, but in humility consider others better than yourselves. Each of you should look not only to your own interests, but also to the interest of others." (Application: Study your husband...what are his interests/his dreams, etc. Line yourself up with him!)

- ♥ Lord, bless this <u>prayer ministry</u>
  - o Matthew 9:38 "Ask the Lord of the harvest, therefore, to send out workers into his harvest field." (Application: of lost and dying marriages!)

- ♥ <u>Praise</u>   We praise You, Lord, that You are the God of Power and Might!

Week 80

- ♥ **Praise**   God is <u>Elohim</u>:   The Triune God, Creator
  - Genesis 1:1 (AMP) "In the beginning God (prepared, formed, fashioned, and) created the heavens and the earth."
  - Psalm 95:1-7 (TLB) "Oh, come, let us sing to the Lord! Give a joyous shout in honor of the Rock of our salvation! Come before him with thankful hearts. Let us sing him psalms of praise. For the Lord is a great God, the great King…He controls the formation of the depths of the earth and the mightiest mountains; all are his. He made the sea and formed the land; they too are his. Come, kneel before the Lord our Maker…We are his sheep and he is our Shepherd. Oh, that you would hear him calling you today and come to him!"
  - Psalm 146:5-6 "Blessed is he whose help is the God of Jacob, whose hope is in the LORD his God, the Maker of heaven and earth, the sea, and everything in them—the LORD, who remains faithful forever."
  - Isaiah 40:25-31 "'To whom will you compare me? Or who is my equal?' says the Holy One. Lift your eyes and look to the heavens: Who created all these? He who brings out the starry host one by one, and calls them each by name. Because of his great power and mighty strength, not one of them is missing. Why do you say, O Jacob, and complain, O Israel, 'My way is hidden from the LORD; my cause is disregarded by my God'? Do you not know? Have you not heard? The LORD is the everlasting God, the Creator of the ends of the earth. He will not grow tired or weary, and his understanding no one can fathom. He gives strength to the weary and increases the power of the weak. Even youths grow tired and weary, and young men stumble and fall; but those who hope in the LORD will renew their strength. They will soar on wings like eagles; they will run and not grow weary, they will walk and not be faint."
  - Isaiah 54:5 "For your Maker is your husband—the LORD Almighty is his name—the Holy One of Israel is your Redeemer; he is called the God of all the earth."
  - Colossians 1:15-20 (TLB) "…He was before all else began and it is his power that holds everything together…It was through what his Son did that God cleared a path for everything to come to him…"

- ♥ **Confession**   Psalm 25:11-15

- ♥ **Thanksgiving**
  1) Thank You, Lord, for the Truth of Your Word.
  2) Thank You, Lord, for Your faithful encouragement.
  3) Thank You, Lord, for loving us and for being so patient with us.
  4) Thank You, Lord, that You are always with us.
  5)_____

- ♥ Lord, bless my husband by giving him a <u>wife</u> who…
  - o does not gossip…
  - o Proverbs 16:28 "A perverse man stirs up dissension, and a gossip separates close friends."
  - o Application: May we especially not gossip regarding our husbands or marriages; may we be close friends with our husbands and honor them with our speech or lack thereof, we pray!
- ♥ Lord, bless our <u>husbands</u>   Salvation (if applicable): Isaiah 55:10-11
  - o We pray the Truth of Your Word for them…
  - o 1 Corinthians 16:13-14 "Be on your guard; stand firm in the faith; be men of courage; be strong. Do everything in love."
- ♥ Lord, bless our <u>marriages</u>
  - o Applying this Scripture to our marriages, may we be compassionate to one another, show God's grace to each other, be slow to anger and abounding in lovingkindness toward one another as husband and wife…
  - o Psalm 103:8 (NASB) "The LORD is compassionate and gracious, Slow to anger and abounding in lovingkindness."
- ♥ Lord, bless our <u>homes</u>
  - o May they be filled with right attitudes…
  - o Psalm 139:23-24 (NASB) "Search me, O God, and know my heart; Try me and know my anxious thoughts; And see if there be any hurtful way in me, And lead me in the everlasting way."
- ♥ <u>Application</u>
  - o 1 Corinthians 7:4a "The wife's body does not belong to her alone but also to her husband." (Application: Lord, ever give me an attitude of the heart, and may I ever live out, that my body is not my own, but rather a gift from myself and from You, Lord, to my husband.)
- ♥ Lord, bless this <u>prayer ministry</u>
  - o Keep it pure from grumbling, complaining, and gossip. May this ministry honor You, Lord, and honor our husbands and families…
  - o Titus 3:1-2 "Remind the people to be subject to rulers and authorities, to be obedient, to be ready to do whatever is good, to slander no one, to be peaceable and considerate, and to show true humility toward all men."
- ♥ **<u>Praise</u>**   We praise You, Lord, that You are the Triune God, Creator!

Week 81

- ❤ **Praise** God is <u>El Elyon</u>: The God Most High
    - o Genesis 14:17-20 (AMP) "...And he blessed him and said, Blessed (favored with blessing, made blissful, joyful) be Abram by God Most High, Possessor *and* Maker of heaven and earth, And blessed, praised, *and* glorified be God Most High, Who has given your foes into your hand! And [Abram] gave him a tenth of all [he had taken]."
    - o Psalm 7:17 (TLB) "Oh, how grateful and thankful I am to the Lord because he is so good. I will sing praise to the name of the Lord who is above all lords."
    - o Psalm 47 "...How awesome is the LORD Most High, the great King over all the earth!...For God is the King of all the earth; sing to him a psalm of praise. God reigns over the nations; God is seated on his holy throne..."
    - o Psalm 92:1-5 (NASB) "It is good to give thanks to the LORD, And to sing praises to Thy name, O Most High; To declare Thy lovingkindness in the morning, And Thy faithfulness by night..."
    - o Psalm 97:9-12 "For you, O LORD, are the Most High over all the earth..."
    - o Psalm 148 (TLB) "...all praise the Lord together. For he alone is worthy. His glory is far greater than all of earth and heaven..."

- ❤ **Confession**   Psalm 130:3-5

- ❤ **Thanksgiving**
    1) Thank You, Lord, for being so good to us.
    2) Thank You, Lord, for loving us.
    3) Thank You, Lord, for Your faithfulness.
    4) Thank You, Lord, that You are always with us.
    5)_____

- ❤ Lord, bless my husband by giving him a <u>wife</u> who...
    - o chooses to not start quarrels...
    - o Proverbs 17:14 "Starting a quarrel is like breaching a dam; so drop the matter before a dispute breaks out."
    - o O Holy Spirit, keep us silent and let us hold our tongues; make us even-tempered, for...
    - o Proverbs 17:27-28 "A man of knowledge uses words with restraint, and a man of understanding is even-tempered. Even a fool is thought wise if he keeps silent, and discerning if he holds his tongue."

- ❤ Lord, bless our <u>husbands</u>   Salvation (if applicable): Ephesians 1:17-18

- o O Heavenly Father, bless them in living out the Truth of Your Word/being obedient to Your Word regarding their role as husbands, that their prayers may not be hindered…
- o 1 Peter 3:7 (NASB) "You husbands likewise, live with your wives in an understanding way, as with a weaker vessel, since she is a woman; and grant her honor as a fellow heir of the grace of life, so that your prayers may not be hindered."

♥ Lord, bless our <u>marriages</u>
- o May we not grow weary in doing good, but may we remember that we will reap a harvest if we do not give up…
- o Galatians 6:9 (NIV) "Let us not become weary in doing good, for at the proper time we will reap a harvest if we do not give up."
- o Galatians 6:9 (NASB) "And let us not lose heart in doing good, for in due time we shall reap if we do not grow weary."
- o Galatians 6:9 (TLB) "And let us not get tired of doing what is right, for after a while we will reap a harvest of blessing if we don't get discouraged and give up."

♥ Lord, bless our <u>homes</u>
- o O Lord, make our homes peaceful dwelling places—secure, undisturbed places of rest…
- o Isaiah 32:17-18 "The fruit of righteousness will be peace; the effect of righteousness will be quietness and confidence forever. My people will live in peaceful dwelling places, in secure homes, in undisturbed places of rest."

♥ <u>Application</u>
- o Luke 6:46–49 May we come to You, Lord, and put Your Word into practice (live it!)…dig down deep that we will stand through the storms of life!
- o Psalm 119:11 "I have hidden your word in my heart that I might not sin against you." May we desire and choose to memorize Your Word, Lord, that we might not sin against You!

♥ Lord, bless this <u>prayer ministry</u>
- o May You do immeasurably more than all we could ever ask or imagine, Lord…
- o Ephesians 3:20-21 "Now to him who is able to do immeasurably more than all we ask or imagine, according to his power that is at work within us, to him be glory in the church and in Christ Jesus throughout all generations, for ever and ever! Amen."

♥ **<u>Praise</u>** We praise You, Lord, that You are the God Most High!

Week 82

- ♥ **Praise**   God is <u>El Shaddai</u>:   The Almighty, All-Sufficient God
    - o Genesis 17:1 (NIV)   "When Abram was ninety-nine years old, the LORD appeared to him and said, 'I am God Almighty; walk before me and be blameless.'" (TLB) "When Abram was ninety-nine years old, God appeared to him and told him, 'I am the Almighty; obey me and live as you should.'"
    - o 1 Chronicles 29:11-13   "...You are the ruler of all things. In your hands are strength and power..."
    - o 2 Corinthians 9:8 (NASB) "And God is able to make all grace abound to you, that always having all sufficiency in everything, you may have an abundance for every good deed." (NIV) "And God is able to make all grace abound to you, so that in all things at all times, having all that you need, you will abound in every good work."
    - o 2 Corinthians 12:9 (NIV) "But he said to me, 'My grace is sufficient for you...'" (TLB) "Each time he said, 'No. But I am with you; that is all you need...'"
    - o Ephesians 1:19-21 (TLB)   "I pray that you will begin to understand how incredibly great his power is to help those who believe him. It is that same mighty power that raised Christ from the dead and seated him in the place of honor at God's right hand in heaven, far, far above any other king or ruler or dictator or leader. Yes, his honor is far more glorious than that of anyone else either in this world or in the world to come."
    - o Hebrews 1:2-3 (NIV)   "...sustaining all things by his powerful word..." (AMP) "...upholding *and* maintaining *and* guiding *and* propelling the universe by His mighty word of power..." (TLB) "...He regulates the universe by the mighty power of his command..."

- ♥ **Confession**   Psalm 103:8-19

- ♥ **Thanksgiving**
    1) Thank You, Lord, for everything!
    2) Thank You, Lord, for providing forgiveness for us through Your Son, Jesus.
    3) Thank You, Lord, for Your kindness, grace, mercy, love, faithfulness, Your hand-picked plan for each of our lives and the abundance of encouragement You give us along the way.
    4) Thank You that You are always with us; You are all we need.

- ♥ **Lord, bless my husband by giving him a <u>wife</u> who...**
    - o is sanctified through and through (may we cooperate with the work of the Holy Spirit in our lives)...
    - o 1 Thessalonians 5:23-24 (NIV) (personalized) May God himself, the God of peace, sanctify us through and through. May our whole spirit, soul, and body be

kept blameless at the coming of our Lord Jesus Christ. The One who calls us is faithful and He will do it.
- o 1 Thessalonians 5:23-24 (TLB) (personalized) May the God of peace Himself make us entirely pure and devoted to God, and may our spirit and soul and body be kept strong and blameless until that day when our Lord Jesus Christ comes back again. God, who called us to become His children, will do all this for us, just as He promised.

♥ **Lord, bless our <u>husbands</u>**   Salvation (if applicable): Jeremiah 32:40
- o May they be rooted and built up in Christ…
- o Colossians 2:6-7 "So then, just as you received Christ Jesus as Lord, continue to live in him, rooted and built up in him, strengthened in the faith as you were taught, and overflowing with thankfulness."

♥ **Lord, bless our <u>marriages</u>**
- o Lord, stand with us to strengthen us in our marriages…
- o 2 Timothy 4:17a "But the Lord stood at my side and gave me strength."

♥ **Lord, bless our <u>homes</u>**
- o May they be a place of encouragement and building up…
- o Ephesians 4:29 (NIV) "Do not let any unwholesome talk come out of your mouths, but only what is helpful for building others up according to their needs, that it may benefit those who listen."
- o Ephesians 4:29 (NASB) "Let no unwholesome word proceed from your mouth, but only such a word as is good for edification according to the need *of the moment*, that it may give grace to those who hear."
- o Ephesians 4:29 (TLB) "Don't use bad language. Say only what is good and helpful to those you are talking to, and what will give them a blessing."
- o Ephesians 4:29 (MSG) "Watch the way you talk. Let nothing foul or dirty come out of your mouth. Say only what helps, each word a gift."

♥ <u>Application</u>
- o Luke 6:46-49 May we live Your Word!
- o Psalm 119:11 May we memorize Your Word!

♥ **Lord, bless this <u>prayer ministry</u>**
- o Romans 12:2b God's good, pleasing, and perfect will be done!

♥ <u>**Praise**</u> We praise You, Lord, that You are the Almighty, All-Sufficient God!

Week 83

- ❤ **Praise**   God is <u>El Olam</u>:   The Everlasting God
  - o Genesis 21:33 "…there he called upon the name of the LORD, the Eternal God."
  - o Psalm 90:1-4 "…Before the mountains were born or you brought forth the earth and the world, from everlasting to everlasting you are God…"
  - o Psalm 102:11-12 (NASB) "My days are like a lengthened shadow; And I wither away like grass. But Thou, O LORD, dost abide forever; And Thy name to all generations."
  - o Psalm 136 (NASB)   "GIVE thanks to the LORD, for He is good; For His lovingkindness is everlasting…"
  - o Hebrews 13:8 (AMP)   "Jesus Christ (the Messiah) is [always] the same, yesterday, today, [yes] and forever (to the ages)."
  - o Revelation 1:17-18 "When I saw him, I fell at his feet as though dead. Then he placed his right hand on me and said: 'Don't be afraid. I am the First and the Last. I am the Living One; I was dead, and behold I am alive for ever and ever! And I hold the keys of death and Hades.'"

- ❤ <u>**Confession**</u>   Psalm 51:4-12

- ❤ <u>**Thanksgiving**</u>   1) Thank You, Lord, that You place Your hand upon us and let us know everything's going to be alright because You are with us and You are in complete control.
  2) Thank You, Lord, for loving us so.
  3) Thank You, Lord, that You know Your plan for our lives and it's a good plan because You are a good God.
  4) Thank You, Lord, that You are always with us; You are all we need.
  5)_____

- ❤ Lord, bless my husband by giving him a <u>wife</u> who…
  - o lives out the Truth of Your Word of…
  - o Psalm 27:14 "Wait for the LORD; be strong and take heart and wait for the LORD." (Personal thought: Hope in the Lord, "braid" my life with Him.) And v. 13: May we be confident that we will see the goodness of the Lord in the land of the living.

- ❤ **Lord, bless our <u>husbands</u>**   Salvation (if applicable): Luke 24:45
  - o May they walk in a manner worthy of You, Lord. May they bear fruit, grow, and be strengthened, that they may have great endurance and patience…
  - o Colossians 1:9-11 "For this reason, since the day we heard about you, we have not stopped praying for you and asking God to fill you with the knowledge of

his will through all spiritual wisdom and understanding. And we pray this in order that you may live a life worthy of the Lord and may please him in every way: bearing fruit in every good work, growing in the knowledge of God, being strengthened with all power according to his glorious might so that you may have great endurance and patience..."

- ♥ Lord, bless our <u>marriages</u>
  - o Lord, may You do immeasurably more than all we could ask or imagine in our marriages, according to Your power that is at work within us. You are able! We give You all the glory, Lord!
  - o Ephesians 3:20-21a (NIV) "Now to him who is able to do immeasurably more than all we ask or imagine, according to his power that is at work within us, to him be glory."
  - o Ephesians 3:20-21a (TLB) "Now glory be to God who by his mighty power at work within us is able to do far more than we would ever dare to ask or even dream of—infinitely beyond our highest prayers, desires, thoughts, or hopes. May he be given glory."

- ♥ Lord, bless our <u>homes</u>
  - o Protect our homes/families. Applying this Scripture to our homes/families, we pray...
  - o Psalm 141:9-10 (NASB) Keep my home/family from the jaws of the trap which [the wicked] have set for us, and from the snares of those who do iniquity. Let the wicked fall into their own nets, while we pass by safely.

- ♥ <u>Application</u>
  - o Luke 18:1b May we always pray and not give up!

- ♥ Lord, bless this <u>prayer ministry</u>
  - o Zechariah 4:6b "'Not by might nor by power, but by my Spirit,' says the LORD Almighty."

- ♥ **<u>Praise</u>** We praise You, Lord, that You are the Everlasting God!

Week 84

- ♥ <u>Praise</u>   God is <u>Adonai</u>:   The Lord and Master
  - o Deuteronomy 10:16-17 "Circumcise your hearts, therefore, and do not be stiff-necked any longer. For the LORD your God is God of gods and Lord, of lords, the great God, mighty and awesome, who shows no partiality and accepts no bribes."
  - o Psalm 16:1-2 (NIV) "Keep me safe, O God, for in you I take refuge. I said to the LORD, 'You are my Lord; apart from you I have no good thing.'" (AMP) "KEEP and protect me, O God, for in You I have found refuge, and in You do I put my trust and hide myself. I say to the Lord, You are my Lord; I have no good beside or beyond You."
  - o Isaiah 45:22 "Turn to me and be saved, all you ends of the earth; for I am God, and there is no other."
  - o Romans 14:7-13   "…For we will all stand before God's judgment seat. It is written: 'As surely as I live, ' says the Lord, 'every knee will bow before me; every tongue will confess to God.' So then, each of us will give an account of himself to God. Therefore let us stop passing judgment on one another. Instead, make up your mind not to put any stumbling block or obstacle in your brother's way."
  - o 1 Corinthians 6:19-20 (AMP) "Do you not know that your body is the temple (the very sanctuary) of the Holy Spirit Who lives within you, Whom you have received [as a Gift] from God? You are not your own, You were bought with a price [purchased with a preciousness and paid for, made His own]. So then, honor God and bring glory to Him in your body."
  - o Revelation 5:9-10 (NASB) "And they sang a new song saying, 'Worthy art Thou to take the book, and to break its seals; for Thou wast slain, and didst purchase for God with Thy blood men from every tribe and tongue and people and nation…'"
- ♥ <u>Confession</u>   Psalm 32:1-5
- ♥ <u>Thanksgiving</u>   1) Thank You, Lord, for the many blessings we have in being Your children.
  2) Thank You, Lord, that You are good and we can trust You.
  3) Thank You that You ever keep on loving us; You are faithful to see us through all things as we cling to You and Your Truths.
  4) Thank You that You are always with us; You are all we need.
- ♥ **Lord, bless my husband by giving him a <u>wife</u> who…**
  - o is willing to suffer for God's glory and through it all commits herself to her faithful Creator and continues to do good…

- o 1 Peter 4:19 (NIV) (see also vv. 12-18) "So then, those who suffer according to God's will should commit themselves to their faithful Creator and continue to do good."
- o 1 Peter 4:19 (TLB) (see also vv. 12-18) "So if you are suffering according to God's will, keep on doing what is right and trust yourself to the God who made you, for he will never fail you."

♥ Lord, bless our <u>husbands</u>   Salvation (if applicable): Psalm 18:16-17
- o May the fruit of Your Spirit fill them…
- o Galatians 5:22-23a (NIV) "But the fruit of the Spirit is love, joy, peace, patience, kindness, goodness, faithfulness, gentleness and self-control."
- o Galatians 5:22-23a (TLB) "But when the Holy Spirit controls our lives he will produce this kind of fruit in us: love, joy, peace, patience, kindness, goodness, faithfulness, gentleness and self-control."

♥ Lord, bless our <u>marriages</u>
- o May our marriages be honored by all; may our marriages be kept pure…
- o Hebrews 13:4 (NIV) "Marriage should be honored by all, and the marriage bed kept pure, for God will judge the adulterer and all the sexually immoral." (Personal thought: Kept pure in our hearts as well; may we not compare in our hearts in any way, for "comparing is a robber of joy.")
- o Hebrews 13:4 (TLB) "Honor your marriage and its vows, and be pure; for God will surely punish all those who are immoral or commit adultery."

♥ Lord, bless our <u>homes</u>
- o May they be a place of truthfulness…
    - o John 8:32 know the truth
    - o John 14:6 Jesus is the truth
    - o Zechariah 8:16 speak the truth to each other
    - o Ephesians 4:15 speak the truth in love

♥ <u>Application</u>
- o Colossians 4:2 (NIV) "Devote yourselves to prayer, being watchful and thankful." (TLB) "Don't be weary in prayer; keep at it; watch for God's answers and remember to be thankful when they come."

♥ Lord, bless this <u>prayer ministry</u>
- o 1 Chronicles 4:10 Bless, enlarge, empower, and keep from harm…this ministry.

♥ <u>**Praise**</u> We praise You, Lord, that You are the Lord and Master!

Always Pray & Don't Give Up (Luke 18:1)

Week 85

- ♥ **Praise**   God is our <u>Father</u>:
  - Matthew 6:8-9 (TLB) "…Remember, your Father knows exactly what you need even before you ask him! Pray…'Our Father in heaven, we honor your holy name.'"
  - John 10:27-30 "My sheep listen to my voice; I know them, and they follow me. I give them eternal life, and they shall never perish; no one can snatch them out of my hand. My Father, who has given them to me, is greater than all; no one can snatch them out of my Father's hand. I and the Father are one."
  - John 14:6-11 "Jesus answered, 'I am the way and the truth and the life. No one comes to the Father except through me…'"
  - Romans 8:15-16 (TLB) "And so we should not be like cringing, fearful slaves, but we should behave like God's very own children, adopted into the bosom of his family, and calling to him, 'Father, Father.' For his Holy Spirit speaks to us deep in our hearts, and tells us that we really are God's children."
  - 2 Corinthians 6:18 "I will be a Father to you, and you will be my sons and daughters, says the Lord Almighty."
  - 1 John 3:1-3 "How great is the love the Father has lavished on us, that we should be called children of God!…"

- ♥ **Confession**   Isaiah 55:6-11

- ♥ **Thanksgiving**
  1) Thank You, Lord, for Your hand-picked blessings for us each one.
  2) Thank You, Lord, that You are always thinking about us.
  3) Thank You, Lord, that You are our provider, protector, and encourager.
  4) Thank You, Lord, that You are always with us; You are all we need.
  5)_____

- ♥ Lord, bless my husband by giving him a <u>wife</u> who…
  - trusts in God's unfailing love; has a heart that rejoices in God's gift of salvation and remembers that God has been good to her …
  - Psalm 13:5-6 "But I trust in your unfailing love; my heart rejoices in your salvation. I will sing to the LORD, for he has been good to me."

- ♥ Lord, bless our <u>husbands</u>   Salvation (if applicable): John 17:3
  - May they be good examples, and may they show integrity. Lord, would You also put men in their lives to set them a good example, men of integrity…

- o Titus 2:6-8a "Similarly, encourage the young men to be self-controlled. In everything set them an example by doing what is good. In your teaching show integrity, seriousness and soundness of speech that cannot be condemned."

♥ **Lord, bless our <u>marriages</u>**
- o Lord, we commit unto You our marriages. May You bring Your plans of success to them…
- o Proverbs 16:3 "Commit to the LORD whatever you do, and your plans will succeed."

♥ **Lord, bless our <u>homes</u>**
- May they be a place of comfort (a fortress where God's love abounds), where all can be themselves, and not a place of perfectionism or materialism, where children or husbands feel that things and/or schedules, checklists, etc., are more important than their hearts! (Ouch!)…
- o Psalm 59:9 "O my Strength, I watch for you; you, O God, are my fortress, my loving God."
- o Psalm 139:1-3 "O LORD, you have searched me and you know me. You know when I sit and when I rise; you perceive my thoughts from afar. You discern my going out and my lying down; you are familiar with all my ways."
- o Isaiah 32:17-18 "The fruit of righteousness will be peace; the effect of righteousness will be quietness and confidence forever. My people will live in peaceful dwelling places, in secure homes, in undisturbed places of rest."

♥ **<u>Application</u>**
- o May we apply what we pray—that our husbands are a hand-picked gift to us from God. May we treat them that way. May our body language, attitude, tone of voice, actions, priorities, and the way we spend our time, etc., display it.

♥ **Lord, bless this <u>prayer ministry</u>**
- o Psalm 91:4b May Your faithfulness shield, protect, and defend this prayer ministry, we pray!

♥ **<u>Praise</u>**   We praise You, Lord, that You are our Father!

Week 86

- ❤ **Praise** God is <u>supreme</u>: Highest in rank, power, authority; superior, highest in degree; utmost.
  - Deuteronomy 10:14-22 "To the LORD your God belong the heavens, even the highest heavens, the earth and everything in it..."
  - Nehemiah 9:6 "You alone are the LORD. You made the heavens...You give life to everything..."
  - Psalm 95:3-7a "For the LORD is the great God, the great King above all gods. In his hand are the depths of the earth, and the mountain peaks belong to him. The sea is his, for he made it, and his hands formed the dry land. Come, let us bow down in worship, let us kneel before the LORD our Maker; for he is our God and we are the people of his pasture, the flock under his care."
  - Isaiah 44:6-8 "This is what the LORD says—Israel's King and Redeemer, the LORD Almighty: I am the first and I am the last; apart from me there is no God. Who then is like me? Let him proclaim it. Let him declare and lay out before me what has happened since I established my ancient people, and what is yet to come—yes, let him foretell what will come. Do not tremble, do not be afraid. Did I not proclaim this and foretell it long ago? You are my witnesses. Is there any God besides me? No, there is no other Rock; I know not one."
  - Colossians 1:15-18 "...He is before all things, and in him all things hold together. And he is the head of the body, the church; he is the beginning and the firstborn from among the dead, so that in everything he might have the supremacy."
  - Revelation 4:11 "You are worthy, our Lord and God, to receive glory and honor and power, for you created all things, and by your will they were created and have their being."
- ❤ **Confession**   1 John 1:8-9 (TLB)
- ❤ **Thanksgiving**   1) Thank You, Lord, for the people You put in our lives.
   2) Thank You, Lord, for all that You have brought us through.
   3) Thank You, Lord, for all that You will bring us through!
   4) Thank You, Lord, that You are always with us; You are all we need.
   5)_____
- ❤ **Lord, bless my husband by giving him a <u>wife</u> who...**
  - knows that though she walks in the midst of trouble, the Lord preserves her life...The Lord will fulfill His purpose for us...His love endures forever...
  - Psalm 138:7-8 "Though I walk in the midst of trouble, you preserve my life; you stretch out your hand against the anger of my foes, with your right hand

you save me. The LORD will fulfill his purpose for me; your love, O LORD, endures forever—do not abandon the works of your hands."

- ❤ **Lord, bless our <u>husbands</u>**   Salvation (if applicable): Romans 10:14-15
  - o May they be forgiving and gentle, not concerned about making a good impression…
  - o Colossians 3:12-14a (TLB) "Since you have been chosen by God who has given you this new kind of life, and because of his deep love and concern for you, you should practice tender-hearted mercy and kindness to others. Don't worry about making a good impression on them but be ready to suffer quietly and patiently. Be gentle and ready to forgive; never hold grudges. Remember, the Lord forgave you, so you must forgive others. Most of all, let love guide your life."

- ❤ **Lord, bless our <u>marriages</u>**
  - o 2 Chronicles 32:7-8 (NASB) (paraphrased/personalized for our marriages) May we be strong and courageous, and not fear the enemy that is all around us trying to destroy our marriages. For God is greater; God is our help and fights our battles. May we rely on Him and the truth of His Word to us.

- ❤ **Lord, bless our <u>homes</u>**
  - o Lord, remove the "idols" from our homes, that our homes will be a place where love for God, and love for each other, flourishes. Make our homes more like how You created them to be in the garden of Eden…
  - o Ezekiel 36:25-27 (TLB) "Then it will be as though I had sprinkled clean water on you, for you will be clean—your filthiness will be washed away, your idol worship gone. And I will give you a new heart—I will give you new and right desires—and put a new spirit within you. I will take out your stony hearts of sin and give you new hearts of love. And I will put my Spirit within you so that you will obey my laws and do whatever I command."

- ❤ **<u>Application</u>**
  - o Genesis 2:22 "Then the LORD God made a woman from the rib he had taken out of the man, and he brought her to the man." Application: Lord, mold us into what our husbands need; make us a gift to them!

- ❤ **Lord, bless this <u>prayer ministry</u>**
  - o Matthew 9:35-38 O Lord God, we call upon You and ask You to send forth workers into the harvest field of hurting, struggling marriages. Please heal and save many souls and marriages through this ministry of praying Your Word, Lord. Thank you and praise you, Lord, that You are a God of compassion!

- ❤ **<u>Praise</u>** We praise You, Lord, that You are supreme!

Week 87

- ♥ <u>Praise</u>   God is <u>sovereign</u>:   Holding the position of ruler, royal, reigning; independent of all others; above or superior to all others; controls everything, can do anything.
    - o Job 42:2 (NIV) "I know that you can do all things; no plan of yours can be thwarted." (AMP) "I know that You can do all things, and that no thought *or* purpose of Yours can be restrained *or* thwarted." (TLB) "I know that you can do anything and that no one can stop you."
    - o Psalm 93 "The LORD reigns, he is robed in majesty and is armed with strength. The world is firmly established; it cannot be moved. Your throne was established long ago; you are from all eternity…"
    - o Isaiah 46:9-10 (AMP) "[Earnestly] remember the former things, [which I did] of old; for I am God, and there is no one else; I am God, and there is none like Me, Declaring the end *and* the result from the beginning, and from ancient times the things that are not yet done, saying, My counsel shall stand, and I will do all My pleasure *and* purpose."
    - o Matthew 10:29-31 (AMP) "Are not two little sparrows sold for a penny? And yet not one of them will fall to the ground without your Father's leave (consent) *and* notice. But even the very hairs of your head are all numbered. Fear not, then; you are of more value than many sparrows."
    - o Romans 8:28 "And we know that in all things God works for the good of those who love him, who have been called according to his purpose."
- ♥ <u>Confession</u>   1 John 2:1-2 (TLB)
- ♥ <u>Thanksgiving</u>   1) Thank You, Lord, for all that You have done for us.
    2) Thank You, Lord, for being in complete control.
    3) Thank You, Lord, for lovingly, powerfully, and sovereignly watching over us and taking care of us.
- ♥ Lord, bless my husband by giving him a <u>wife</u> who…
    - o trusts in the Lord at all times…
    - o Psalm 62:8 (NIV) "Trust in him at all times, O people; pour out your hearts to him, for God is our refuge."
    - o Psalm 62:8 (TLB) "O my people, trust him all the time. Pour out your longings before him, for he can help!"
    - o Psalm 62:8 (AMP) "Trust in, lean on, rely on, *and* have confidence in Him at all times, you people; pour out your hearts before Him. God is a refuge for us (a fortress and a high tower). Selah [pause, and calmly think of that]!"
- ♥ Lord, bless our <u>husbands</u>   Salvation (if applicable): John 14:6

- May they have no unwholesome talk come out of their mouths, but only what is helpful for building others up…
- Ephesians 4:29 "Do not let any unwholesome talk come out of your mouths, but only what is helpful for building others up according to their needs, that it may benefit those who listen."

♥ **Lord, bless our <u>marriages</u>**
- Scatter the enemies of our marriages with Your mighty arm…
- Psalm 89:10b (NASB) "Thou didst scatter Thine enemies with Thy mighty arm."

♥ **Lord, bless our <u>homes</u>**
- Lord, may Your Word and obeying/honoring it be the foundation of our homes/families…
- Deuteronomy 6:17-18a (NIV) "Be sure to keep the commands of the LORD your God and the stipulations and decrees he has given you. Do what is right and good in the LORD's sight, so that it may go well with you…"
- Deuteronomy 6:17-18a (TLB) "You must actively obey him in everything he commands. Only then will you be doing what is right and good in the Lord's eyes. If you obey him, all will go well for you…"

♥ **<u>Application</u>**
- Lesson I learned from the book *A Woman After God's Own Heart* by Elizabeth George…
  - The better follower I am, the better leader my husband will be![64]
  - O Lord, I pray that You will make me a better follower!

♥ **Lord, bless this <u>prayer ministry</u>**
- Please keep it pure from gossip, complaining, and grumbling. May this prayer ministry honor You, Lord, and honor our husbands and families…
- Titus 3:1-2 "Remind the people to be subject to rulers and authorities, to be obedient, to be ready to do whatever is good, to slander no one, to be peaceable and considerate, and to show true humility toward all men."

♥ **<u>Praise</u>** We praise You, Lord, that You are sovereign!

---

[64] Elizabeth George, *A Woman After God's Own Heart*, (Eugene, Oregon, Harvest House Publishers, 1997), 60-62.

Week 88

- ♥ **Praise**   God is <u>omnipotent</u>:   All powerful; having unlimited power or authority; almighty.
    - o Psalm 147:3-5a "He heals the brokenhearted and binds up their wounds. He determines the number of stars and calls them each by name. Great is our LORD and mighty in power."
    - o Jeremiah 32:17 (AMP) "Alas, Lord God! Behold, You have made the heavens and the earth by Your great power and by Your outstretched arm! There is nothing too hard *or* too wonderful for You."
    - o Ephesians 1:19-20 (TLB) "I pray that you will begin to understand how incredibly great his power is to help those who believe him. It is that same mighty power that raised Christ from the dead and seated him in the place of honor at God's right hand in heaven."
    - o Hebrews 1:3 (TLB) "God's Son shines out with God's glory, and all that God's Son is and does marks him as God. He regulates the universe by the mighty power of his command. He is the one who died to cleanse us and clear our record of all sin, and then sat down in highest honor beside the great God of heaven."

- ♥ **Confession**   Psalm 86:5

- ♥ **Thanksgiving**
    1) Thank You, Lord, that You never grow weary or tired.
    2) Thank You, Lord, for being so patient with us.
    3) Thank You, Lord, that You are there on the mountaintops and in the valleys; knowing You, Lord, is such a precious gift!
    4) Thank You, Lord, that You are always with us; You are all we need.
    5)_____

- ♥ **Lord, bless my husband by giving him a <u>wife</u> who...**
    - o lives out the Truth of Your Word of...
    - o Psalm 37:34a (NIV) "Wait for the LORD and keep his way."
    - o Psalm 37:34a (AMP) "Wait for *and* expect the Lord and keep *and* heed His way."
    - o Psalm 37:34a (MSG) "Wait passionately for God, don't leave the path."
    - o Psalm 37:34a (TLB) "Don't be impatient for the Lord to act! Keep traveling steadily along his pathway."

- ♥ **Lord, bless our <u>husbands</u>**   Salvation (if applicable): John 6:64-65
    - o May they not hold on to their anger...

- o Ephesians 4:26-27 (TLB) "If you are angry, don't sin by nursing your grudge. Don't let the sun go down with you still angry—get over it quickly; for when you are angry you give a mighty foothold to the devil."

♥ **Lord, bless our <u>marriages</u>**
- o May we wait on the Lord and gain new strength to persevere in our marriages...
- o Isaiah 40:31a (NASB) "Yet those who wait for (hope in) the LORD Will gain new strength."

♥ **Lord, bless our <u>homes</u>**
- o May our homes be a place where special memories are made, where the Lord is feared and His name is honored. May a precious scroll of remembrance be written in Your presence, Lord...
- o Malachi 3:16 "Then those who feared the LORD talked with each other, and the LORD listened and heard. A scroll of remembrance was written in his presence concerning those who feared the LORD and honored his name."

♥ **<u>Application</u>**
- o Further applications from lessons I learned from the book *A Woman After God's Own Heart* by Elizabeth George...
  O Lord, please help me to...
- o Be a blessing and not a burden to my husband daily!
- o Be a help and not a hindrance to my husband daily!
- o Fit into my husband's plans daily and not fight for my own way![65]

♥ **Lord, bless this <u>prayer ministry</u>**
- o May You do immeasurably more than we could ever ask or imagine, Lord, through the power of Your Holy Spirit, throughout the generations, we pray...
- o Ephesians 3:20-21 "Now to him who is able to do immeasurably more than all we ask or imagine, according to his power that is at work within us, to him be glory in the church and in Christ Jesus throughout all generations, for ever and ever! Amen."

♥ **<u>Praise</u>** We praise You, Lord, that You are omnipotent!

---

[65] Ibid.

Week 89

- ♥ **Praise** God is <u>omniscient</u>: Having infinite knowledge; knowing all things.
  - o Psalm 139:1-6 (TLB) "O Lord, you have examined my heart and know everything about me…Every moment, you know where I am…You both precede and follow me, and place your hand of blessing on my head…"
  - o Isaiah 65:24 (TLB) "I will answer them before they even call to me. While they are still talking to me about their needs, I will go ahead and answer their prayers!"
  - o Romans 11:33-36 (TLB) "Oh, what a wonderful God we have! How great are his wisdom and knowledge and riches! How impossible it is for us to understand his decisions and his methods!…For everything comes from God alone. Everything lives by his power, and everything is for his glory. To him be glory evermore."
  - o Hebrews 4:13 "Nothing in all creation is hidden from God's sight. Everything is uncovered and laid bare before the eyes of him to whom we must give account."

- ♥ **Confession**   Romans 5:20b

- ♥ **Thanksgiving**   1) Thank You, Lord, for everything—for who You are.
  2) Thank You, Lord, for all that You are doing in our lives and our marriages.
  3) Thank You, Lord, that You are ever faithful.
  4) Thank You, Lord, that You are always with us; You are all we need.
  5)_____

- ♥ **Lord, bless my husband by giving him a <u>wife</u> who…**
  - o tries to walk a blameless path, with Your help…
  - o Psalm 101:2 (TLB) "I will try to walk a blameless path, but how I need your help, especially in my own home, where I long to act as I should."

- ♥ **Lord, bless our <u>husbands</u>**   Salvation (if applicable): Romans 1:20
  - o May Your Word not come back void, but may it sink in and accomplish Your purposes in their lives, Lord…
  - o Isaiah 55:10-11 "As the rain and the snow come down from heaven, and do not return to it without watering the earth and making it bud and flourish, so that it yields seed for the sower and bread for the eater, so is my word that goes out from my mouth; It will not return to me empty, but will accomplish what I desire and achieve the purpose for which I sent it."

- ❤ Lord, bless our <u>marriages</u>
    - o May we ever remember that nothing is too difficult for God; that includes whatever struggle we may be having in our marriages right now! God is bigger than any of our problems...
    - o Jeremiah 32:17 (NASB) "Ah Lord GOD! Behold, Thou hast made the heavens and the earth by Thy great power and by Thine outstretched arm! Nothing is too difficult for Thee."

- ❤ Lord, bless our <u>homes</u>
    - o May our homes be a place where love for God and the Truths of His Word are passed down...
    - o Deuteronomy 6:4-9 "Hear, O Israel: The LORD our God, the LORD is one. Love the LORD your God with all your heart and with all your soul and with all your strength. These commandments that I give you today are to be upon your hearts. Impress them on your children. Talk about them when you sit at home and when you walk along the road, when you lie down and when you get up. Tie them as symbols on your hands and bind them on your foreheads. Write them on the doorframes of your houses and on your gates."

- ❤ <u>Application</u>
    - o 1 John 3:18 (TLB) "Little children, let us stop just *saying* we love people; let us *really* love them, and *show it* by our *actions.*"
        - o Applying this Scripture to our marriages...
        - o O Lord, please help us not just to say that we love our husbands; let us really love them and show it by our actions!

- ❤ Lord, bless this <u>prayer ministry</u>
    - o We commit this prayer ministry to You, Lord; bring Your plans of success to it, we pray...
    - o Proverbs 16:3 "Commit to the LORD whatever you do, and your plans will succeed."
    - o Ever for Your glory, Lord, ever for Your glory!

- ❤ <u>**Praise**</u> **We praise You, Lord, that You are omniscient!**

7

Blank Prayer Sheets

Meeting together to pray and release
God's power into our lives, our husbands,
our marriages, our homes…

Always Pray & Don't Give Up (Luke 18:1)

Date: _____

♥ <u>Praise</u>   God is _____
_____

    o   Verse: _____
    o   Verse: _____

♥ <u>Confession</u>
_____

♥ <u>Thanksgiving</u>   1) Thank You, Lord, for
    _____

    2) Thank You, Lord, for
    _____

♥ Lord, bless my husband by giving him a <u>wife</u> who…

    o   _____
    o   Verse: _____

♥ Lord, bless our <u>husbands</u>   Salvation (if applicable):_____

    o   _____
    o   Verse: _____

♥ Lord, bless our <u>marriages</u>

    o   _____
    o   Verse: _____

♥ Lord, bless our <u>homes</u>

    o   _____
    o   Verse: _____

♥ <u>Application</u>

    o   1 John 3:18 Let us love with action and in truth by
    _____

    o   Luke 18:1 May we always pray and not give up!

    o   _____

- ❤ Lord, bless this <u>prayer ministry</u>
    - o   Zechariah 4:6b Bless, protect, and grow it, Lord, by your Spirit!
    - o   1 Chronicles 4:10 Bless, enlarge, and empower it; keep it free from sin.
    - o   Psalm 91:4b May Your faithfulness be its shield and rampart, Lord.
    - o   Matthew 9:38 Lord, raise up prayer warriors for marriages.
    - o   Romans 12:2b God's good, pleasing, and perfect will be done.
    - o   _____

- ❤ <u>**Praise**</u>   We praise You, Lord, that You are _____

Always Pray & Don't Give Up (Luke 18:1)

Date: _____

- ♥ <u>Praise</u>   God is _____
  _____
  - o   Verse: _____
  - o   Verse: _____
- ♥ <u>Confession</u>
  _____
- ♥ <u>Thanksgiving</u>   1) Thank You, Lord, for
  _____

  2) Thank You, Lord, for
  _____
- ♥ Lord, bless my husband by giving him a <u>wife</u> who…
  - o   _____
  - o   Verse: _____
- ♥ Lord, bless our <u>husbands</u>   Salvation (if applicable): _____
  - o   _____
  - o   Verse: _____
- ♥ Lord, bless our <u>marriages</u>
  - o   _____
  - o   Verse: _____
  - o
- ♥ Lord, bless our <u>homes</u>
  - o   _____
  - o   Verse: _____
- ♥ <u>Application</u>
  - o   1 John 3:18 Let us love with action and in truth by _____
  - o   Luke 18:1 May we always pray and not give up!
  - o   _____

- ♥ **Lord, bless this <u>prayer ministry</u>**
    - o   Zechariah 4:6b Bless, protect, and grow it, Lord, by your Spirit!
    - o   1 Chronicles 4:10 Bless, enlarge, and empower it; keep it free from sin.
    - o   Psalm 91:4b May Your faithfulness be its shield and rampart, Lord.
    - o   Matthew 9:38 Lord, raise up prayer warriors for marriages.
    - o   Romans 12:2b God's good, pleasing, and perfect will be done.
    - o   _____

- ♥ <u>**Praise**</u>   We praise You, Lord, that You are _____

Always Pray & Don't Give Up (Luke 18:1)

Date: _____

- ♥ <u>Praise</u>   God is _____
  _____
  - o   Verse: _____
  - o   Verse: _____
- ♥ <u>Confession</u>
  _____
- ♥ <u>Thanksgiving</u>   1) Thank You, Lord, for
  _____
  2) Thank You, Lord, for
  _____
- ♥ Lord, bless my husband by giving him a <u>wife</u> who…
  - o   _____
  - o   Verse: _____
- ♥ Lord, bless our <u>husbands</u> Salvation (if applicable): _____
  - o   _____
  - o   Verse: _____
- ♥ Lord, bless our <u>marriages</u>
  - o   _____
  - o   Verse: _____
  - o
- ♥ Lord, bless our <u>homes</u>
  - o   _____
  - o   Verse: _____
- ♥ <u>Application</u>
  - o   1 John 3:18 Let us love with action and in truth by
    _____
  - o   Luke 18:1 May we always pray and not give up!
  - o   _____

- ❤ **Lord, bless this <u>prayer ministry</u>**
    - o Zechariah 4:6b Bless, protect, and grow it, Lord, by your Spirit!
    - o 1 Chronicles 4:10 Bless, enlarge, and empower it; keep it free from sin.
    - o Psalm 91:4b May Your faithfulness be its shield and rampart, Lord.
    - o Matthew 9:38 Lord, raise up prayer warriors for marriages.
    - o Romans 12:2b God's good, pleasing, and perfect will be done.
    - o _____

- ❤ <u>**Praise**</u>   We praise You, Lord, that You are _____

Always Pray & Don't Give Up (Luke 18:1)

Note: Last blank prayer sheet; make copies prior to using!

Date: _____

♥ **Praise**   God is _____
_____

- Verse: _____
- Verse: _____

♥ **Confession**
_____

♥ **Thanksgiving**   1) Thank You, Lord, for
_____

2) Thank You, Lord, for
_____

♥ Lord, bless my husband by giving him a <u>wife</u> who…

- _____
- Verse: _____

♥ Lord, bless our <u>husbands</u> Salvation (if applicable): _____

- _____
- Verse: _____

♥ Lord, bless our <u>marriages</u>

- _____
- Verse: _____

♥ Lord, bless our <u>homes</u>

- _____
- Verse: _____

♥ **Application**

- 1 John 3:18   Let us love with action and in truth by
_____
- Luke 18:1   May we always pray and not give up!
- _____

Always Pray & Don't Give Up (Luke 18:1)

- ♥ **Lord, bless this <u>prayer ministry</u>**
    - o   Zechariah 4:6b Bless, protect, and grow it, Lord, by your Spirit!
    - o   1 Chronicles 4:10 Bless, enlarge, and empower it; keep it free from sin.
    - o   Psalm 91:4b May Your faithfulness be its shield and rampart, Lord.
    - o   Matthew 9:38 Lord, raise up prayer warriors for marriages.
    - o   Romans 12:2b God's good, pleasing, and perfect will be done.
    - o   _____

- ♥ <u>**Praise**</u>   We praise You, Lord, that You are _____

Suggested Reading

These books have helped me as a woman, a wife, and a mom. Enjoy!

1) *31 Days to a Happy Husband: What a Man Needs Most from His Wife*
    by Arlene Pellicane

2) *A Housewife Desperate for God: A Look at the Proverbs 31 Woman*
    by Mariel Davenport

3) *A Woman After God's Own Heart*
    by Elizabeth George

4) *Beautiful in God's Eyes: The Treasures of the Proverbs 31 Woman*
    by Elizabeth George

5) *Beauty by the Book: Seeing Yourself as God Sees You*
    by Nancy Stafford

6) *Becoming Your Spouse's Better Half: Why Differences Make a Marriage Great*
    by Rick Johnson

7) *Captivating: Unveiling the Mystery of a Woman's Soul*
    by John & Stasi Eldredge

8) *For I Know the Plans I Have for You (Butterfly): Pocket Inspirations*
    compiled by Marilyn Jansen

9) *God Knows My Name: Never Forgotten, Forever Loved*
    by Beth Redman

10) *His Princess: Love Letters from Your King*
    by Sheri Rose Shepherd

11) *Jesus Calling: Enjoying Peace in His Presence*
      by Sarah Young

12) *Keep Your Love On!: Connection, Communication & Boundaries*
      by Danny Silk

13) *Knowing God Through His Names: A Ten Week Study With Our Unchanging God*
      by Mariel Davenport

14) *Life of the Beloved: Spiritual Living in a Secular World*
      by Henri J. M. Nouwen

15) *Love & Respect: The Love She Most Desires; The Respect He Desperately Needs*
      by Emerson Eggerichs

16) *Loving God with All Your Mind*
      by Elizabeth George

17) *Me? Obey Him?: The Obedient Wife and God's Way of Happiness and Blessing in the Home*
      by Elizabeth Rice Handford

18) *Overcoming Mediocrity: Courageous Women*
      by Christie Lee Ruffino

19) *Prayers from a Mom's Heart: Asking God's Blessing and Protection for Your Children*
      by Fern Nichols

20) *Streams in the Desert: 366 Daily Devotional Readings*
      by L. B. Cowman

21) *The 4:8 Principle: The Secret to a Joy-Filled Life*
      by Tommy Newberry

22) *The Christian Family*
      by Larry Christenson

23) *The Power of a Praying Parent*
      by Stormie Omartian

24) *The Power of a Praying Wife*
      by Stormie Omartian

25) *The Power of Praying for Your Adult Children*
      by Stormie Omartian

26) *The Prayer of Jabez: Breaking Through to the Blessed Life*
      by Bruce Wilkinson

27) *To Train Up a Child*
      by Michael & Debi Pearl

28) *With God All Things Are Possible*
      by Joanne Fink

29) *Words That Hurt, Words That Heal: Speaking the Truth in Love*
      by Carole Mayhall

30) *You're Made for a God-Sized Dream: Opening the Door to All God Has for You*
      by Holley Gerth

Works Cited

George, Elizabeth. *A Woman After God's Own Heart.* Eugene: Harvest House Publishers, 1997.

Moms In Touch International, compiler. *Moms in Touch International Leader's Guide and Personal Quiet Time,* 3rd printing. San Marcos: Printed and Distributed by Ad Pak, 1997 revised.

Morris, William, ed. *The American Heritage Dictionary of the English Language.* New College Edition. Boston: Houghton Mifflin Company, 1976.

Omartian, Stormie. *The Power of Praying for Your Adult Children: Book of Prayers.* Eugene: Harvest House Publishers, 2009.

Webster, A. Merriam. *Webster's Collegiate Dictionary.* Fifth Edition. Springfield: G. & C. Merriam Co., Publishers, 1943.

About Tammy

Tammy has lived out the journey of always praying and not giving up! God and His Word are her anchor. She is a prayer warrior. An ordinary person through whom God is doing extraordinary things. Her love for God is beautiful. Her enthusiasm for God and His Word is contagious. She is real. She is transparent. Her story will touch your heart and give you hope that God *is* real. He is good. He loves you more than you can imagine, and He *will* work everything out, if you just *Always Pray & Don't Give Up!*

To learn more about Tammy, visit her insightful author's blog at JuaniaBooks.com.

For more information about Tammy's speaking ministry, please contact her at: TammyRentsch@juaniabooks.com.

Made in the USA
Lexington, KY
16 April 2018